DATE DUE

APR 3 1992	
Nov. 22 '97	

BRODART   Cat. No. 23-221

CHILDREN OF
COLONIAL DESPOTISM

CHILDREN OF COLONIAL DESPOTISM

Press, Politics, and Culture in Cuba, 1790–1840

Larry R. Jensen

UNIVERSITY PRESSES OF FLORIDA

University of South Florida Press / Tampa

Printed in the U.S.A. on acid-free paper. ∞

Library of Congress Cataloging in Publication Data

Jensen, Larry R.
    Children of colonial despotism.

    "A University of South Florida book."
    Bibliography: p.
    Includes index.
    1. Cuba—Politics and government.2. Press and
politics—Cuba—History—19th century. 3. Freedom of the
Press—Cuba—History—19th century. 4. Cuba—
Intellectual life. I. Title.
F1779.J46   1987   972.91'04'68282'09729   87–10384
ISBN 0-8130-0868-9

UNIVERSITY PRESSES OF FLORIDA is the central agency for scholarly
publishing of the State of Florida's university system, producing books selected
for publication by the faculty editorial committees of Florida's nine public
universities: Florida A&M University (Tallahassee), Florida Atlantic University
(Boca Raton), Florida International University (Miami), Florida State University
(Tallahassee), University of Central Florida (Orlando), University of Florida
(Gainesville), University of North Florida (Jacksonville), University of South
Florida (Tampa), University of West Florida (Pensacola).

ORDERS for books published by all member presses should be addressed to
University Presses of Florida, 15 NW 15th Street, Gainesville, FL 32603.

Nosotros los de la Isla de Cuba . . . hijos del despotismo colonial, nietos de la Inquisición y descendientes legítimos de aquellos valientes y nobles, pero ciegos y extraviados devastadores de Flandes y América. . . .

—*Domingo del Monte to Tomás Gener*
Matanzas, 4 June 1834[1]

CONTENTS

LIST OF FIGURES

PREFACE

THIS BOOK grew out of the conviction that the periodical press constitutes a neglected source for Cuban history and that its very evolution exemplifies the island's fate. As a source, the press puts flesh on the political narrative, allowing closer scrutiny of Cuba's reputation as the "ever-faithful isle." The impact of continued colonialism upon the island and the vagaries of this relationship are also apparent in the development of the press. For most of the period under study, creoles countenanced Spain's restrictive press policies; they sacrificed expressive freedom at the altar of sugar profits and social stability. But continued loyalty also meant that events in Spain could disturb the political equilibrium of the island. On three occasions—1811–14, 1820–23, and 1836—the imposition of constitutionalism and a free press in Spain produced dramatic changes in Cuba. These intervals are like flashes of light that reveal the evolution of the press, the political issues, and the internal pressures for ideological compromise in a booming plantation society.

The interludes of constitutionalism and a free press dictate the book's organization. An initial chapter offers background on developments prior to the declaration of a free press on

18 February 1811. In the two decades after the founding of the *Papel Periódico de la Habana* in 1790, the first generation of "public writers" dedicated the new medium to the progress of sugar prosperity. These elite men of letters sought to establish their own literary guidelines within the limits defined by royal legislation. Even after a successful struggle against the censorial ambitions of the bishop of Havana, they had sufficient stake in the economic and political status quo to adhere to a vision of the press not drastically different from the episcopal view. Their self-imposed content standards restricted the development of the periodical press and the literary career associated with it.

The international reverberations of Napoleon's invasion of Spain changed the function of the periodical press on the island. The second chapter focuses on the first interlude of free press and, after 13 July 1812, constitutionalism. Free press legislation and the Constitution of 1812 developed out of the peculiar situation of Cádiz, the last bastion of Spanish resistance against the French. The free press legislation of 10 November 1810 abolished all previous prepublication censorship procedures and panels and required prior censorship only for writings on doctrinal or ecclesiastical matters. In Cuba, publications became more numerous, more people than ever served as editors or writers or contributed letters or patriotic poetry, but postpublication censorship records demonstrate that the preconstitutional literary consensus did not collapse. The discovery in March 1812 of a major conspiracy by the "population of color" only reinforced a strategy of cautious experimentation with a free press and other constitutional liberties. Controversy in the press, although considerable by standards of the previous decade, was largely restricted to acrimonious debates over personal reputation.

The third and fourth chapters cover the second constitutional period, 1820–23. The *trienio* featured a dramatic challenge to the sugarocracy and its allies in officialdom by *piñeristas*—Spaniards and disaffected creoles who sought revenge through constitutional means: elections to representational institutions and the use of a free press. An informal alliance of *piñerista* editors demanded full implementation of the Constitution of 1812. They were aided in their campaign by their unexpected control of the postpublication censorship juries established by the new press legislation of 22 October 1820.

Protected from prosecution by partisan juries, these editors contributed to the removal of Cuba's two top officials; their press assault was contained only by a concerted campaign of official prosecution and extraofficial violence.

The fourth chapter emphasizes the second phase of the constitutional *trienio:* political recovery of the sugarocracy. General Nicolás Mahy's offensive against the *piñeristas* produced a marked moderation in the Cuban press by June 1822, and stimulated wider creole support for constitutionalism, a position previously dominated by the students of the San Carlos Seminary and their progressive educators. Whereas the constitution had appeared a weapon in the hands of the *piñeristas,* it now seemed a blueprint for substantial self-government: all the constitutional institutions—provincial deputation, municipal council, judiciary (and censorship juries)—could now further elite creole interests. Moderate constitutionalists argued that neither restoration nor revolution could ensure greater creole political autonomy without disastrous social dislocation. This forthright expression of Cuban self-interest in constitutionalism coincided with the latest success of the sugarocracy—permission from the Spanish Cortes (parliamentary assembly) for Cuba to establish its own tariff legislation. Loyalty to constitutionalism, then, was born of a peculiar blend of idealism and self-interest: admiration for the theoretical basis of constitutionalism mixed with fear of political innovation, an ironical coincidence of a new assertive "americanism" and a deepened identification with peninsular politics.

Moderate constitutionalism, however, rested on the foundation of peninsular politics, which was even more unstable now that France had invaded Spain to restore Ferdinand VII to full power. The prospect of a return to royal absolutism tested the ideological mettle of a new generation of creoles that had emerged from the classrooms of philosophy and constitutional law in the San Carlos Seminary. José Antonio Saco, Domingo del Monte, and José de la Luz are only the most notable of a cohort, born around the turn of the century, who came of age in the last year of the constitutional *trienio*, and for this reason may be termed the generation of '23. They expressed their firm adherence to the constitution with a cry of loyalty emanating, they said, from their "impassioned liberalism." Their ardent *periódicos*, however, could not counteract the ever-present specter of Haiti and the growing perception of an intimate connection between constitutionalism and conspiracy. The Soles y Rayos de Bolívar conspiracy of 1823, added to the uprising of 1812, effectively silenced the adherents of moderate constitutionalism. It revealed the contradiction of an elite that desired greater political autonomy under a system of constitutional liberties that, at the same time, threatened the structure of Cuban society, skewed as it was by race and class distinctions. Creoles accepted the restoration of royal absolutism in 1823 with emotions ranging from relief to resignation; they offered few protests against new legislation that further restricted their participation in politics. By 1825 the captain general of Cuba enjoyed all the powers normally delegated to governors under a state of siege, although an unofficial understanding with the sugarocracy softened the impact of this legislation.

The return of constitutionalism to Spain in 1836 revealed Cuba's true status as a colony. For the first time a constitutional government declared that the island was not part of the Spanish "nation" and prohibited the proclamation of constitutionalism in Cuba. Chapter Five devotes considerable attention to factors leading to this decision, with special attention to the role played by the periodical press. After the second Restoration, absolutist censorship had prohibited politics but tolerated literature, and creoles who had come of literary age in 1823 found refuge in romanticism. With its mandate to indulge imagination at the expense of artistic canons, romanticism served as a surrogate manifesto of political liberation. An outpouring of creole literary activity, 1829–34, undermined the mutual accommodation between sugarocracy and officialdom and contributed to the suppression of constitutionalism in Cuba in 1836. Captain General Miguel Tacón crushed a constitutional rebellion in the eastern end of the island but not before a free press in Santiago de Cuba revealed creole support for constitutionalism as the best balance between political rights and the socioeconomic status quo—some self-governance and participation in "national" politics without risking the side effects of political independence. When the Spanish Cortes formally approved a special status for the island in 1837, Cubans finally realized that they could no longer place their political hopes on peninsular constitutionalism.

In the conclusion I reconsider the interaction of press, politics, and culture in light of the curious juxtaposition of the political trauma of 1836–37 with the major literary boom of

1838–39. Cuban writers exacted their revenge on Tacón by contributing to his recall, but their victory was limited to the reinstatement of literary publication in 1838. Subsequent officials did not stray from Tacón's vision of the island's second-class status, and censorship remained intransigent. The persistence of absolutist press standards became a crucial issue for a new generation of creoles: Ramón de Palma, Cirilo Villaverde, Anselmo Suárez y Romero—in all more than fifteen young creoles who stepped into the literary spotlight in 1838.

Unlike del Monte, Luz, and Saco, this generation of writers—the generation of '38—had never known the stimulus of a free press or the pull of public debate over political issues. The protective hothouse of the *tertulia* had nurtured them to be passionate partisans of literature—poetry, drama, essay, and narrative. Consequently there was one question that preyed on their minds: could literature flourish in a repressive climate? The simple answer was no, as illustrated by the quick collapse of Cuban literature's "first moment of splendor." Yet I suggest that colonial press restrictions and creole literary production should not be viewed simply as antithetical. In the first place, the Cuban sugar oligarchy and many creole men of letters had supported press restrictions as necessary in a volatile slave society. Even more importantly, the history of the periodical press since 1790 demonstrates that protracted colonialism deserves some of the credit for the impressive emergence of Cuban literature in the 1830s. Colonial proscriptions on political discussion in the press repeatedly turned creole energies from politics to literature. By 1838–39, however, it should have been clear that writers could not exceed certain limits or colonial authorities would intervene. Moreover, licensing and censorship imposed content restrictions that circumscribed readership, making the career of letters economically unviable. This was the final disillusionment for the "children of colonial despotism."

ACKNOWLEDGMENTS

I **WAS** able to pursue research because of a fellowship from the Social Sciences and Humanities Research Council of Canada, with an additional grant from the Yale Concilium on Latin American Studies. I acknowledge support for dissertation completion from the Weter Fund, Latin American Studies at Stanford University, the Center for Research in International Studies (Stanford University), and the History Department of Stanford University. The University Research Council of Vanderbilt University provided additional funds to revise the manuscript.

I would express my appreciation and gratitude to the staffs of various archives and libraries, but particularly to the Archivo General de Indias (Seville), the Archivo Histórico Nacional (Madrid), and the Biblioteca Nacional José Martí (Havana). Many colleagues gave counsel and encouragement at critical stages of my work: Richard E. Boyer, Jacques A. Barbier, Jeffrey D. Needell, John D. Wirth, Gavin I. Langmuir, Donald L. Winters, Dewey W. Grantham, and Paul H. Freedman. I am especially grateful to Samuel T. McSeveney, Franklin W. Knight, J. León Helguera, Allan J. Kuethe, and Paul K. Conkin for their detailed comments. The greatest debt for intellectual stimulation and example is owed to my mentor, Richard M. Morse. Finally, I would like to thank Wylann Solomon for substantive editorial suggestions.

xiv

A NOTE ON SOURCES

RESEARCH INTO Cuban history is bedeviled by deteriorating relations between the United States and Cuba. North American scholars must design projects to compensate for restricted access to Cuban archives and libraries. For those interested in the period 1790–1840, Spanish archives hold an overwhelming bounty. This is due in part to actions that the *literati* of my study would certainly have deemed "despotic." In 1888 and 1889 a Spanish delegation selectively extracted from the archives of the governors and captains general of Cuba more than eight hundred *legajos* (bundles) pertaining to the period between 1790 and 1840. These documents, now *Sección XI. Papeles de Cuba* in the Archivo General de Indias (Seville), joined the already voluminous collections of colonial remissions and imperial paperwork in metropolitan archives. For my purposes, the most valuable holdings in the Archivo General de Indias are *Sección V. Gobierno. Audiencia de Santo Domingo* (more than two hundred *legajos*) and *Sección X. Ultramar* (more than four hundred *legajos*), featuring letters, petitions, and memorials from private citizens and public officials as well as the deliberations of Spanish authorities over this information. The Ultramar materials date primarily from the period of constitutionalism and colonial revolt; part of this collection never reached the Archivo General de Indias and is housed as the Ultramar Section of the Archivo Histórico Nacional in Madrid. The Madrid collection assumes primary importance beginning in the period of the 1830s.

If Spanish actions achieved a concentration of archival materials in Spain, the same cannot be said for the other major source for this study: the periodical press. The Archivo General de Indias contains a significant collection of the Cuban press; for much of the period of my study colonial printers were required to submit to authorities copies of all items printed. I also used the considerable resources of the Biblioteca Nacional (Madrid), the Library of Congress, the New York Public Library, the Harvard University Library, and the Boston Public Library.[1] Finally, after nearly two years of research, I used the collection of the Biblioteca Nacional José Martí to fill the gaps in my reading of the Cuban periodical press. It was possible to exploit this collection efficiently by consulting Teresita Batista Villareal, et al., *Catálogo de publicaciones periódicas cubanas de los siglos XVIII y XIX* (Havana, 1965).

Secondary sources on the Hispanic periodical press and its Cuban variant are a mixed blessing. For the most part, the historiography features a litany of names, titles, and dates of uncertain veracity.[2] For Spanish America in general, the numerous titles of José Toribio Medina are the most reliable place to start, and many subsequent studies merely rework his diligent research into the libraries of nineteenth-century men of letters. Medina's sources, however, were often repeating rumors or folklore. The best overview of accumulated tradition is José Torre Revello, *El libro, la imprenta y el periodismo en América durante la dominación española* (Buenos Aires, 1940). Less reliable is Gustavo Adolfo Otero, *El periodismo en América* (Lima, 1946).

Only one significant secondary work pertains exclusively to the history of the Cuban periodical press: Joaquín Llaverías y Martínez's *Contribución a la historia de la prensa periódica* (2 vols., Havana, 1957–59). *Contribución* is neither an analysis nor an overview of the subject; rather, it is an unsystematic collection of short articles first published in the *Boletín del Archivo Nacional* (Havana) from 1916 to 1941. The series began as a study of "nuestros grabados" ("our masthead engravings") but acquired a larger perspective by 1923. Typically, each article featured a summary of all the information Llaverías y Martínez (director of the Archivo Nacional from 1922 to 1956) could uncover on a particular title, and several reproduced front pages. *Contribución* is especially valuable for the many documents transcribed from the Archivo Nacional. In light of current restricted access to that archive, Llaverías y Martínez provides an inestimable service to anyone interested in the Cuban press.

Valuable information can also be found in secondary writings on the larger Cuban literary and intellectual scene. For the Cuban press to 1840, the best place to begin is Antonio Bachiller y Morales's *Apuntes para la historia de las letras y de la instrucción pública en la isla de Cuba* (3 vols., Havana, 1936–1937). This work is a rich vein of information that subsequent investigators have repeatedly appropriated. Francisco Calcagno's *Diccionario biográfico cubano* (New York, 1878) organized Bachiller y Morales's data and added other sources to create a biographical dictionary; José T. Medina's *La imprenta en la Habana, 1707–1810, notas bibliográficas* (Santiago de Chile, 1904) wedded the extensive bibliographical expertise of its author to Bachiller y Morales's material and replicated the year-by-year format of the *Apuntes;* Aurelio Mitjan's *Estudio sobre el movimiento científico y literario de Cuba* (Havana, 1890) deliberately chose a thematic organization but relied upon Bachiller y Morales even more than its footnotes indicate.[3]

Since the publication of these works, the historiography of Cuban literary life has become more complex—one might argue redundant as well—with every subsequent synthesis. Mitjans, for example, set the trend by citing Bachiller y Morales and Calcagno without acknowledging that the latter was often relying upon the former. Thus was born the incestuous quality of Cuban literary history that has continued into the twentieth century.[4] Three recent publications provide valuable clarification. A helpful bibliographical introduction to major literary protagonists is now available in David William Foster, *Cuban Literature: A Research Guide* (New York, 1985). The Instituto de Literatura y Lingüística de la Academia de Ciencias de Cuba has recently published encyclopedic and summary overviews of Cuban literature: *Diccionario de la literatura cubana* (2 vols., Havana, 1980, 1984); *Perfil histórico de las letras cubanas desde los orígenes hasta 1898* (Havana, 1983).

I have standardized to modern usage the capitalization of the titles of the periodical press. I have not attempted to translate all Spanish terms because many have no accurate English equivalent or deserve a particular connotation during the period of my study. *Periódico*, for example, cannot be translated as newspaper, for at the beginning of the nineteenth century the word identified items as diverse as serialized booklets, official gazettes, newspapers (weeklies to dailies), and literary reviews (or *revistas*)—literally any *impreso*, or printed item, that issued periodically.

ABBREVIATIONS

AAH   *Anales de la Academia de la Historia*

AGI   Archivo General de Indias (Seville)

AHN   Archivo Histórico Nacional (Madrid)

APHL   Antonio Bachiller y Morales, *Apuntes para la historia de las letras y de la instrucción pública en la isla de Cuba*. 3 vols. Havana, 1936–1937.

BAN   *Boletín del Archivo Nacional* (Havana)

BNJM   Biblioteca Nacional José Martí (Havana)

BNM   Biblioteca Nacional (Madrid)

CAT   Teresita Batista Villareal et al. *Catálogo de publicaciones periódicas cubanas de los siglos XVIII y XIX*. Havana, 1965.

CEDM   *Centón epistolario de Domingo del Monte*. 7 vols. Havana, 1923–57.

CHPP   Joaquín Llaverías y Martínez. *Contribución a la historia de la prensa periódica*. 2 vols. Havana, 1957–59.

DBC   Francisco Calcagno. *Diccionario biográfico cubano*. New York, 1878.

DLC   Instituto de Literatura y Lingüística de la Academia de Ciencias de Cuba. *Diccionario de la literatura cubana*. 2 vols. Havana, 1980, 1984.

PHLC   Instituto de Literatura y Lingüística de la Academia de Ciencias de Cuba. *Perfil histórico de las letras cubanas desde los orígenes hasta 1898*. Havana, 1983.

RBN   *Revista de la Biblioteca Nacional* (Havana)

xix

CHAPTER 1

Secularization and
Self-Censorship,
1790–1810

MUD AND PALACES, dried beef and opera—Havana in the
1790s presented a study in contrasts. A new role in imperial defense and communications, foreign demand for sugar and coffee, and relaxed commercial legislation vitalized a city that had
subsisted for two centuries as port and provisioner for the annual visit of the Spanish fleet.[1] Havana's swelling population—
51,307 residents in 1792 made it the fourth largest city in the
Americas—spilled over the walls and fortifications of the old
city into hastily erected suburbs constantly menaced by fire
and tempest.[2] Everywhere the sights and sounds of the city testified to the growing contribution of African slaves to prosperity; by 1792 the "population of color" (*gente de color*) outnumbered the island's white inhabitants.[3]

Most histories of Cuba trace the origins of prosperity to the
British occupation of Havana (12 August 1762–6 July 1763): a
devastating defeat for the Spanish in the Seven Years' War became, in this interpretation, an opportunity for Cuban sugar
producers to break the stranglehold of colonial regulations, to
exploit new markets and sources of slaves. The Cuban historian Manuel Moreno Fraginals has pointed out that this interpretation rested uncritically upon nineteenth-century sources

1

hostile to imperial economic restrictions; he documented substantial sugar development before 1762, a development somewhat obscured by the extralegal status of much of the sugar production and export. Moreno Fraginals did find a role for the British to play: he stressed the energizing effect of British slave imports at a stage in the sugar economy where manpower, not technology or land, stood as the most forbidding obstacle to increased output. Recently, John R. McNeill challenged even this concession to the traditional emphasis on the British impact. He demonstrated not only that sugar and slavery were considerably developed before 1762, but that the number of slaves introduced by the British had been grossly exaggerated. McNeill concluded that "in the slave trade, as in other respects, the British occupation of 1762–63 affected Cuban society much less than historians have supposed: rather than radically increasing the volume of trade, the occupation merely made legal and visible what had formerly been covert commerce."[4]

Spanish reaction to the military humiliations of the Seven Years' War did have a dramatic impact upon Cuba. Spain rejuvenated colonial defenses, but limited resources forced increased reliance upon American Spaniards (creoles).[5] Charles III created disciplined militias to supplement the regular army, and Cuba's strategic importance persuaded him to offer creole militia officers the exclusive judicial status (*fuero*) attached to similar positions in the peninsular army. Perhaps even more important, the crown rewarded creoles with commercial freedoms in recognition of their greater financial responsibility for the island's garrison.[6] This expanded opportunity for status and wealth gave an important impetus to a creole elite that in leaner times had managed to develop a stranglehold over land and office holding, most recently through sugar production. Even before the Seven Years' War, "most if not all of the titled nobles had begun to convert to sugar production," and the subsequent sugar revolution accelerated the process of gaining titles, thus reinforcing and intensifying the connection between sugar and social status. By 1796, for example, the number of titles of nobility jumped to twenty-three from five in 1763. The increased number, however, did not change the tightly knit character of the sugar elite. The case of Juan O'Farrill, an important sugar planter, demonstrates both the interconnectedness of the sugarocracy as well as its ability to embrace a second-generation "outsider." O'Farrill became the son-in-law of a marquis, the brother-in-law of a count, and eventually saw four sons-in-law gain titles.[7]

Reform of imperial communications after the English occupation also redounded to Havana's favor. The Crown selected Havana as the pivotal point in a reorganized mail system designed to integrate those areas most vulnerable to foreign encroachment. By 1764, cargo-supplemented mailboats were plying the Atlantic between Spain and Havana. As printed gazettes were already an essential element in mail communication, it is no surprise that this innovation prompted the first application to publish a gazette in Cuba. That year the captain general, Conde de Ricla, approached the printer Blas de Olivos[8] with a proposal for a bimonthly gazette and a yearly *Guía de Forrasteros*, a Who's Who of colonial bureaucrats and prominent citizens. To back Olivos's application for the title of royal printer, the captain general wrote a covering letter emphasizing the dismal state of the city's printing facilities, even noting that the island "often lacked the most necessary books for Christian education and primary instruction." The Council of the Indies, however, rejected Olivos's petition, apparently on the advice of Francisco Manuel de Mena, who, as printer of the Madrid gazette, hardly qualified as a disinterested party. This is apparent, for example, in his argument that colonial gazettes should be suppressed to safeguard paper stocks administered through the royal paper monopoly.[9]

It was not until 1782 that Olivos's son-in-law, Francisco Seguí, finally gained permission to publish *La Gaceta de Havana*. Unfortunately, little is known about this short-lived gazette.[10] It was issued on 8 November under the direction of Diego de la Barrera,[11] who had edited the first Cuban *Guía de Forasteros* the previous year. Of some interest is a critique of the first issue by the Venezuelan Francisco de Miranda, resident in Havana at that time. Miranda defended the gazette against criticism that it was a "jumble of things, without beginning or end, or method, or order," while admitting that it bore the marks of hasty assembly. In offering his suggestions for a more logical organization for subsequent issues, Miranda revealed that the first issue was a miscellany which included lists of current consumer prices and port traffic, an essay on the utility of gazettes, suggestions for remedial actions against runaway slaves, news items ranging from a store fire in Jamaica to public disturbances in England and Scotland, and an item on the medicinal value of coffee.[12] Other readers may not have been so charitable, and the gazette's failure in 1783 postponed the advent of the Cuban periodical press until the next decade.

The intimate relationship between the Cuban periodical press and the political and cultural life of the island began in earnest on 24 October 1790 with the publication of the first issue of the *Papel Periódico de la Habana*. A weekly gazette of four small pages, the paper featured the official communications of the colonial bureaucracy, precensored news of the European capitals, and several advertisements.

It was a modest beginning by standards of the time. By contrast, in France, the literary measure of the century, a virtually uncensored press was playing a pivotal role in the restructuring of political life. Shortly after the fall of the Bastille, the National Assembly decreed freedom of the press. Whereas France had but twenty-seven *périodiques* in 1779 (including only three important newspapers), over fourteen hundred titles appeared in the years 1789–1799.[13] A new function for the revolutionary press proved as threatening as its numerical increase: in the absence of official political factions, editors provided rallying points for competing visions of a new society. Jean-Paul Marat, like other editors of the Parisian radical press, elaborated an ideology of popular sovereignty in the pages of *Ami du Peuple* that would soon be appropriated by the Jacobin faction. For a watching (or more accurately, reading) world, the subsequent excesses of the Terror seemed but an aftershock of the explosion of a free press.[14]

The revolutionary press of France represented a clear departure from the Hispanic vision of the periodical press. Until the French Revolution, Hispanic *periódicos* had evolved in a manner comparable to those of most European areas despite the vigilance of the Inquisition and the seminal legislation regulating the printing press promulgated by the Catholic Kings on 8 July 1502.[15] In the seventeenth century the broadsheet, a single sheet of paper printed on one side announcing great discoveries, disasters, or battles, or championing determined orthodoxy in an era of religious controversy, yielded to the more regular gazette format—several pages of officially sanctioned foreign news and legislative decrees. The gazette dominated the Hispanic periodical press until the relaxed statutes on book publishing issued by Charles III on 14 November 1762 apparently prompted a potpourri of publications on literature, customs, and foreign ideas in general.[16] The editors of these new publications had gauged accurately the temper of the new king, for Charles III saw the periodical press, in league with the reformed universities and the fledgling Societies of *Amigos del País*, as the appropriate vehicle for disseminating ideas on rebuilding Spanish wealth and prestige.[17]

As his reign progressed, however, Charles III found printers and editors to be incontinent allies. Numerous publications emulated Spain's first patently *afrancesado* weekly, *El Censor* (Madrid, 1781–85). *El Censor*'s editor, Luis Cañuelo, while a lawyer for the Royal Council, was also an outspoken Francophile, a Mason, and an enthusiast of Voltaire, Rousseau, and Montesquieu.[18] Charles III suppressed *El Censor* on 29 November 1785, but the subsequent excesses of its imitators, coupled with disturbing rumors of political unrest in France, led the king to issue on 2 October 1788 the first detailed guidelines for the periodical press.[19] Prepublication censorship became the responsibility of censors appointed by a *juez de imprentas.* The legislation made no mention of the qualifications necessary for the position of censor; like book censorship, *periódico* censorship demanded only reputation and learning unless an article dealt with ecclesiastical or doctrinal matters, the exclusive preserve of the episcopacy. The legislation revealed no alarmism about the new medium but merely outlined procedures more appropriate than the existing strictures on book publication.

These explicit guidelines were welcomed by the most prolific and dominant editor of the day, Francisco Sebastián Nipho. He predicted relief from the recriminations of authors offended by rejection of partisan or controversial contributions.[20] From the tone of the legislation and editorial reaction, then, it appears that the periodical press was a medium for a "literate and well-to-do minority [who] were by the 1780s becoming scientific amateurs in the manner of cultured groups of more enlightened countries."[21] Two of these productions—*El Correo Literario de la Europa* (1780–81, 1786–87) and the *Espíritu de los Mejores Diarios que se Publican en Europa* (1787–14 February 1791)—were exemplary in their commitment "to make known in Spain the state of sciences, arts, literature, and commerce of the century, which was the 'most scientific of all that compose the lengthy epoch of seven thousand years'."[22]

The French Revolution challenged this optimistic vision of

the role of the periodical press. While a free press survived only three years in France,[23] the brief effusion came to epitomize the potential and peril of the medium for decades thereafter. It also provoked a new phase in the Hispanic press early in the reign of Charles IV. The architect of this revision, the conde de Floridablanca,[24] also first secretary for Charles III, concentrated initially on mobilizing customs officials and the Inquisition to impose a news blackout on events across the Pyrenees.[25] Although these measures required discretion on the part of peninsular editors, the Spanish press continued to flourish into 1790. The *Correo de Madrid* featured a series on modern philosophers while political economy dominated issues of the *Espíritu*.[26] As events in France unfolded and Spain became a target of French revolutionary propaganda, Floridablanca finally moved to shackle the peninsular press as well. The legislation of 24 February 1791 ordered the termination of all *periódicos* except the official *Gaceta de Madrid* and the *Diario de Madrid*. This coincided with Inquisition efforts to censor retroactively the Spanish press of the previous several years and with royal orders to the directors of the Societies of Amigos del País "to slacken their activities and to permit no more discussions of questions of political economy."[27]

These measures form the basis for the persistent interpretation that the era of Charles IV marked a step backward in the development of the Hispanic periodical press.[28] In fact, the edict had limited impact beyond Madrid itself, where censorship subjected the *Diario de Madrid* to a close surveillance. Outside the capital, for example, the *Diario de Valencia*, founded on 22 February 1790, suffered at most a short interruption and continued to 1835. Further, while apprehension about the French press resulted in the closing of the border in June 1792, the conde de Aranda,[29] newly appointed to succeed Floridablanca, had already intimated a revised policy on press freedom that would encourage important new *periódicos* to appear by the fall.[30] The legislation of 1791, then, did not reverse the evolution of the Hispanic periodical press. While official sensitivities to the danger of the new medium were heightened by the example of the French press, the utility of a carefully monitored press still overshadowed the menace of its revolutionary potential. This was the decidedly ambivalent attitude that would dominate the early history of the Cuban press.

The appearance of the *Papel Periódico de la Habana* on

24 October 1790 also coincided with the beginning of a new cycle of Cuban prosperity based upon several factors: the royal decision of 28 February 1789 that allowed open introduction of slaves into Havana, provoking a deluge of importations estimated as high as twenty thousand between 1789 and 1792;[31] the revolutionary violence in Saint-Domingue that destroyed the Caribbean's leading sugar producer and sent prices rocketing, financing a rapid expansion of Cuban production; and the war with France (1793) that disrupted communication between Spain and the colonies and necessitated the much-desired expedient of neutral shipping.[32] Ambitious creole sugar producers in league with the highest Spanish official on the island, Captain General Luis de las Casas y Aragorri,[33] rose to the challenge. Government and sugarocracy cooperated to found appropriate institutions: a mercantile guild and commercial court (*consulado*)[34] to regulate all facets of the world of sugar, an academy (Sociedad Económica de Amigos del País)[35] to promote useful knowledge on economic matters, and a gazette to facilitate flow of information.[36]

The most significant innovation of the first decade of the *Papel Periódico* (biweekly, 1791–1805) occurred in 1793, once again at the instigation of Las Casas. To ensure financial and editorial stability the captain general recommended that proprietary and editorial rights be assumed by the newly formed Patriotic Society.[37] Comprised of top colonial officials, sugar planters ranging from the titled aristocracy to the merely wealthy, and reputable professional men—lawyers, professors, physicians, and ecclesiastics—the Patriotic Society promoted the interests of Cuban sugar producers, often to the detriment of peninsular commercial interests still associated with the principle of monopoly. This correlation between sugarocracy and Patriotic Society was immediately apparent: an analysis of a 1787 petition to establish a *consulado*, for example, reveals that all five individuals listed as sugar planters would be Society members by 1795; by contrast, only one of six individuals identified as a merchant on the petition later became a Patriotic Society member.[38]

The Patriotic Society accepted Las Casas's suggestion and established an editorial board. In 1793, members who served monthly terms included such prominent citizens as Agustín Ibarra (artillery captain), Tomás Romay y Chacón (physician and researcher/teacher), José Agustín Caballero y de la Torre

Figure 1-1. Cuban Periódicos, 1790–1810

1800	1801	1802	1803	1804	1805	1806	1807	1808	1809	1810

Papel Periódico de la Habana / Aviso / Aviso de la Habana / Diario de la Habana

(24 Oct 1790)

Aurora. Correo Político-Económico de la Habana

3 Sep   Mar

Lonja Mercantil

12 Sep   12 Dec

Regañón de·la Habana

30 Sep   13 Apr

Enciclopedia

Criticón

16 Oct   4 Dec

Amigo de los Cubanos

Miscelánea Literaria

Mensagero Político-Económico-Literario de la Habana

Jan

KEY

——————— Publication verified
------------ Incomplete publication data
(SC)   Santiago de Cuba

(theologian, philosopher, and professor at the seminary), Domingo Mendoza (cleric and professor at the seminary), and Francisco de Arango y Parreño (the most important ideologue of Cuban sugar producers, and the island's main lobbyist with Spain for the next thirty years). Almost immediately, the pages of the *Papel Periódico* mirrored the Patriotic Society's priorities; space devoted to economic information increased to nearly half of the four-page issue.[39] The enterprise prospered. On 2 September 1794, a Patriotic Society report disclosed a subscription list of 126 individuals, each paying six *reales* per month.[40] Shortly thereafter the income from 196 subscriptions (plus individual sales) enabled the Society to begin purchases of books from Spain destined for a new public library.[41]

The content of the *Papel Periódico* was not exclusively official edicts and economic data; the literary possibilities of the new medium encouraged a few Cubans to publish exhortatory essays in the genre known as *costumbrismo*. As early as 5 February 1792, Diego de la Barrera published what amounted to a *costumbrista* manifesto, indicating a deliberate editorial policy against "pernicious customs and practices," promising to "correct vices by portraying them in their true colors" and by juxtaposing the "appreciable charm of virtue."[42] Common targets were gambling, idleness, and vanity in women.[43] While moralistic and tiresome at its worst, *costumbrismo* in its focus on Cuban society initiated a literary tradition which subsequently produced incisive essays about local customs.[44]

By 1794, the Patriotic Society felt that the *Papel Periódico* had already stimulated the island's sciences, arts, and letters and would promote a "degree of enlightenment" to rival European standards.[45] Their confidence was not without foundation; for almost two decades the *Papel Periódico* would devote space to the "useful" items of information that typified much of the eighteenth-century press after the publication of the *Encyclopédie*. In addition to lists of commodity prices and *costumbrista* essays on virtue and vice, it included articles on scientific discoveries, meteorological and geographical data, and natural history ("The Life Expectancy of Some Animals and Insects").[46] But the pages of this official publication did not encompass the intellectual world of elite members of the Patriotic Society. Prepublication censors, elected by the Society and answerable to the captain general, monitored content carefully. After the French Revolution, the perceived connection between "enlightened" ideas and revolution provoked an even closer examination of "useful" information. The result was a narrowing of acceptable topics: the scientific miracle of vaccine and the importance of public cemeteries were two that became almost mundane through repetition. Nor did letters to the editor promote controversy, even when they claimed to be recounting discord within literary gatherings or *tertulias*—a dispute over the scientific properties of moon rays, for example.[47]

The most significant constraint on content, however, did not come from the Society's censors. The bishop of Havana, Felipe Joseph de Trespalacios y Verdeja, had appropriated considerable authority over the content of the publication. He demonstrated his resolve in a controversy over ecclesiastical censorship in November 1792. At issue was an article, published without episcopal approval, that contained a questionable reference to the scriptures after a spectacular series of winds and rains had battered Havana for several days, an anonymous author mused over the Great Flood from the perspective of a son of Noah.[48] The bishop judged the article an abuse of the scriptures and charged that he could not depend upon royal officials to enforce his legal right to censor any items that fell within his ecclesiastical jurisdiction; in response, he directly informed the printers of the city of his authority.[49] Bishop Trespalacios resented Las Casas's insistence that he did not know the identity of the anonymous author; it was rumored that the author was Nicolás Calvo y O'Farril, one of the founders of the Patriotic Society and a relative of the captain general.[50]

The following year, a more serious confrontation developed over the bishop's refusal to approve the printing of Tomás Romay's acceptance speech for an award for his *Discurso sobre los cuatro sugetos que por buenas obras son mas acreedores a la gratitud de toda la Isla de Cuba.*[51] Captain General Las Casas attempted to mediate the dispute, allowing the bishop to document his past stewardship over the press. The resulting *expediente* shows the ample scope of ecclesiastical censure. Of seventeen examples of recent episcopal censorship cited, nine seem outside ecclesiastical or doctrinal concerns. An article suggesting that city lighting be financed by a tax on flour imports, for example, was rejected by the bishop as impractical. Using the argument that such suggestions affronted those exercising legislative functions, he prohibited articles on bankruptcy, urban lighting, and street cleaning. Similarly, he prohibited an article decrying the impact of foreign commerce, stating that such suggestions were unacceptable in a society where sovereignty and legislative initiative descended from the Crown to the nation. Pointing to the specter of "equality," the "philosophy of the day," and contrasting this "detestable" principle with the affirmation of hierarchy evidenced in heaven and the church, the bishop was compelled to defend secular authority as well. In this view, the bishop felt his ecclesiastical jurisdiction threatened by discussions of republicanism or equality, or even the most innocent assault on the perquisites of monarchy; for example, the bishop disallowed an article recounting the efforts of the grandfather of China's emperor to improve the rice strain because it implied constraints on royal conduct.

The bishop also defined his limits on the ideology of "las luces" (the Enlightenment), so prominent in the rhetorical statements of the Patriotic Society and its periodical mouthpiece. The bishop prohibited articles on the importance of philosophical study and the wisdom of the Greeks. He rejected an article citing Plato as an authority for arguing the importance of the Catholic religion as the bulwark of the state with the comment "This is not a paper for everyone's eyes." While maintaining that there was no more useful occupation for the printing press than the publication of *periódicos*, the bishop cautioned that articles should be less abstract and should serve to stimulate agriculture, arts, and commerce "in the service of God and to the good of the State." In rejecting an article that held liberty to be the necessary environment for authors, the bishop remarked that restricting liberty would ensure less "corruption of our customs and fewer revolutions." The periodical press, then, was for him a potential carrier of the germs of heresy and revolution. The flow of ideas, he believed, had to be strictly curtailed by authorities of the church and the state, and this prohibition extended to articles deemed appropriate for peninsular audiences after a supposedly similar censorship procedure. Like most colonial officials (Las Casas was an exception), the bishop viewed the Cuban intellectual environment as distinct from that of Spain, bereft of European sophistication and menaced by a diverse population and the precedents of the French and Haitian revolutions.

The Patriotic Society lost its battle to print Romay's speech— it was finally published in the Society's *Memorias* in 1839.[52]

Other efforts to diminish episcopal influence encountered, case by case, similarly intransigent resistance from the bishop for the remainder of the decade. The next year, for example, the bishop disallowed an article satirizing a plan for voluntary contributions to the Royal Treasury. Despite repeated requests from Las Casas, the bishop refused to specify the reasons for this verdict or to say whether it was based upon his 9 February 1793 legislative mandate over "el dogma y moral Evangélica."[53] By this point the bishop's vigilance over the press was part of a larger campaign against Las Casas and his collaborators. Jurisdictional sensitivities between a bishop jealous of his spiritual authority and a zealous secular official degenerated into a war of letters and representations to Madrid over the bishop's behavior and mental and physical capacities. Bishop Trespalacios, in defense of his refusal to resign in April 1795, cited the machinations of elite creoles and Las Casas to replace him with the *habanero* Luis de Peñalver, first director of the Patriotic Society and bishop-elect of Louisiana. Indeed, such lobbying *was* taking place, casting doubts on the authenticity of reports about episcopal malfeasance and eventually persuading the Consejo to absolve the bishop of charges of improprieties and physical incapacity.[54]

Only the bishop's death on 16 October 1799 broke this impasse. After the vicar-general appointed José Agustín Caballero as ecclesiastical censor, the Patriotic Society petitioned the captain general (now the recently arrived Salvador de Muro, Marqués de Someruelos) to terminate the exceptional powers of the ecclesiastical censor which had so often impeded publication.[55] The Society argued that the bishop's extensive authority over the periodical press had been purely personal and did not reflect the intent of royal legislation. While no specific response to their request has been uncovered, the captain general supported important gains for creole *literatos* during the next year; by September 1800, Havana enjoyed three new publications. When the Patriotic Society elected Manuel de Zequeira y Arango[56] as editor of the *Papel Periódico* in July 1800, three disappointed candidates took advantage of Havana's expanding and competitive printing scene to found their own *periódicos*. Antonio Robredo, one of the original editors of the *Papel Periódico* in 1793, founded the *Aurora: Correo Político-económico de la Habana* (3 September 1800–March 1810) in the belief that the periodical press was the most effective way "to develop informed citizens."[57] Félix Fernández de Veranés, priest, professor *texto aristotélico*, "public writer," and director of the 1795 *Memorias*, was the probable editor of *La Lonja Mercantil de la Habana* (12 September–12 December 1800), a weekly devoted to economic information.[58] Buenaventura Pascual Ferrer's *El Regañón de la Habana* (30 September 1800–13 April 1802)[59] provided the standard of excellence for this surge of publications, for its pages consciously elaborated the potential of the periodical press and guidelines for its practitioners. Medina calculated that "of all the Spanish American papers of the colonial period," *El Regañón* was "the best written."[60]

For the *literatos* of the Patriotic Society this productive interval following the death of Bishop Trespalacios proved crucial. No individual or institution assumed the bishop's mantle, and his replacement did not arrive for two years. Further, Society literati enjoyed Captain General Someruelos's cooperation; for example, he offered the editors of the *Aurora* not only access to his sources of information on international events but also authorization to print without ecclesiastical clearance.[61] By the time the new bishop, Juan José Díaz de Espada y Landa,[62] arrived in Havana on 25 February 1802, it is uncertain whether he could have recovered the personal prerogatives of his predecessor;[63] in fact, he did not immediately show any inclination to do so. The new bishop presented an entirely different attitude toward the sugarocracy and officialdom. He not only sought membership in the Patriotic Society at its annual meeting in December 1802, but also accepted the directorship for 1803.[64] In the meantime, Bishop Espada reappointed José Agustín Caballero as ecclesiastical censor.

The explanation of the new bishop's very different attitude to the creoles of the Patriotic Society may lie in his peninsular background, his education at the progressive University of Salamanca, or his sponsorship by Manuel Godoy, the controversial royal favorite and careful patron of the Spanish Enlightenment.[65] It is equally possible that his attitude stemmed from more immediate circumstances. In his first summer in Havana, the bishop was saved from yellow fever by the medical intervention of Tomás Romay, who would subsequently become his collaborator in public health advances such as vaccination and public cemeteries.[66] In turn, the Patriotic Society enthusiastically embraced the new prelate. José de Arango y Núñez del Castillo,[67] introducing Espada as president on 13 January 1803, expressed the confidence that the bishop would "know how to harmonize, even integrate, Christian charity and public economy [economía pública]."[68]

The mood of mutual goodwill lasted for several years, allowing Society writers to consolidate their control over press content. This hegemony was publicly paraded in articles published by the Patriotic Society's censors—two prominent members elected at the annual meeting. The censors reviewed submissions that the Society's editor viewed as questionable and published their decisions on rejected items for the edification of contributors and readers. Once again, the censors' reports provide insight into what was considered unacceptable for publication. Twenty-nine examples of censored submissions, 1805–6, outline the range of rejected items.[69] It is striking that controversial items constituted a small minority: a discussion of religion deemed inappropriate for a general audience; a discourse on the subject of beauty accused of containing profane and seductive ideas; several thinly disguised personal attacks on individuals (authors and officials) or powerful groups (*hacendados* charged with usury). The censors rejected the vast majority of items not for dangerous ideas or libelous charges but for failings in style and content. Transgressions of style— word usage, orthography, errors in Latin epigrams—figured in seventeen negative decisions. The censors proscribed twelve items for uninstructive, derivative, or trite content. In rejecting a comparison of the ladies of Havana with their foreign counterparts, for example, they argued that "this type of light composition, since it does not contain an important moral or expose a social vice, must at least have grace and style. . . ." The Society's censors were not only standing guard against "dangerous" ideas; they were also outlining standards of "taste" for the periodical press.

The years 1807–8 witnessed a souring of relations between the bishop and Society *literatos* and his final, unsuccessful attempt to recover episcopal influence over press content. The confrontation seems to have started out as a personal squabble between the ecclesiastical censor, José Agustín Caballero, and Antonio Robredo, editor of *El Aviso* (formerly the *Papel Periódico*). Robredo had marked as "uncivil" certain passages of one of Caballero's verdicts and returned it to the ecclesiastical censor. Caballero was a man of reputation, and on 25 May 1807 he asked Captain General Someruelos to apprise Robredo of the respect due his censorial judgments. In this atmosphere of alerted sensitivities, it is also possible that Caballero finally felt constrained to complain about the eroding authority of his position. He charged that *El Aviso* often published items without ecclesiastical clearance (he cited six specific instances for 1806) and that the *Aurora* had avoided episcopal censure since its inception in 1800. Caballero's ambiguous position as ecclesiastical censor certainly complicated the situation; while he took his position seriously, he was also a prominent member of the Patriotic Society (a member of the 1793 editorial panel and civil censor in 1795–96), a philosophy professor at the San Carlos Seminary, and a progressive intellectual—he introduced the works of Locke and Newton into the highly scholastic curriculum he inherited.[70]

By January 1808 the bishop had joined the controversy, claiming that the impossibility of distinguishing the secular from the ecclesiastical required an overarching ecclesiastical censorship. To illustrate his point, the bishop recounted to Someruelos how the ecclesiastical censor had prevented a doctrinal error in a recent *Aviso* article by substituting the word "benefactions" for "miracles" in an account of the sinking of a frigate. Someruelos rejected this argument and exempted from ecclesiastical censorship "political matters"—news items or published legislation—and reprints from peninsular sources.[71] In effect, the captain general reaffirmed the literary gains of the period since Bishop Trespalacios's death.

The weakness of imperial mechanisms of control (already evident in the inefficacy of Floridablanca's 24 February 1791 legislation) also facilitated the Patriotic Society's control over press content. Although the debility of royal press legislation went unacknowledged until 11 April 1805,[72] the Crown had already recognized the demise of Inquisition vigilance by 1802.[73] The Spanish Inquisition's censures were postpublication, designed to prevent the reprinting of items that either evaded prepublication censorship in the Hispanic press or came from foreign sources with different censorship standards. In the eighteenth century the intellectual grasp of the Spanish Inquisition seems to have declined even as it continued to exceed the standards set by the Roman Inquisition. Marcelin Defourneaux suggests that one result was more *in totem* prohibitions of targeted material rather than selective expurgations.[74] In addition to the writings of Rousseau and Raynal, bawdy tales, and overzealous devotionals, the periodical press was a notable target. Records kept by the Cuban agent of the Inquisition of Cartagena de Indias provide a general idea of the Holy Office's role in the supervision of the periodical press.[75] A May 1791 edict, for example, prohibited, *in totem, El Duende de Madrid* (1735–36) and *El Corresponsal del Censor* (1787). The Cuban records of Inquisition activities, however, suggest that energies waned in the 1790s and collapsed in the following decade. The last substantial entry is dated 19 May 1804; another impediment to local, secular control over press content had been removed.[76]

Despite the eclipse of ecclesiastical censorship, elite monopoly of the medium ensured a fundamental consistency in the regimen of censorship—an awareness of information that could not be printed in a medium that (at least potentially) was "*para todas manos.*" While Patriotic Society members might wish, to the discomfiture of the bishop, to indulge in literary allusions to the Ancients in the press, or to rail privately against the "sonorous stupidities of rancid scholasticism,"[77] they argued that the new medium should, as the bishop suggested, be restricted to promoting agriculture, the useful arts, and commerce.[78] The *Papel Periódico* (under its several names) specialized in governmental edicts, minutes of official bodies such as the *consulado,* and advertisements relating to sugar, slaves, and property. The *Aurora* concentrated upon international events, primarily wars and natural disasters, and the gossip of the European courts. Its editors' close collaboration with the captain general ensured a content as discreet as the Patriotic Society's own paper.[79]

For most of a decade, noted the editors of the *Aurora* in 1808, their publication had successfully gratified public curiosity about international affairs while simultaneously "guiding public opinion on public affairs without recourse to coercive means, toward ends agreeable to the Government."[80] The complicity of elite litterateur and colonial official typifies the first phase of the Cuban press, although this does not seem to be true for the colonial Hispanic press[81] in general: the *Diario de México* endured direct viceregal censorship, the *Telégrafo Mercantil* (Buenos Aires) ceased publication because of official disapproval, and the *Gaceta de Guatemala* lost an editor to the prisons of the Inquisition.[82] In Cuba, however, a happy congruence of priorities produced a significant, elite-monitored periodical press.[83] Only the sensational crisis of 1808 in Spain eventually disturbed this equilibrium.

The crisis represented the bitter harvest of the alliance with France. French troops crossed the Pyrenees in 1807 to battle the Portuguese and the British and then refused to leave the peninsula. By February 1808, Napoleon's armies had captured Barcelona and were marching on Madrid. Partisans of the royal heir, Ferdinand, took advantage of the political crisis and compelled Charles IV to abdicate in favor of his son on 19 March. On 2 May 1808 French troops brutally crushed a popular uprising in Madrid and on 10 May forced Ferdinand to renounce the throne and join his father in exile in Bayonne. On 6 July 1808, Napoleon presented the Spanish nation with the Constitution of Bayonne, and on 25 July, he placed his brother, Joseph Bonaparte, on the throne of Spain.[84]

Official word of the royal family's capture circulated in Havana by 17 July 1808, although the news already had become commonplace. The situation was explosive, aggravated by deteriorating economic conditions occasioned by international conflicts, particularly the British maritime retaliation for Spain's 1804 alliance with the French. When United States President Thomas Jefferson responded to French and English attacks on U.S. neutral shipping by freezing foreign commerce in December 1807, the island became almost completely isolated. The cost of imports soared, the sugar harvest remained unsold, and sugar and coffee prices plummeted.[85] The island began to experience the negative implications of sugar monoculture. Planters, in the rush for expansion, had cut down forests, seized tobacco fields, and eliminated slave gardens. While these and other measures promoted greater and more concentrated production, they also made Cuba much more vulnerable to volatile foreign markets, uncertain foreign imports, and expensive credit arrangements.

In this context of economic crisis, seventy-three citizens led by Francisco de Arango and Deputy Governor José Ilincheta petitioned the Havana city council on 26 July 1808 to form a Junta Suprema de Gobierno in emulation of the peninsular juntas that had appeared to confront the French invader in the name of Ferdinand VII. This proved to be a decisive moment, for the formation of such juntas in other colonial centers contributed to the momentum for political independence. The petition, not unexpectedly, ran into opposition from many colonial officials—Royal Finance, the tobacco monopoly, the naval establishment, all bureaucracies directly responsible to the Ministry of the Indies—and peninsular mercantile interests. The key to its failure, however, lay in the opposition from the military, specifically the many Cuban creoles who had risen in the ranks of the regular army and the militia during the reform of colonial defenses; they identified their prestige and corporate privileges with the imperial system.[86]

Arango and Ilincheta, faced with their failure to mobilize sufficient support, withdrew their petition, and Cuba took the first step toward its reputation as the "ever-faithful isle." It was an auspicious first step because it indicated that Cuban loyalty was not merely the product of fears of political innovation—the specter of Saint-Domingue—but also was purchased with the hard currency of imperial concessions and nurtured by the actions of such colonial officials as Las Casas and Someruelos. In 1793 and 1805, and against imperial wishes in 1799, 1801, and 1808, the captains general of Cuba had proved themselves sensitive to creole demands for freer trade.[87] Of course there were the other, less positive motivations for loyalty. The events surrounding the expulsion of French residents from the island in 1809 proved particularly instructive to the island's white population. Members of the militia had to be mustered to suppress the violence and vandalism attributed to the "population of color." In this environment, there were few individuals willing to challenge the structures of authority, particularly the corporate privileges of the military.[88]

The status quo, however, did not go unchallenged from outside Cuba, and here the periodical press assumed a crucial and contradictory role. The periodical press had become increasingly vital to Captain General Someruelos's attempts to stay abreast of events during his protracted governance. While predecessors like Las Casas had relied primarily upon ship captains, passengers, and personal correspondence to anticipate or flesh out official communiqués,[89] Someruelos relied more upon the periodical press. In both instances the information often came to the captain general through the governor of Santiago de Cuba, whose jurisdiction placed him in much closer proximity to Jamaica, a primary source of world news. In the time of Las Casas, the governor might send letters synthesizing the latest intelligence gleaned from a slaver returning from Kingston.[90] By 1806, newspapers, primarily from Jamaica but also from New York, New Orleans, and London, dominated the remissions of Governor Kindelán.[91] Santiago de Cuba was a particularly valuable funnel of information during periods when the international situation reduced foreign trade, for the Jamaican papers still arrived through the surreptitious agency of Danish shipping, French pirates, or contrabandists.[92] Someruelos's dependence upon the periodical press intensified during the events surrounding the collapse of Spanish resistance to Napoleon—the flight of the Central Junta from Madrid in early December 1808, the convocation of delegates from the Americas the following month, and the military reverses of November 1809 to January 1810 that finally reduced the loyalist jurisdiction to the virtually impregnable port city of Cádiz.

At the same time, however, the press constituted a major threat to the island's determined tranquility. On 1 February 1809, Someruelos decreed vigilance so that neither foreigners nor "incendiary papers" should penetrate the island as a by-product of the economic expediency of neutral shipping.[93] It was a generalized concern of colonial officialdom, heightened even further after July 1809 by news of Joseph Napoleon's scheme to promote revolution in the Americas by "seditious" and "inflammatory" "gazettes and other papers."[94] Events of 1810 vastly complicated the situation: American creoles proclaimed provincial juntas in Caracas on 19 April and in Santiago de Chile on 18 September, deposed the viceroys of Buenos Aires and New Granada in May and July, triggered a popular uprising in Mexico in September, and initiated a second insurrection in Quito in October. Suddenly, the sources of contagion had multiplied. Some, like the superintendent of the tobacco monopoly and former intendant, Rafael Gómez Roubaud, claimed that Someruelos exploited this paranoia about the press to gain even more authority over the island.[95] This charge contained a grain of truth, for during some periods of his lengthy tenure (13 May 1799–14 April 1812), Someruelos virtually governed without advice from Spain. Yet it is clear that the Jamaican press, for example, did seek to subvert the political order in Cuba. Most often this involved erroneous accounts of political unrest or imminent political transformation and on occasion blatant appeals for the formation of patriotic juntas in emulation of mainland precedents. The most notable instance was the article "Proclamation/Caracas á Cuba," which appeared in the *Jamaica Courant,* 10 November 1810.[96] The proclamation, inviting Cubans to "reform the Ancient Government" and "establish a Junta to govern the island" in the name of Ferdinand VII, was also printed in the *St. Jago Gazette,* 3–10 November 1810.[97]

The sugarocracy and the periodical press pointedly ignored the Jamaican challenge and made a determined effort to link the island's political fate to Spain. Sentiment as well as expediency supported this position. Cubans, perhaps more than any other group of American Spaniards, felt a transatlantic bond to Mother Spain. In recent decades *habaneros* had taken quickly to European travel and participated in politics at the Spanish court.[98] After the abortive attempt to establish a junta, creoles reaffirmed their ties to Spain. In October 1808 Arango and the Havana municipal council pledged loyalty to Ferdinand VII and the newly created Junta Central but asked that Cuba be considered not a colony but the equal of any peninsular province.[99] This remained their position even after it became apparent that the Junta Central would not implement the promised equality of New World possessions within the Spanish "nation." Peninsular delegates to the Junta Central, chosen by a different representational formula, outnumbered American delegates twenty-six to ten.[100] Still, any representation seemed flattering and held the promise of further political gains. Cuban loyalty may have been shortsighted but no more so than the sugarocracy's eager embrace of sugar monoculture. Indeed, as always, there was a connection: political resolve was strengthened by the recovery of economic prosperity resulting from Spain's alliance with Britain and the end of the United States embargo on foreign trade.

The Cuban absorption in peninsular politics also affected the press. Public curiosity regarding the events in Spain and Europe prompted a new officially sanctioned source, *El Mensagero Político Económico-literario de la Habana.* Issued in January 1809 by Manuel de Zequeira and the naturalist and government official José Antonio de la Ossa,[101] this biweekly originated as a patriotic contribution to the Spanish resistance to Napoleon. Its editors personally donated funds for the relief of the survivors of the Battle of Zaragoza by selling two thousand copies of Zequeira's poem mourning those who had died resisting the French.[102] By focusing on coverage of peninsular news, they hoped to stimulate similar acts of patriotism from other Cubans. Of course, they also aimed at supplanting the

Aurora (it did fail in March 1810). Zequeira later admitted that public curiosity about events in the peninsula gave *El Mensagero* six hundred subscribers within the first three months.[103]

By late 1810, *El Mensagero* and the original *Papel Periódico*, now a daily titled the *Diario de la Habana*, were the only newspapers in Cuba, and Patriotic Society writers had dominated the press for two decades. It is important to appreciate the implications of this restricted literary situation. The press furnished elite Cuban creoles with a vehicle to express, if not a sense of national identity, at least an agenda of self-interest—free trade, increased sugar production, and slave imports. Yet this monopoly also froze the evolution of the medium and limited its impact upon Cuban society. It allowed a literary elite to define the acceptable boundaries of public expression and to suppress topics that might have attracted a larger readership.

In arguing that content defined the circulation and impact of the Cuban periodical press prior to 1811, it is not necessary to dismiss all other factors. There were economic obstacles. Paper costs and paper shortages were constant concerns reflecting the royal paper monopoly's inability to adjust to unprecedented demand. On 27 and 28 January 1809, *El Aviso*'s new editor, Tomás Agustín Cervantes, reported to the Patriotic Society that the main impediment to expanding circulation to cover the entire island was the mail rate which lumped printed matter in the same category as private letters, despite the fact that differential rates were already the norm in Spain.[104] Literacy might seem an even more substantial factor. Though high by Spanish American standards, Cuban literacy rates were indeed low in comparison to Western European rates. Jorge Domínguez has calculated that "not more than 10–12 percent of adult Cubans [fifteen years and older] would have been literate before 1820."[105] Literacy statistics reflected the exclusion of the "population of color" from primary schools and the slow development of primary schools prior to the dramatic increases of the 1820s (39 schools and 731 students in 1793; 71 schools and more than 2,000 students in 1801; and 2,793 enrolled in 1817).[106]

Yet for all the importance of literacy, circulation levels of the Cuban press were well below even conservative estimates of the literate population of the island, suggesting that other factors must be considered. Tomás Agustín Cervantes, who assumed editorship of the Society's paper in 1808, recognized the connection between content and circulation. Although subscriptions had risen from 126 in 1794 to just fewer than 400 by 1802, they had fallen to 277 by the beginning of his term, and Cervantes diagnosed the problem as content. As a remedy he added a number of features—increased detail about shipping and ship passengers, deaths and burials, and astrological and religious features—and these changes, coupled with increased curiosity about events in the peninsula, raised subscriptions to 500 by November 1810.[107] Cervantes's analysis was practical and limited in scope; restricted by censorship and self-interest, he did not contemplate the possibility of dramatically increasing readership by substantially altering the fare of the *Diario*.

Comparative press studies also argue for the importance of content in certain literary situations. Here it is important not to treat the English development as typical. Enjoying a tradition of greater press freedom and less dominated by a literary elite, English newspapers geared themselves to the concerns of a population that was more than 50 percent literate. In this situation, the upper limits of readership might be constrained only by literacy or printing technology. France, by contrast, conformed to the more restrictive continental pattern of press evolution that applies to the Hispanic press before 1811. French literacy was at least 10 percent below the English level, but this cannot account for the significantly smaller number of newspapers and readers in a country with a substantially larger population. Rather, it was the aristocratic control of the press, or at least the projection of aristocratic values by those involved in the heavily censored press, that set a literary fare beyond the scope of all but the aristocracy and those who aspired to that status: "Instead of appearing responsive to the daily interest of ordinary Frenchmen, these editors presumed to know what sophisticated readers might find uplifting."[108] Indeed, studies of French printing reveal a "narrow circle of affluent, reliable, and respectable publishers [whose business] . . . was apt to be more oriented toward achieving monopolistic advantage than toward winning the favor of additional consumers."[109] The same principle seems to have been operating in the Cuban case.

If the Patriotic Society's literary monopoly determined the function of the Cuban periodical press to 1810, it also defined the career associated with it. For the most part, on the eve of the first free press experiment, the job of *periodista* was still just one outlet of the Cuban man of letters and not his means of support. Oratorical skills were equally valued, and they extensively influenced writing style and in fact provided the basis for many *impresos:* elegies, discourses, and sermons.[110] The typical profile of fifteen men of letters[111] who made substantial editorial and creative contributions would reveal someone born in Havana in the 1760s or early 1770s, educated at the San Carlos Seminary and the University of Havana, accepted as a Patriotic Society member by 1795, and employed as a public official or university professor.[112] A composite sketch is an appropriate representative of this group, which might be considered Cuba's first literary generation; in addition to shared values and literary conventions, the extensive practice of anonymous and pseudonymous publication obscured their individuality. By 1810, only the *Diario*'s editor, Tomás Agustín Cervantes, diverged significantly from this pattern. Cervantes represented a new generation—he was born in 1782 and would not become a Society member until 1808. He might also be considered the island's first and only full-time journalist, although he would later assume his father's position in the finance bureaucracy.[113] Still, in all other ways the editor of the official daily emulated his literary elders, particularly in his view that a closely edited periodical press was crucial to "fixing public opinion."[114]

Cervantes inherited the literary gains and boundaries of the first two decades of periodical press evolution. Through a fortuitous combination of local initiative, episcopal eclipse, and imperial ineffectiveness, the Patriotic Society, abetted by an amenable colonial official, captured control over press content during the first decade of the nineteenth century.[115] However, the vigilance of the Patriotic Society's own censorship mechanisms meant that the transition from episcopal to Society dominance could only be glimpsed dimly in the pages of the periodical press. There was justice in the observation that *habaneros* subscribed to the Society's paper for "no other reason than to know what slave was for sale, what house to rent, or what ship had entered port." Literary content did not exceed "an insipid letter, a poetic delirium, or at best, a fragment of the first book that came into the hands of the editor."[116] Yet this judgment was less a comment on literary talents than on the deliberate restraint of Society literati. The content of the printed page and the relative absence of controversial items in the censorship materials argue that they demonstrated a refined sensitivity to consensual limitations on periodical press content. This is nowhere more evident than in the contrast between the Cuban press and newspapers from the United States, England, and Europe, which circulated in select circles on the island either in their original form or as reprints in the increasingly pervasive Jamaican press.[117]

That Cuban men of letters did not exploit their literary monopoly for more spectacular achievements does not deny the significance of their struggle for control over censorship. With caution it seems possible to interpret the Patriotic Society's efforts as an aspect of the secularization of a sugar elite whose single-minded pursuit of efficient production led to conflict with ecclesiastical interests. Episcopal interference in the publishing of useful information was as unacceptable as other obstacles to sugar production: meatless Fridays, religious holidays, and tithing on the profits from new sugar mills.[118]

Yet the meaning and scope of the term "secularization" should be carefully qualified. The Patriotic Society's assault on episcopal prerogative does indicate secularization in the sense of a growing separation of church/state realms of influence. The evidence does not necessarily confirm a new secular worldview or even an anticlerical bias. For example, the confrontation between the Patriotic Society and Bishop Trespalacios, 1793–95, might be just as appropriately viewed as political—the local elite and allies in officialdom opposing an intransigent "outsider" and his intimate coterie. Nor does the Patriotic Society's tutelage after 1800 correspond to the classic pattern of the periodical press and secularization in Europe during the second half of the century—the mass-production steam press which expanded readership and, as Owen Chadwick has speculated, intensified divergent opinions to the detriment of "established moral agreements upon which the consensus of European society rested."[119] The secularization of the Cuban periodical press to 1810, then, primarily signified the quest of a literary elite for self-censorship.

CHAPTER 2

Free Press:
Libel and Exoneration,
1811–1814

FOR CUBA, the peninsular political crisis acquired new dimensions when the Spanish Cortes approved free press legislation on 10 November 1810. This legislation guaranteed the right of Spaniards to "write, print and publish their political ideas . . . not only as a brake on the arbitrariness of those who govern, but also as a means of enlightening the nation in general, and as the only means of knowledge of true public opinion."[1] It abolished all previous prepublication censorship procedures and panels, and required prior censorship only for writings on doctrinal or ecclesiastical matters.

The free press legislation was a priority of the Cortes that gathered for its first session on 24 September 1810. In this policy it deviated both from its medieval predecessors and from the initial plans of its convener, the Central Junta, which summoned it to unify Spaniards against the French.[2] The logistical impediments to reconstituting the Cortes on the basis of estates[3] led the Central Junta, on 1 January 1810, to impose a straight representational formula,[4] but subsequent military reverses, the collapse of the Central Junta, and the retreat of patriotic forces to Cádiz further complicated the selection process and restricted the pool of potential representatives. It was decided that areas too distant from Cádiz (the Americas) or under foreign occupation (Castile, Catalonia) would be represented temporarily by substitute deputies—native sons resident in Cádiz. This expedient also proved decisive for the political composition of the Cortes: not only had the nobility and clergy lost their customary influence, but the deputies would be "largely liberals, patriots, and surprisingly young, because the people who had fled to Cádiz were largely liberals, patriots, and young enough to have undertaken the arduous journey to what was thought of as a last enclave of free Spain."[5] Once assembled, the Cortes assumed the role of a constituent congress and began to work on legislation for a free press and a constitution to limit the power of the monarchy.

The peculiar circumstances of the deputies, and the intimate connection of French and Spanish history since the French Revolution, left their mark on the free press legislation. While acknowledging the positive example of the French revolutionary press, the legislators confronted the more immediate experience of the Napoleonic occupation. The French immediately took over Spanish publications in captured territory, imposed the death penalty for authors or sellers of seditious *impresos*, and used the press to mount a propaganda campaign. French actions against the Hispanic press, therefore, linked periodical press freedom to the cause of resistance to Napoleon. Spanish patriots countered the French press offensive with *periódicos* of their own. The weekly *Semanario Patriótico*, for example, appeared in Madrid on 1 September 1808, during a period when the city was once again under Spanish control. When Napoleon led his troops into Madrid on 4 December 1808, however, the editors of the *Semanario* had already fled with their presses to Seville. The *periódico* was reestablished there on 4 May 1809 only to retreat to Cádiz after the 31 August 1809 issue. In Cádiz, Manuel José Quintana, one of the editors of the peripatetic *periódico*, led the agitation for free press legislation. The minority of delegates who backed this proposal won the day by superior oratory in the Cortes and the support of the intimidating public gallery that attended these sessions.[6]

In Havana, the *Diario de la Habana*'s unauthorized publication of the text of the free press legislation on 21 January 1811 placed the captain general in a difficult position.[7] Someruelos had become increasingly preoccupied with the rumors of political turmoil in Cuba published by the Jamaican press,[8] and now he faced the probability of similarly "irresponsible" items printed locally. He was therefore tempted to delay implementation of a free press by using a loophole in the legislation that declared free press conditional upon the creation of a supreme censorship board and regional counterparts in Spain and the Americas. Indeed, this stipulation became one of the pretexts used to suspend free press legislation in other parts of the American possessions. Faced with popular insurrection in New Spain, Viceroy Francisco Javier Venegas delayed implementation until the promulgation of the constitution on 30 September 1812 (press freedom lasted only until December),[9] while Peruvian Viceroy José de Abascal technically "adhered to the free press decree, but . . . intervened personally whenever he found a publication to be dangerous and made the writing of dissident literature so risky that few persons in Peru attempted it."[10] Once again, Cuba pursued a unique course. After consultation with the ranking judge of the Audiencia (high court of justice) on 8 February, Someruelos decided he could not risk public reaction to such a stalling tactic; he appointed an interim censorship panel and declared free press on 18 February 1811.[11]

The first test of the new literary environment came from an unlikely source: members of the interim censorship panel appointed by Someruelos. Domingo Mendoza, professor at the San Carlos Seminary and one of the original editors of the *Papel Periódico* in 1793, and José Agustín Caballero, last noted in his role as ecclesiastical censor, had recently received permission to publish a *periódico* to discuss whether the sword or the pen might contribute most to the "destruction of French vandalism." Shorn of rhetoric, *El Lince* (1 February 1811–1 May 1812?) was the effort of these two prominent literary men to raise contributions for the Spanish resistance to Napoleon. Problems arose when they refused to abandon their *periódico* after their appointment to the interim censorship board. To reduce conflict of interest, they began to rely upon reprints from other sources. Publishing a free press editorial from the *Tertulia de Cádiz*, or an excerpt from the writings of Baron Humboldt criticizing the excessive financial burdens of superfluous colonial bureaucrats, removed Mendoza and Caballero from the dangerous position of seeing an original article denounced before a censorship panel to which they belonged.

Their strategy did not appease Someruelos,[12] and they com-

Figure 2-1. Major Cuban Periódicos, 1811–1814

1811	1812	1813	1814
J F M A M J J A S O N D	J F M A M J J A S O N D	J F M A M J J A S O N D	J F M A M J J A S O N D

Diario de la Habana

Mensagero / Gaceta Diaria
8

Patriota Americano

Lince

1   1 (May)
Semanario Mercantil / Noticioso   /
6   12
Correo
16   4
Censor Universal
7   27
Eco (SC)
10 24
Tertulia
23
Frayle
4   26
Reparón
13   29
Perinola
25 29
Ramillete (SC)
18   9
Cena
14   31
Diario Cívico
1
Centinela
8   26
Espejo de Puerto Príncipe

Actas (SC)
3   18
Filósofo Verdadero
15   22
Esquife
1   30
Patriota (M)
22   17
Miscelánea (SC)
13   24
Café
1 31

KEY
——————— Publication verified
------------- Incomplete publication data
(SC) Santiago de Cuba
(M) Matanzas

pounded their unpopularity by boycotting the censorship board to protest an accusation of partisanship aired in the Havana municipal council.[13] The controversy revolved around the censorship board's debate over an article critical of ecclesiastical management of burial grounds.[14] "To make a profit with the ashes of the dead" was one of the phrases denounced by Antonio Eusebio Ramos on behalf of the bishop. The three secular censors voted that the article did not constitute libel against the bishop, yet they agreed that all copies should be collected and detained. Mendoza and Caballero, undoubtedly frustrated by this inconsistent verdict, tried to win an amendment acknowledging an affront to episcopal authority. They were not successful; the controversy was left unsettled, prompting the suggestion in the municipal council that Mendoza and Caballero were the bishop's henchmen. Mendoza and Caballero felt particularly insulted that Someruelos, who presided over the meeting, had not defended their reputations. They refused to attend further meetings of the censorship board until the issue was settled, and their absence effectively halted censorial supervision of the Havana press. Such a stalemate only invited further abuse of the free press, and Someruelos appealed to the bishop to intervene. Considering the nature of the accusation, it is not surprising that the bishop declined. Fortunately for Someruelos, the arrival of the official appointments to the censorship panel ended the stalemate.[15]

The incident illustrates the fragility of the new press procedures—a single controversy within the supervisory panel paralyzed the process of postpublication censorship. When Mendoza and Caballero began to print all correspondence relating to the affair in *El Lince,* including confidential minutes of the censorship panel and Someruelos's ultimatums, the confrontation took on new proportions. Someruelos's mounting anger reflected a colonial official's difficult adjustment to new standards of public expression and structures of control. The publication of official and confidential documents shocked him and intensified his concerns about the disruptive potential of a free press.

Despite these early inefficiencies of the censorship process, the coming of free press to Havana did not produce the literary chaos of Cádiz—what one anonymous author termed the "Diarrhea of the Presses."[16] Postpublication censorship, though less efficient than its prepublication variant, was still in the hands of the sugarocracy: the provincial censorship board comprised five individuals of sufficient reputation to be nominated by the Supreme Censorship Board and appointed by the Cortes. As long as the *literatos* of the Patriotic Society still dominated the periodical press, the opportunity for radically expanded expression in the press did not erase the constraints that had conditioned two decades of literary life. Major political innovation, inviting economic ruin and racial conflagration on the model of Haiti, remained unthinkable. Cubans who desired greater political participation, as well as those who opposed already existing innovations, studiously avoided direct criticism of the new political status quo. This unofficial literary truce meant that the Cuban free press at this point generally eschewed explicit clashes of ideology. New energies activated by the opportunity of a free press found expression instead in surrogate battles between literary personalities and other outbursts of personal attack and vindication.

To appreciate the scope of problems precipitated by these battles over personal reputation, it is necessary to understand the broad connotations given to the crime of libel. Libel was not confined to cases involving clear defamation of local citizens. For example, on 21 October 1811, José Rafael de Ugarte denounced an item in the *Diario de la Habana* (No. 417) for denigrating the effectiveness and safety of a product he was using in his medical practice. As the item enjoyed a royal patent, Ugarte accused the author of libeling the product's unnamed inventor. On 7 December 1811, the censorship board agreed, finding the article's criticism insulting to the patent holder "because it judged him to be ignorant." They ordered the recall of all copies within two days. [17]

Most accusations of libel, however, did derive from more personal attacks, often expressed in pamphlet form, typically four to sixteen printed pages published to air a single theme or grievance. Heir to the handwritten *anónimo*, a sheet of paper which might be posted furtively in a prominent place in the city, pamphlets were favored by "public writers" and private individuals who sought to influence public opinion without the larger commitment required by a regularly issued *periódico*. There were moderate voices, like José de Arango, whose writing cautioned authorities not to overreact to the problem of libel or to create protected categories for officialdom within the free press legislation. [18] More often, however, pamphlets targeted the powerful, reflecting the aspirations of those individuals who wished to replace them with only minimal change to the overall system. This represented a dramatic assault on the social hierarchy. Those who formerly had found protection in wealth and power now learned that their prominence invited public discussion of both their public and private behavior.

The declaration of a free press initiated a period of experimentation with the new boundaries of legal expression and libel. In the vanguard was Tomás Gutiérrez de Piñeres, a peninsular cleric and lawyer for the previous episcopal administration,[19] who could not forgive the sugarocracy's opposition to his mentor, Bishop Trespalacios. More specifically, as Piñeres was candid enough to admit, he blamed the judiciary for more than eleven years of litigation over the dissolution of a sugar mill partnership. Piñeres achieved notoriety with a series of pamphlets that charged the Audiencia with judicial inefficiency and incompetence. *Declamación primera contra el despotismo del poder judicial*, dated 12 November 1811, charged Regent Luis de Chaves with nepotism and intimidation of other members of the court. Official reaction was not long in coming; on 14 December 1811, the *Diario* broadcast the censorship board's verdict of libel against Piñeres.

The censors' ruling did not intimidate the cleric, for he claimed that only the bishop was legally competent to judge his literary production.[20] As Piñeres followed with further charges against the highest court on the island, he found a powerful, if unofficial, ally in the captain general. Someruelos had his own motivations for permitting attacks on the Audiencia, for he desired to see the court transferred from Puerto Príncipe to Havana, where it could be controlled more effectively, and to date the Audiencia had stubbornly and successfully resisted this move. In private correspondence with the justice minister, Ignacio de Pezuela, Someruelos corroborated certain charges of judicial irregularity; while praising Regent Chaves as a "great legist and very incorrupt," he admitted that Chaves was despotic (*voluntarioso*) and should be retired.[21] At the same time, Someruelos tolerated Piñeres's subsequent accusations against the Audiencia. On 20 March 1812, *Declamación nona* criticized the court's persecution of the cadet Mariano Acosta for allegedly affixing an *anónimo* to the door of one of the judges. Four days later, the next pamphlet attacked the court for infringing on legal jurisdictions outlined by the free press legislation. Piñeres praised Someruelos for overruling the Audiencia and limiting its access to the *Diario*.[22] The praise was well earned. On 28 March 1812, the Audiencia complained that the captain general still had not responded to its 19 February letter recommending that the bishop silence Piñeres; noting the cleric's continued offenses, they reiterated their demand that Piñeres be expelled from the island as "an incorrigible cleric."[23]

Piñeres's pamphlets illustrate some of the problems with libel at this stage of free press development. Controversy usually started over a question of reputation or litigation and widened into an attack upon those in public office or the judiciary. Typically, an author like Piñeres would justify his attacks upon authority by citing the preamble of the free press legislation—the free press's mission to counteract arbitrary acts of the powerful and to enlighten public opinion—and would argue, with some justification, that local authorities were only paying lip service to this legislative intent.[24] Local authorities, such as the Audiencia, would respond by bemoaning a literary state of war in which the system of censorship appeals (one to the provincial board and two to the Supreme Censorship Board in Spain) allowed guilty parties to compound their crimes before a final judgment could be rendered on their first offense.[25] At the same time, Piñeres's case was exceptional because he argued successfully for some time that his clerical status removed him from the jurisdiction of the provincial censorship board, and because the captain general apparently tolerated attacks on the Audiencia for his own reasons.

Neither clerical status nor official toleration protected most authors, including the most controversial *periodista* of the first constitutional period—Simón Bergaño y Villegas. It is ironic that this individual, who would dominate the periodical press from 1811 to 1814, was in Havana only as a prisoner in transit to Spain. The Guatemalan Audiencia had indicted him as a "libertine and corruptor" for opinions expressed as author and editor (1802?–1806) of the official gazette of the Guatemalan capital. Biographical detail is sketchy, but John Tate Lanning has speculated that Bergaño's physical infirmities (he was crippled by a childhood fall from a tree), his indeterminate social origins, and his reading of Feijóo combined to form the "ideal revolutionary ingredients."[26] Although this portrait is highly conjectural, there is no doubt that the young editor ran afoul of the archbishop of Guatemala.

On 8 January 1806, the archbishop denounced six examples of Bergaño's writing published between July 1803 and January 1806. These articles ranged in subject from a medical discourse on hermaphrodites to an attack on the efficacy of prayer. Bergaño's pretensions to classical poetry also offended the archbishop. Three of the six items involved Bergaño's devotion to Venus and Bacchus. One article compared the turbulent emotions of a young lover at the approach of his beloved to those felt by the sinner at the tolling of the church bells.[27] The Guatemalan Audiencia ruled in favor of the archbishop and decreed Bergaño's removal to Spain; for lack of a ship bound directly to Spain, however, they sent him to Havana to await passage. The Audiencia warned Someruelos that despite the prisoner's poor health, they considered him dangerous enough to be held incommunicado.[28]

By 16 May 1809, Someruelos had accepted the Guatemalan Audiencia's conditions that he be responsible for remitting the prisoner to Spain. In practical terms, this meant assuring that Bergaño was in satisfactory health to make the ocean crossing. Medical reports were not good, however; the lower half of Bergaño's body was completely paralyzed, he had lost control over bowel and bladder, and he suffered from two exposed ulcers.[29] On 24 July, the inspector of hospitals speculated that the prisoner might never recover sufficiently to make the ocean voyage, further delaying Bergaño's deportation. By the following year, however, Bergaño's health had improved, and doctors recommended fresh air to build up his strength for a series of operations. As this plan involved even less confinement for the prisoner, they sought Someruelos's permission. He granted it but also asked the intendant to investigate which ships were ready to leave for Spain. As there were no ships that could accommodate the prisoner's need for space and medical supervision, deportation was postponed again. Once again Bergaño won a reprieve by his precarious balance between the danger of death and the "safety" of illness. Meanwhile, he enjoyed his carriage rides and sought to enlarge his literary reputation.[30]

Bergaño's vehicle was *El Patriota Americano* (January 1811–December 1812), the second *periódico* launched shortly before the formal declaration of a free press on 18 February 1811.[31] *El Patriota Americano* was a collaborative effort on the part of Bergaño, José del Castillo (a young creole educated in

Baltimore and admitted that year to the Patriotic Society), and Nicolás Ruiz (a litterateur who by September would also be editing *El Mensagero*).[32] Filled with the image of themselves as "public writers" contributing to the common good, the editors of *El Patriota* avoided the news items and international gossip that were the province of *El Mensagero*. In a *revista* format designed for eventual binding into book form, they discoursed on key issues for creoles who linked their fate to the peninsular political transformation: the nature of patriotism, the functioning of the projected constitution, and the legal status of the American possessions within the Spanish nation. This selective focus, coupled with a project to collect data for a history of the island, ensured *El Patriota*'s reputation with subsequent generations of Society members. It did not guarantee popular success, however, especially when a free press opened wider options for attracting readers. Bergaño soon abandoned *El Patriota* to experiment with press freedom.[33]

Bergaño's new publication, the *Correo de las Damas*, issued on 16 March 1811 in collaboration with the litterateur and translator Joaquín José García,[34] became the first innovative *periódico* to be published under the new free press guidelines. Maintaining that the female populace was not "born condemned to ignorance," the *Correo* offered its pages to compensate for the male monopoly over education beyond the primary level.[35] A periodical publication addressed to a female audience signified an important new trend in the Hispanic press.[36] Still, female readership is difficult to measure—of 204 subscribers listed by issue 14, only 69 were women—and the publication often seemed directed to the male populace of Havana. One editorial asked, "Will we not be content with caging [women] like dangerous animals, imprisoned in body and spirit, without wishing to tyrannize their minds as well?"[37] The general content of the *Correo*, however, makes it obvious that its male editors sought not to educate their readers but to entertain, to develop their own reputations for wit and literary style on the larger scale allowed by a free press. Sensational topics such as "violence, seduction, and other excesses" allowed Bergaño to satisfy a penchant for moralizing. Ironically, his columns of counsel and correction under the pseudonym *La vieja* shared space with reprints of the torrid poetry that had so offended the archbishop of Guatemala.

It is difficult to judge which aspect of this ambivalent literary style catalyzed Bergaño's adversaries into attacking his ambiguous position as a criminal outside prison walls. The most vocal critic at this stage may have been the *Tertulia de las Damas* (30 April 1811–August 1812); Bergaño's satiric obituary for the *Tertulia*, diagnosing "a great weakness and scarcity of nourishment," was almost certainly the cause.[38] The *Tertulia* responded with a satiric funeral for the *Correo*, unleashing a series of rejoinders that would end with the publication of documents revealing Bergaño's prosecution in Guatemala.[39] Bergaño's journalism was also attracting more dangerous opponents—the captain general, the bishop, and the censorship panel. Already on 8 June 1811, Someruelos's legal advisor, Juan Ignacio Rendón, suggested that Bergaño could be denounced to the Inquisition for blaspheming the virgin birth and denying the existence of eternal hellfire. Judging from the captain general's favorable reaction to this proposal, he already regretted having accepted charge of the prisoner.[40]

The bishop of Havana joined Bergaño's detractors after issues 47 and 48 of the *Correo* featured a story about the seduction of a young woman. The bishop reacted immediately with a printed pastoral on 2 September, but the censorship panel still had not passed judgment when issue 63 of the *Correo* compounded the offense with a review of the Havana press that referred explicitly to episcopal interference with press freedom.[41] The bishop decided to take matters into his own hands, and the *Diario* on 3 November contained an episcopal prohibition on all three issues. Apparently, the bishop also applied some pressure on the printer Lorenzo Palmer, for when Bergaño attempted to print issue 67 of the *Correo*, which contained new accusations against the bishop, he found Palmer unwilling to do so. Bergaño had to appeal to Someruelos and cite the letter of the free press legislation before Palmer could be persuaded, one day later, to print the number.[42] Under episcopal pressure, the censorship panel finally condemned the story as contrary to public decency and accepted custom (*buenas costumbres*). They ruled that "both papers are filled with a thousand specious reflections, promoting immodesty and prostitution, and they lack the decency with which one should address the public."[43]

Despite this judgment, the bishop had to wait nearly three months for his personal vindication; on 22 February 1812, the censorship panel finally found two of Bergaño's writings to be injurious and libelous to the bishop's reputation, especially those passages in which Bergaño had presumed to instruct the bishop in the meaning of the scriptures.[44] The timing and the fashionable anti-French language in the verdict—Bergaño's actions were compared to the harassment of the archbishop of Paris by "the libertine, obscene and proscribed Rousseau"—indicate that the censorship board had joined the bishop as one of Bergaño's targets and now had a larger stake in prosecuting him. Indeed, they overstepped their jurisdiction by recommending penalties to the captain general. Someruelos's legal advisor, Leonardo del Monte, had to point out that only the judiciary could assess penalties, but having said that, del Monte was forced to admit that the judiciary was stymied by Bergaño's peculiar status: his poor physical condition and absolute poverty meant that he could be punished "neither through the body nor the purse."[45]

The literary antics of Bergaño and the sensational charges of Piñeres tend to distract attention from the full dimensions and tone of literary production during the first year of free press. Whereas the periodical press in the previous decade had been largely limited to the *Papel Periódico* (biweekly to 1805, triweekly from 1805 to 1810) and the *Aurora* (weekly), by the beginning of the second year of free press Havana boasted ten *periódicos:* two dailies, one triweekly, and seven weeklies.[46] The multiplication of pamphlets was equally impressive.[47] Prior to 1808, the yearly number featuring royal orders, episcopal pastorals, and Patriotic Society memorials may not have exceeded ten. Beginning in 1808, the peninsular crisis more than doubled this number by adding patriotic publications against the French, orations for fallen heroes, and official communiqués about European events (twenty-five in 1808, nineteen in 1809). The number dropped precipitously in 1810 (six) but recovered the following year (twenty-six) as the free press encouraged individuals like Piñeres to put their grievances into print. This new function of the press was in even greater evidence in 1812, when more than one hundred pamphlets were published.

Despite the increased number of publications in general (and of personal-reputation pamphlets in particular), a final reckoning of the first year of literary freedom suggests a relatively subdued press. For every assassination of character there were many more stirring defenses of reputation. Pamphlets also publicized official notices, religious admonitions, and earnest discussions about the new political landscape, such as José de

Arango's *Breve análisis de la voluntad popular y bosquejo de falso patriotismo* (1812). Once Bergaño's *Correo* ceased publication in November 1811, the restraint of the periodical press was quite noticeable. *El Patriota Americano* began its second volume with an editorial that characterized the Spanish political experience as "regeneration," not to be confused with the revolutionary experience of countries that stifled political reform.[48] Three newly founded publications evinced moderate stances: *El Frayle* (4 January–26 September 1812), edited by Mariscal de Campo Francisco Montalvo y Amboludi, countered criticism of religious institutions in *El Patriota Americano;*[49] *El Reparón* (13 February 1812–29 May 1813) promised to wed the conservative reformism of the *costumbrista* tradition to a wider range of topics, including politics, public order, education, and the theater;[50] and *La Perinola* (25 February–29 April 1812) offered an irregular weekly outlet to José de Arazoza, one of the most active *costumbristas* after 1807.[51]

Although concerned officials continued to complain about press abuse, the dominant tone in the press itself after one year of experimentation was neither relief nor anxiety, but a mild disappointment. Manuel Zequeira's farewell editorial on 24 March 1812 judged editorship to be a demanding task with often unrewarding results. The *Gaceta Diaria* (formerly *El Mensagero,* now a daily) had not lived up to his expectations: "the multitude of papers being printed, the scarcity of presses and good operators, made our efforts useless, and frustrated our hopes."[52] It is important to note that disappointment did not stem from external constraints; as *El Hablador,* Zequeira's literary alter ego, noted: "it seemed a time when the threat of censorship did not impede Havana's public writers from speaking their mind."[53] This did not mean that writers, or those few who were beginning to style themselves as *periodistas,* openly expressed their thoughts. The majority of editors were still members of the literary elite of the Patriotic Society,[54] and Zequeira's comment did not address the informal mechanism of self-censorship that still conditioned much of the press.

In March 1812, just as the second year of press freedom began, an aborted uprising of free blacks and slaves disturbed the literary equilibrium. Spread through the medium of African rituals and brotherhoods, the conspiracy was betrayed by one of the white merchants recruited by José Antonio Aponte, a free black. This intelligence, coinciding with the appearance of threatening *anónimos*, and the 15 March attack by slaves on the plantation Peñas Altas in Havana province, led Someruelos to order preemptive arrests on 19 March. On 9 April 1812, Aponte and eight of his closest collaborators were executed.[55]

The events of March and April deprived the white population of any complacency they might have felt as they witnessed the growing political chaos of the mainland colonies. Aponte's conspiracy challenged the very basis of Cuban society and prosperity. Unlike a previous conspiracy in 1810, organized by a group of disaffected whites unhappy with colonial restrictions on commerce, Aponte's conspiracy was a rebellion against slavery, organized by blacks of all shades of skin and servitude.[56] This was the nightmare that had haunted the Cuban sugar oligarchy since the Haitian Revolution.

Aponte's conspiracy derived from tensions within Cuban slave society, but its timing may have been influenced by peninsular politics. The debate in the Cortes on the future of slavery and the slave trade had an impact, despite Someruelos's attempts to suppress the news by prohibiting the introduction or reprinting of numbers 37 and 38 of the *Diario de sesiones de Cortes*. In fact, the strategy may have backfired, for rumors of the debate became rumors of legislation abolishing slavery, and the government's silence only fueled the suspicions and grievances of the "population of color."[57] It is equally possible that the presence in Havana of the famed black brigadier Gil Narciso of Santo Domingo (Someruelos deliberately housed him and his retinue in the suburbs) and the crowning of Henri Christophe as king of Haiti (Christophe's portrait hung in Aponte's house) were also inspirations for action.[58]

Regardless of the immediate motives of Aponte, there was no doubt about the impact of his actions and prosecution. The conspiracy reminded the white population that peninsular political innovations, such as free press and the projected constitution, might not be appropriate for a society based upon slavery. While they shared the political goals of American creoles—an 1811 petition of thirty-three American deputies to the Cortes[59] listed free trade and internal production and equality within the various structures of empire—they also appreciated the vulnerability of their slave-based prosperity and the considerable *de facto* concessions they had received under political absolutism. Most specifically, the sugarocracy responded with a vigorous defense of Cuban slavery: *Representación de la ciudad de la Habana a las cortes españoles.* In the view of Moreno Fraginals, *Representación* demonstrated "for the first time the absolute crisis of sugarocrat political values, the renunciation of all political liberty on the altar of sugar, the sacrifice of the nation to the plantation."[60]

In the aftermath of Aponte's conspiracy, Cubans were advised to equate their self-interest with the status quo.[61] A series of *impresos* by *El tierradentro amigo del taquígrafo* analyzed the intellectual mood of the island. The dialogue between Don Lucas, a resident of Havana, and his friend Don Luis, who had just returned to the city after a lengthy absence, allowed the author to characterize Havana society at that moment. Don Lucas noted that Havana had lost some of its easy conviviality. There were ominous indications that the Audiencia intended to intensify its prosecution of writers and editors. From this trend Don Lucas predicted dire consequences for press freedom in Cuba.[62]

Don Lucas should have included Someruelos in his discussion, for the Audiencia was not alone in its darkening assessment of the impact of the periodical press on social peace. Here the aftershock of Aponte's conspiracy is quite apparent, for as late as February 1812 the captain general insisted that press abuse was not a menace to the tranquility of the island. Shortly after the failed conspiracy, however, the captain general offered a less sanguine appraisal: press abuse "could cause more harm than secret Napoleonic emissaries, for these could be hung, while seductive *impresos* circulated in the hands of everyone." Someruelos concluded that press restrictions were appropriate in countries where press freedom was poorly understood.[63]

The restraint of the Havana press in the succeeding months cannot be attributed to intensified official vigilance, however, because Juan Ruiz de Apodaca replaced the confident and autocratic Someruelos as captain general on 14 April 1812. Apodaca, a soldier and diplomat, proved tentative, continually appealing to higher authorities. He allowed the censorship procedure to become bogged down in controversies between the censorship board and the judiciary and between the board and the Audiencia.[64] While Apodaca's indecisiveness may have been politically astute in terms of career advancement, his irresolute attitude toward the press made the restraint of editors and writers even more crucial.

To be fair, Apodaca also faced a significant new task—to implement the Constitution of 1812, the result of the Cortes's deliberations since 1810.[65] The constitution outlined significant changes in the structure of Spanish politics. Royal power remained hereditary but was strictly limited by the legislative authority of the Cortes. Equally significant was the complicated sequence of indirect votes for representatives to municipal councils, provincial deputations (delegations to advise the viceroy or captain general, who was now referred to as the *jefe político superior*, or superior political chief),[66] and the Cortes. However, it should be noted that the revolutionary potential of the move to electoral politics was avoided: despite the elaborate procedure, "the constitution itself never clearly specified who possessed the vote," meaning that "each viceroyalty, and in truth probably each locality, set its own standards."[67]

Apodaca proclaimed the constitution on 13 July 1812, and the rowdy celebrations in Havana that evening only increased the apprehension of those whose vested interests in the political and economic status quo had already been threatened by Aponte's conspiracy.[68] The fear of political crisis and the continued domination by elite men of letters seem the best explanations for a Cuban press that, despite the transition to constitutionalism, could only manage three new *periódicos* in Havana during the remainder of 1812.[69] The ascendency of the new, conservative press of José de Arazoza and his partner, José de Soler, played a role in the deliberate moderation of the press. Arazoza and Soler built their business so circumspectly that they were able, after the end of free press in 1814, to assert that their press had never known freedom of the press.[70] On 29 May 1812, the Patriotic Society chose Arazoza and Soler as its official printer, which meant, among other things, printing rights to the *Diario de la Habana*. On 22 June, Apodaca ordered all government notices printed in the *Diario*. This action, which increased the *Diario*'s status and revenues, struck a terrible blow to Mariano Seguí's pretensions to be government printer; on 19 October 1812, Seguí officially lost this title.[71]

The editorial policy of Arazoza and Soler was not unique. The moderateness of *La Cena* (14? July 1812–31 October 1814?)—a new publication by Antonio José Valdés, from the new press that came to bear its name—is all the more remarkable for the undoubtedly liberal leanings of its editor. Valdés, an orphan of unknown parentage, had distinguished himself by opening a primary school in 1803. Despite his publication of the first Spanish grammar produced in Cuba (1806), Valdés could not secure approval of his work from the Patriotic Society. This disappointment probably convinced him to travel to the United States around 1808–9 and subsequently to reside in Mexico until he returned to found his press. The moderation of his press—as few issues of *La Cena* have survived, this argument is based upon the absence of censorial prosecution—seems surprising in light of his resentment against the Patriotic Society[72] and the items he chose to illustrate samples of his type library: a fragment from Rousseau, a speech by George Washington to Congress in 1783, and the free press legislation of 1810.[73]

Valdés, like other authors and editors, apparently took the lesson of Aponte's conspiracy to heart. As a consequence, the constitutionally sanctioned free press on the island remained a pale facsimile of its peninsular counterpart. There were no Cuban equivalents of Cádiz *periódicos* such as *El Robespierre Español, Amigo de las Leyes* (1811–13), which espoused radical Jacobin ideas, or the *Diario de la Tarde* (1811–13), which openly attacked the Cortes and the Constitution of 1812.[74] The Havana press studiously avoided the great issues of political and economic change and continued to provide a forum for libel and exoneration. As controversy centered less on the form of government than on the struggle to monopolize the new structures of political power, most confrontations in the press debate continued to appear as personal or sectarian squabbling.

El Centinela en la Habana (8 October 1812–26 February 1814) illustrates the role of the periodical press as protector of personal and corporate reputation. *El Centinela* was founded by Antonio del Valle Hernández, the secretary of the Havana *consulado*, to counter a threat to this key sugar institution.[75] The challenger was the newly elected municipal council, sworn in on 19 August 1812, which intended to assume its constitutional responsibility for urban services and funds that the *consulado* had collected for this purpose. As the new municipal council had a periodical mouthpiece in *El Censor Universal*, Valle Hernández responded in kind. Judging official channels of appeal and redress to be insufficient, he sought a verdict in the court of public opinion by publishing all the documents relating to the jurisdictional dispute.[76] Although the new constitution was the primary cause of the conflict, constitutionalism was not addressed as an issue by *El Centinela*. Only in the strident attacks on the constitutional municipal council did it vary from the self-censored and class-censored publications promoted by the creole literary elite before 1811.

In the second year of free press, the case of Simón Bergaño y Villegas remained the most controversial example of the press as a forum for the discussion of personal reputation. Ironically, it was official harassment that thrust Bergaño back into the spotlight. Bergaño had terminated the *Correo de las Damas* and had been so unobtrusive in the last days of Someruelos's governance that when Apodaca sought a medical report on the prisoner, he found that he had to launch an investigation to find him. Apparently, Bergaño had convinced the Guatemalan Audiencia that he was too ill for the ocean crossing, for they had granted him permission to convalesce at a local hot springs. Ordered by Apodaca on 2 July to return to Havana, Bergaño railed against the "multitude of hidden enemies" whom he held responsible for the captain general's curiosity.[77]

The medical examinations that Bergaño underwent upon his return could only have increased his paranoia. A panel of experts agreed that the prisoner could survive the ocean crossing with medical attendance. That five medical men could now unanimously wish Bergaño Godspeed in spite of evidence of deteriorating health is an accurate barometer of the postconspiracy conservatism that viewed a free press with suspicion.[78] Bergaño, his departure imminent, clutched at all straws. On 12 July 1812, he requested a personal interview with Apodaca so that the captain general might witness his poor health firsthand. On 20 July he wrote claiming to be included within the royal pardon of 25 May, although in fact such a pardon was merely a rumor at that moment. It proved to be a successful ploy, and just in time, for final arrangements had been made on the eighteenth for his deportation. Once again, when faced with a potentially controversial decision, Apodaca chose to defer the issue. Until he could consult with the Guatemalan Audiencia, Apodaca canceled plans to remit the prisoner.[79]

In the interim, Bergaño founded another *periódico*, the *Diario Cívico*, on 1 September 1812. The new publication proved to be very subdued. Filling a daily publication required extensive reprinting from other sources, and Bergaño seemed bent on selecting innocuous articles on topics such as the positive correlation between education and national customs.[80] Articles signed by Bergaño demonstrated similar restraint. His admiration for the recently deceased Spanish statesman, Gaspar de Jovellanos, in some ways typified the *Diario Cívico*. Like Jovellanos, Bergaño suggested enlightened reforms promoted by a progressive monarchy (he was particularly influenced by Jovellanos's advocacy of land redistribution as a strategy for increasing public prosperity).[81] Reform was the password. No radical political change should prejudice the limited electoral franchise granted by the constitution to the propertied classes. The image of American delegates participating in the Cortes seemed to formalize the equality of the ultramarine provinces. Given such advances, Bergaño deemed greater political innovation not only foolhardy but unnecessary.[82]

Bergaño's editorials in the *Diario Cívico* seem so securely within the boundaries of creole orthodoxy and postconspiracy press conservatism that the persistent hostility he endured seems difficult to explain. Criticism, especially through letters to editors, appeared widespread in the Havana press, but *El Reparón* (13 February 1812–29 May 1813) proved to be the most intransigent critic. It lavished sarcasm in anecdotes, such as one submitted by Tataratitatata, that related how a certain editor, D. Simón Siríndico, fraudulently claimed to speak Italian.[83] To Bergaño's assertion that "my system is that of moderation," *El Reparón* responded with a special supplement suggesting that Bergaño's "moderate" behavior in Guatemala had led to his arrest and expulsion.[84]

Towards the end of the second year of free press, the debate over Bergaño's reputation continued to provide a spark of controversy in an otherwise uneventful year.[85] A number of *periódicos* ceased publication: *El Lince, El Frayle,* and *El Patriota Americano,* the latter ending after the second volume for lack of subscribers.[86] Two other developments deserve brief mention. For the first time, other centers on the island challenged Havana's monopoly of the periodical press. Santiago de Cuba boasted three *periódicos* in 1812, and by October 1812 and January 1813, respectively, Puerto Príncipe and Matanzas also enjoyed publications.[87] The proliferation of provincial *periódicos* swelled the ranks of moderate publications: for example, the prospectus of *La Sabatina* (a weekly published in Santiago de Cuba, 18 November 1812–?), praised man's gift for rational thought and dedicated the publication to expanding the boundaries of human knowledge.[88] Here was the language of the Enlightenment as if the Age of Revolution had not intervened.

The amended press legislation of 10 June 1813[89] also reinforced the moderation of the Cuban press. Several innovations were particularly relevant: writings by ecclesiastics on nonecclesiastical matters were subject to ordinary jurisdiction; public figures could only be held up to scrutiny for their actions in the service of the state; authors found guilty by the provincial censorship board were now limited to one appeal to the Supreme Censorship Board. Finally, in a move calculated to counter ecclesiastical opposition to constitutionalism, the political chiefs in the Americas were given the power to remove any ecclesiastical *impreso* before a judicial verdict had been reached. While a process of appeal to Spain remained available, this procedure enabled officials to react quickly to controversial items and limit their impact.

The new press restrictions might have produced an even more restrained press in the third year of free press but for Bergaño. Although the Guatemalan Audiencia had ruled him ineligible for the royal pardon of 25 May 1812, Leonardo del Monte, now *juez letrado* or constitutional magistrate, argued that it would be morally impossible to transfer the ailing prisoner. On 8 April 1813, Apodaca accepted this recommendation and suspended all plans to move Bergaño until he received orders from Cádiz.[90]

Saved once more from deportation by the delicate state of his health, Bergaño continued his literary efforts in the face of mounting press criticism. Another key to the motivation of Bergaño's detractors became apparent after the founding of *El Filósofo Verdadero* on 15 March 1813. Though mediocre by literary standards, *El Filósofo* played an important part in the press dialogue because of its decidedly conservative tone. Its editor championed the "Christian" reaction to the philosophies of "materialism and deism,"[91] indicted Rousseau's *Social Contract* for the horrors of the French Revolution, and found Bergaño a convenient target. Significantly, both editors deplored revolutionary equality and emphasized the mutuality of society's unequal but complementary parts. Bergaño's anticlericalism provided the controversy, for he rejected the church as exemplary of the principle of hierarchy in society, choosing instead to argue from his perception of nature. While *El Filósofo*'s editor saw hierarchy in a world ordered by God, Bergaño sought his examples in the imagery of musical harmony.[92]

Bergaño reacted to his reprieve by testing the effectiveness of the new press regulations with another publication. The format of *El Esquife* (1 September 1813–30 June 1814) was purely satirical, an innovation in itself and an important precedent.[93] Satire may have been a response to the continued abuse of his detractors; it certainly ended his period of "moderation." Bergaño defended *El Esquife* with the following motto: "Light-hearted wit reproves more fully than serious and bitter invective." He cleverly manipulated the naval allegory, populating his crew with outstanding defenders of the constitution, like the ship's captain, Liberato Antiservilio, who fearlessly engaged enemies in his ship, *Arranchador*. *El Esquife* cruised the "streets and plazas of Havana and environs," searching for enemies flying the colors of political reaction. Favorite targets were the church hierarchy, the tobacco monopoly, and the conservative press. Yet even in this outlandish format Bergaño did not concentrate on issues or arguments but rather fired clever verbal salvos and allegorical allusions at prominent officials and *habaneros*.[94]

For all the criticism of journalistic detractors and worried officials, the attitude of elite *habaneros* toward Bergaño seems to have been more tolerant. Carriage rides and a country convalescence suggest that the indigent Bergaño had attracted some supporters. This also appears to be the lesson of the controversy surrounding Bergaño's application for membership in the Patriotic Society. On 11 December 1813, the Patriotic Society voted fifteen to four to admit him. The minutes of that meeting, referring to Bergaño only as the editor of "various periodical papers,"[95] offer no comment on the motivations for this favorable vote. Clearly, the Patriotic Society was not unchanged. That only nineteen members attended the annual meeting suggests institutional debility (an impression verified by reorganizational efforts after the Restoration). Finally, one cannot rule out the possibility that the vote was a challenge to Apodaca, who, although president of the Patriotic Society, was noticeably absent from the meeting.

Apodaca responded with uncharacteristic resolution. He informed the members that he was convoking an extraordinary Sunday session in his quarters. Eighteen members attended on the following day, and Apodaca bolstered his support by recruiting José de Arazoza and Juan Agustín Ferrety as well. Apodaca, unexpectedly dressed in all the finery of his office, reminded the meeting that Bergaño had been sentenced, not merely accused, and that consequently he had forfeited his rights as a citizen. This, Apodaca argued, would exclude him from Society membership.

Censor Francisco Filomeno championed Bergaño's cause. He insisted that the Cortes had issued legislation to eliminate political interference in Society affairs, and as the election had followed the Patriotic Society's charter, the verdict was irrevocable. Apodaca reportedly interrupted Filomeno and asked him if he was trying to further the spirit of sedition. Apparently this threat intimidated most members. Denied further discussion, all but two members voted to suspend Bergaño's admission until he was cleared of criminal charges.

Although the incident humiliated the Patriotic Society, it was essentially directed at Bergaño for his satires in *El Esquife*, and Apodaca was not content with one victory. He wrested a statement of support for his action from the provincial deputation on 16 December.[96] On the following day, Apodaca presided over the Havana municipal council and received a similar endorsement. The municipal council specifically criticized *El Esquife* as "a vexatious newspaper that has heaped injury on men and women, estates and conditions, without exception."[97] The provincial deputation, however, also pointed out the bottleneck in the captain general's renewed efforts to expel Bergaño from the island: the *juez letrado*, Leonardo del Monte, held jurisdiction over Bergaño's case. It was del Monte who authorized a second panel of doctors to contradict claims that the prisoner was fit for ocean travel.[98] Del Monte's protection proved more crucial than ever, for under Apodaca's urging, the municipal council offered an expanded analysis of Bergaño's detrimental impact upon the city. The exposition ended with the plea "Free us from Don Simón Bergaño," a sentiment echoed in *anónimos* that began to appear throughout the city.[99]

But once again, and for the final time, Bergaño's health frustrated his opponents' hopes. On 16 January 1814, Apodaca learned that Bergaño had suffered an epileptic fit, causing one of his ulcers to hemorrhage. The prisoner's cries for a confessor reached the ears of the commander of the Cabaña prison, who authorized a last will and testament. Still, Bergaño clung to life and refused to be transferred to any of several hospitals that reluctantly agreed to take him. Towards the end of January, Bergaño broke the stalemate by requesting to convalesce in the countryside near Jesús del Monte. The provincial deputation adamantly opposed this suggestion, stating that if Bergaño wanted better medical treatment he should be transferred to a hospital, but if pure air was the only issue, La Cabaña should suit him fine. However, reports indicated that the prisoner was hemorrhaging continually now, and Apodaca knew that the medical attention in the prison was occasionally lax. Not wishing to be liable for negligence, and undoubtedly tired of the whole affair, Apodaca agreed to Bergaño's request on 2 February 1814. Soon thereafter, Bergaño arrived in Jesús del Monte, and there he remained for the remaining months of a free press.[100]

Bergaño's departure deprived the Havana press of its last controversial contributor. Now, the *Diario Cívico* and *El Esquife*, probably edited by Joaquín José García or compiled by the printer Feliciano Romay, featured content as derivative as the three Havana dailies (the *Diario*, *La Cena*, and the *Noticioso*)[101] or as subdued as provincial publications like *El Patriota* (Matanzas, 22 September 1813–17 September 1814?), *La Miscelánea de Cuba* (Santiago de Cuba, 13 November 1813–24 July 1814?), and *El Canastillo* (Santiago de Cuba, 5 March–1 July 1814). Bergaño's collaborators did emphasize the founder's preferred themes, but now articles defending a free press, for example, were reprints from a Cádiz *periódico*.[102] A similar strategy dominated other publications, in part reflecting their editors' concerns about the political uncertainties occasioned by Ferdinand VII's recovery of his crown in December 1813.

With the king's return, constitutionalism became an endangered option. It had been the work of the liberal, extraordinary Cortes[103] that had seized power in Cádiz under exceptional circumstances. The elimination of the French threat revealed the rifts between "liberal" and "servile" factions throughout the peninsula. As defined by their respective enemies, "liberal" designated "godless, agitator, and contemner of our customs," while "servile" signified "ignorant, egotistical, and content with abuses." One side charged that the liberal, in his fantasies of equality, was oblivious to authority, while the other side accused the *serviles* of a pessimistic view of history that admitted no greater good than social peace.[104] It should be emphasized, however, that the liberal cause was endangered even before the restoration of the monarchy: the new, ordinary Cortes was composed of a majority of royalists, or *serviles*.[105]

The peninsular political uncertainties found expression in the Havana press. On 27 and 28 May 1814, the press proclaimed the news of Ferdinand's return to Spain. Although the king had to share the "vivas" in *La Cena*'s headline with the constitution and the Spanish nation,[106] few felt that he would willingly share the spotlight for any length of time. Authors and editors, as well as public officials, scurried to implement strategies to exploit the political transition or to soften its impact. While the substitute editor of the *Diario Cívico* filled the June issues with pleas that the true patriots of the struggle against Napoleon not be overlooked or punished as the balance of power moved away from the constitutionalists, Bergaño himself advertised his withdrawal from controversy. On 25 June 1814, the *Diario Cívico* announced the availability of Bergaño's new poem, "El Desengaño, o sea despedida de la corte y elogio de la vida del campo."[107]

In this atmosphere of uncertainty and rumor, a ship arrived in port on 5 July 1814 with news from the peninsula. The captain general of Andalusia informed Apodaca that Ferdinand had abolished the constitution on 4 May, calling it an assault on his prerogatives patterned on the "revolutionary and democratic French constitution of 1791." The king charged that there was only one explanation why this legislation, so foreign to Spanish tradition, had been accepted—a press campaign "to prepare minds to receive so great an innovation." Now that he was finally free to act, Ferdinand desired to erase the constitutional experience by decreeing the *status quo ante*.[108]

Given the king's bitterness toward the press, it is not surprising that his Valencia decree of 4 May was augmented by new guidelines for the press. The edict specified that it was illegal to "affix any handbill, distribute any announcement, or to print papers or any writings," without previous censorship by appointed officials. All writings were to be stripped of partisan sentiment to avoid offending authority, custom, and individual reputation. Instead, the edict continued, the press should be dedicated "to the progress of the sciences and the arts, to the enlightenment of the government, and to the maintenance of the mutual respect that must exist between all members of society."[109]

This information from Spain placed Apodaca in a dangerous predicament.[110] To begin with, the news had not arrived through official channels, despite the credibility of the source. Further, the city was explosively awash with rumors and Apodaca feared that the "population of color" might take advantage of any transitional political turmoil. Finally, more than thirty foreign ships crowded the Havana harbor. The ships were mostly English, and therefore, Apodaca reasoned, the port was teeming with "sailors with democratic ideas, like all commoners," who might influence the local population to resist the restoration of absolute monarchy.

The captain general decided to move slowly and without a show of force. His first priority was to prepare public opinion, and for advice he consulted the Havana municipal council on 7 July 1814. Though no details of the meeting were revealed, Apodaca launched a press campaign two days later. Through an unspecified printer, he arranged for copies of the 4 May decree. Meanwhile, Arazoza and Soler published a description of the king's triumphal entry into Valencia. On the tenth, Apodaca broadcast this news to all the jurisdictions and corporations of the island, yet there was still no mention of his intention to proclaim the Restoration. Two factors finally tipped his hand: wildly accelerating rumors and the departure of the foreign convoy. Apodaca convened the municipal council and obtained a plurality in favor of proclaiming the royal decree of 4 May prior to official receipt of the legislation. This decision was published in the *Diario* of 21 July 1814.

Freedom of the press ended with scarcely a whisper of public protest, despite the reimposition of regulations that required printers to renew their licenses and editors to submit their publications to prepublication censorship. The full impact of the decree was probably muted by the disappearance of the *Diario Cívico* and *El Esquife* earlier in the month. In Havana, the *Diario*, the *Noticioso*, *La Cena*, and *El Filósofo Verdadero* attempted to survive the transition, although the latter folded on 22 August because its editor found the prepublication censorship procedures to be too onerous for a single individual.[111] *El Espejo de Puerto Príncipe* provided the only exception to this uneventful transition. Five days after receiving Apodaca's proclamation, *El Espejo* printed an article praising the submission of the Swedish king to the constitutional sovereignty of the people. Constitutional monarchy on the English model was proposed as approaching the "degree of culture suggested by philosophy and reason."[112] In response to this article, the Audiencia's lawyer recommended that the printer, Mariano Seguí, be imprisoned and his press confiscated. If Seguí had still been printing in Havana, that undoubtedly would have been his fate. However, the Audiencia ruled that disciplinary action was the province of the lieutenant governor of Puerto Príncipe, and this official merely warned Seguí that the new press regulations had to be followed to the letter.[113]

The Restoration's impact on the press can be illustrated by the transformation of *La Cena* and the founding of *El Café del Comercio*. The transition to stricter publication standards might have been acceptable to *La Cena*'s editor, Antonio José Valdés, who had on occasion noted press freedom as a divisive factor.[114] On 13 May, perhaps foreseeing the restoration of absolute monarchy, Valdés had been more severe in his assessment. Nowhere, he lamented, had authority been so flagrantly attacked as in Havana. He cited the press abuses of the "*exaltados*" who sought to "suffocate the progress of the enlightenment." These sentiments, so worthy of the preconstitutional era, may have stood Valdés in good stead after 21 July. Regardless, the content of *La Cena* changed. Gone were Valdés's editorials, however moderate they might have been.[115] Instead, extensive foreign news and diverting features, such as cautionary tales about snuff-taking, filled *La Cena*'s pages.[116]

El Café del Comercio, the only new *periódico* founded in the remaining months of 1814, epitomized Ferdinand VII's vision of the Restoration press. Issued on 1 September 1814 by Valdés's son, Antonio María, *El Café* promised to publish anything relating to "our patron," commerce. The publication represented a return to a stress on the "public utility" of the periodical press. Daily publication pressures, however, forced the younger Valdés to offer space-filling general essays on commerce and agriculture (there was a series on raising poultry, for example) and to borrow extensively from the *Diario*, the *Noticioso*, and *La Cena*. Both father and son soon admitted that there was only a limited currency of information that the Restoration press could print, and both *El Café* and *La Cena* "declared bankruptcy" on 31 October 1814.[117]

By the end of 1814, only the *Diario*, the *Noticioso*, and *El Espejo* survived. It seemed as if the free press interlude could be forgotten or even denied, in part because Cuba had not really experimented with the full potential of the free press legislation. Concern about sugar prosperity and the shock of Aponte's conspiracy pressured the press to continue much of the self-censorship of the previous two decades. Publications became more numerous, more people than ever served as editors or writers or contributed letters to the editor or patriotic poetry, but the literary consensus that reached back to the 1790s did not collapse. The only intemperate performances had come from those who might be considered outside the sugarocracy's influence: some members of the elected municipal council who attacked the perquisites of the *consulado* and expressed resentment against the literary elite of the Patriotic Society ("*el sector de los Cultos*");[118] Piñeres, whose frustrations were rooted in his relationship with another foe of the sugar elite, Bishop Trespalacios; and Bergaño, whose temperament, legal circumstances, and poor health made him a literary outcast. While "outsiders" felt fewer compunctions about experimenting with press freedom, they also represented a minority among press contributors, a minority that remained preoccupied with partisan defenses of reputation and self-interest.

With the Restoration, the *literatos* of the Patriotic Society recovered their monopoly over the periodical press. They sought rewards for their literary moderation during the preceding three years,[119] and returned to their former literary activities: poetry, *costumbrismo*, letters to the editor on fine points of language. On the surface, literature merely replaced politics in the Restoration press—for example, in the "Variety" section of the *Noticioso*. Yet literature was not merely substituting for politics; it could also be political, and the political subtext of literature had been set by year's end. From a favorite peninsular source (*El Mercurio Gaditano*), the *Noticioso* filled several issues with a denunciation of August Wilhelm Schlegel's contention that inspiration should be freed from classical regulations on form and content. This critique of Schlegel and the "corruption of modern literature" placed the blame squarely on the current romantic vogue of "abandoning oneself to all the disorders of the imagination."[120] The article equated the artistic excesses of imagination with the political excesses of the constitutional period and praised the order and stability inherent in the restoration of monarchy and the literary standards in force before the advent of free press. This series may be seen as the literary manifesto of the Restoration. For the next five years, colonial officials would ensure that literary expression mirrored the social and political order of royal absolutism.

CHAPTER 3

Constitutional Reprise (I): The Flota Press Offensive, 1820–1822

IN 1820 events in Spain once again disturbed Cuba's political equilibrium. To subdue his rebellious New World possessions, Ferdinand VII assembled over thirty thousand men on the island of León near Cádiz to wait for ships promised by the czar of Russia. Restless and dissatisfied with their treatment since the end of the Napoleonic Wars, the men turned on the peninsula instead. The revolt, initiated by Major Rafael Riego in Cádiz on New Year's Day, 1820, soon gained momentum within the military. On 7 March 1820, a group of generals forced Ferdinand VII to swear allegiance to the Constitution of 1812; once again, Spain and her remaining colonies became a constitutional monarchy.[1]

A peninsular newspaper brought news of the convocation of the Cortes to Havana on 14 April 1820. Captain General Juan Manuel de Cagigal (29 August 1819–3 March 1821) attempted to delay the political transition until he received official orders, but this decision angered the peninsular garrison, particularly the Catalan battalion whose former commander (Antonio Quiroga) was one of the heroes of the military revolt. Two days later, a threatening crowd of soldiers, peninsular residents, and others eager for a new political order gathered in the

Plaza de Armas to demand the immediate proclamation of the Constitution of 1812. For the sake of public order, Cagigal reluctantly came down to the plaza and swore loyalty to the constitution.[2]

This innovation was decidedly unwelcome to the sugar-ocracy. The years 1815–19 had been the most buoyant period to date in the history of Cuban sugar. Peace in Europe and North America had stimulated demand, and slave importations increased dramatically despite growing British pressure to end the slave trade.[3] The Crown's appointment of José Cienfuegos Jovellanos (nephew and partisan of the Spanish statesman and economist whose writings had so influenced Francisco Arango and other creole ideologues) as captain general in 1816 seemed to promise continued benevolent neglect. With the additional appointment of Alejandro Ramírez as intendant in the same year, Cuban sugar producers once again enjoyed the benefit of a fully cooperative colonial bureaucracy.

Royal legislation on economic matters in this period also strengthened the position of the sugarocracy. On 23 July 1817, the Crown abolished the last remaining symbol of colonial economic protectionism and peninsular interference, the royal tobacco monopoly; on 10 February 1818, Cuba won the right to trade freely with any foreign country; the royal order of 16 July 1819 validated old municipal land grants, giving sugar planters "full bourgeois possession of their land, including the right to evict the remaining small-scale cultivators of tobacco," many of them recent immigrants, who were now completely unprotected after the dismantling of the tobacco monopoly.[4]

The years since the Restoration had also allowed the Patriotic Society to recover its monopoly over intellectual life. With the reimposition of prepublication censorship, elite literati dominated not only the sanctioned *periódicos*—the official *Diario de la Habana*, Palmer's *Noticioso*, and, after January 1817, the Society's *Memorias*[5]—but also other aspects of culture, such as the theater. Every word of the periodical press and every word, song, and gesture on the stage had to be approved by censors (most often Society members) appointed by the captain general.[6] The Englishman Robert Jameson remembered the censorship as oppressive:

No community was ever kept more completely out of hearing of all that could interest them, than this. Public news came thoroughly sifted of every particle of antidespotism, through the government press; and, though a free trade necessarily brought information, it rested, like the *miasmata* of fever, chiefly on the seashore.[7]

In this restrictive literary atmosphere, some *literatos* sought other outlets, championing reforms in the welfare of abandoned children or in cholera prevention. Most effort, however, focused on public education. Several *periodistas* of the first constitutional period, such as José Antonio de la Ossa and José de Arazoza, served as school inspectors. Two other Society members, Félix Varela, priest and philosophy professor at the San Carlos Seminary,[8] and Justo Vélez, law professor at the same institution, wrote instructional booklets that were printed by Arazoza and Soler's press at Society expense.[9] Educational reform also occurred at the San Carlos Seminary with the encouragement of Bishop Espada. In 1813, Félix Varela began to teach in Spanish rather than Latin, and subsequently offered a course in experimental physics. The seminary, with its youthful faculty of predominantly secular priests and Cubans, provided a stark contrast to the University of Havana, staffed by older, scholastic, regular clerics.[10]

There were indications, however, that the Patriotic Society had not completely recovered its former vitality. While membership climbed—to over 350 members by April 1817[11]—participation did not. To address this problem, the Society faithful decided that year to require an initiatory discourse of all new members. They hoped that this would help "the Society to close its doors to those who seek no other honor than seeing their name on the membership roll."[12] Nevertheless, the problem of participation persisted. At the annual meeting of 22 December 1819, Secretary José María Peñalver noted that although fewer meetings had been held the past year, attendance had continued to fall off, and he admitted that "the patriotic spirit of the Society was concentrated in a few members." Despite the decline of creole involvement, however, the Patriotic Society still championed the interests of Cuban sugar. The most significant achievement of the year was the success of the Chair of Political Economy established at the Colegio Seminario in October 1818 and filled by Justo Vélez. During 1819, Vélez lectured from his edition of the works of Jean Baptiste Say, the French partisan of Adam Smith. Examinations on 20 June

1819 required the first class to discuss the contribution of the island to the metropolis under the current regime of unrestricted commerce and the disasters that could result from a return to restrictive policies.[13]

The sugar oligarchy, content with its recent economic gains, did not welcome a return to constitutionalism. Constitutionalism brought back different legal standards, representational formulas, and most immediately, a free press. Prepublication censorship yielded to postpublication censorship by censorship boards (initially the surviving members of the 1814 panels supplemented by new interim appointments).[14] The "pouring forth [of] odes, sonnets, advices, essays, and every species of composition by every species of author"[15] became the immediate preoccupation of planters and officials. For example, Francisco Sedano, the lieutenant governor of Puerto Príncipe, complained that the editor of the *Gaceta de Puerto Príncipe* had reprinted items from the *Diario Constitucional de Barcelona* containing all manner of antimonarchist sentiments. Sedano felt powerless to intervene, not only because the constitution protected the rights of Spaniards to publish, but also because the articles were nothing less than the proclamations of the generals who had made the revolution. Sedano feared that the patriotic rhetoric of liberalism and constitutionalism originating in Spain could have unsettling effects in Cuba if publicized by the local periodical press.[16]

The first *periódicos* to appear, however, still bore the marks of Restoration strictures. On 27 April, lawyer and litterateur Ignacio Valdés Machuca issued *El Mosquito* (27 April–24 August 1820), but the *costumbrista*'s traditional concern for individual and social morality overshadowed the satirical device of a mosquito's insatiable probing into human affairs.[17] One week later, Valdés Machuca published his second offering, a weekly written entirely in verse, entitled *La Lira de Apolo* (4 May–1 July 1820).[18] *La Lira* featured contributions from most of the prominent Cuban poets, including Manuel de Zequeira, yet this collection of sonnets and odes had the savor of musty poetic productions that had languished unpublished for some time. Like *El Mosquito*'s satire, *La Lira*'s poetry represented the spring cleaning of a literary household not aired since 1814.

La Mosca (14 May–13 June 1820), edited by the Argentine poet and proconstitutional patriot José Antonio Miralla,[19] was also retrospective in tone, for its epigram declaring light-

Figure 3-1. Major Cuban Periódicos, 1820–1822

1820 J F M A M J J A S O N D	1821 J F M A M J J A S O N D	1822 J F M A M J J A S O N D	1823 J F M A M J J A S O N D

Diario de la Habana

Noticioso

Memorias

Observador de la Isla (SC)   Papel Oficial
           12   14

Gaceta de Puerto Príncipe

   Mosquito
27   24
   Lira de Apolo
4   1
   Mosca
14 13
    Esquife Arranchador
       1   19   2   29
    Indicador Constitucional

    Tío Bartolo
           28
   Argos
5   5
    Observador Habanero
15
     Botiquín / Impertérrito
               1
    Tía Catana

    Correo Semanal (TR)

    Galera
12   29
      Navío Arranchador
      7   30
      Minerva (SC)
31   1
       Miscelánea Liberal (SC)
1
        Falucho Vigía
10
        Amigo del Pueblo / Amante de Sí Mismo
2   6 9   25
      Sábelo Todo
5   21

KEY

—————— Publication verified	(SC)	Santiago de Cuba
- - - - - - - - Incomplete publication data	(TR)	Trinidad

hearted criticism superior to harsh invective paraphrased the masthead of Bergaño's *El Esquife. La Mosca* claimed to share *El Mosquito's* curiosity about the ways of men, being particularly intrigued by a conversation overheard among a table of *campesinos* at a local cafe. These peasants expressed disbelief that, despite the proclamation of the constitution, the political situation of the island still favored the "hungry cats" of the colonial administration. *La Mosca* pledged to investigate their grievances.[20]

In fact, political transformation was proceeding, but at a restrained pace established by Cagigal (now referred to as the superior political chief) and a preparatory junta composed of seven prominent citizens including Intendant Ramírez and Juan Bernardo O'Gaban, who represented Bishop Espada.[21] The junta assumed responsibility for organizing elections for *ayuntamientos*, provincial deputations, and deputies to the Cortes. The junta divided the province of Havana into eleven districts or *partidos* comprising numerous parishes (the city of Havana contained twelve parishes).[22] Eligible citizens—once again there were no explicit definitions mentioned, but residency, race, and class figured prominently—exercised their franchise at the parish level. To elect the Cortes deputies, for example, citizens elected a parish representative to a meeting at the *partido* level; these delegates would elect a representative to a provincial electoral junta that would in turn choose the deputies and their substitutes.[23]

Both planters and officials anxiously awaited the outcome of elections. Other aspects of the constitutional transformation had already produced mixed results for the political equilibrium of the island. For example, the formation of the "national militia" legislated by the Constitution of 1812 reversed the creole preponderance in the "urban" and "rural" militias; the new militia was composed predominantly of peninsular Spaniards attracted by the uniform and prestige of the military and the chance to feel superior to the local creoles.[24] On the other hand, the constitution also revived provincial deputations to supervise municipal councils, commerce, agriculture, revenues, and public education; in the previous constitutional period, provincial deputations had been notorious strongholds of the sugarocracy.

The return of the electoral process and press freedom soon produced the island's first major crisis. During the parish elections of 18 June 1820 for municipal council positions, voters in the parish of Santo Cristo del Buen Viaje protested when the overseeing committee ended the voting after only four hours. Arguing that legislation specified the voting should continue daily from 8:00 a.m. to 2:00 p.m. until all had voted, they appealed to Cagigal, who turned to the provincial deputation for advice. The provincial deputation decided to reopen the polls, but this only heightened the controversy. On 21 June 1820, Tomás Gutiérrez de Piñeres, the outspoken cleric of the first constitutional period, published *Sobre elecciones parroquiales,* a denunciation of the provincial deputation. Piñeres insisted that the local parish decision to terminate the elections could not be overturned because it was at this level that the people exercised their constitutional sovereignty.[25] Further, he charged that the deputation's willingness to dissolve itself in 1814 had deprived it of legitimacy until new elections could be held the following month. Now even the provincial deputation, through its secretary, Tomás Romay, felt the need for public exoneration, and the tempo of contentious *impresos* increased prior to the impending elections for deputies to the Cortes.[26]

Impresos did not monopolize controversy, however; three new *periódicos* printed by the Imprenta Liberal took long strides toward the dreaded prospect of a combative press. Two of these, *El Indicador Constitucional* (1 June 1820–1 November 1823?) and *El Esquife Arranchador* (1 June 1820–29 May 1822),[27] initially shared editorial staff. Evaristo Sánchez,[28] the main editor of *El Indicador Constitucional,* soon usurped his collaborator, Joaquín José García, at *El Esquife Arranchador* as well. García, it will be remembered, was Bergaño's collaborator during the previous free press interlude.

El Indicador Constitucional and *El Esquife Arranchador* epitomized two divergent avenues to a reputation as a *periodista. El Indicador* was a daily, offering an opportunity for continuous editorial influence and even a modest revenue. To meet the arduous task of filling a daily paper, *El Indicador* offered a summary of the best items from rival dailies and borrowed extensively from the peninsular press. Reprints, as noted earlier, saved editorial energy and presented a relatively safe strategy for printing controversial items. Reprinting peninsular items was also an ideological statement. Sánchez refused to recognize any distinction between Cuba and the peninsular provinces. This was an important assumption, for the political benefits of equal status had to be measured against the contagion of peninsular factionalism. *El Indicador's* byline insisted that perilous liberty was preferable to pacific slavery. Sánchez and García declared their unequivocal loyalty to the constitutional regime and swore to criticize even the most respected personages or publications if necessary.[29]

In contrast, *El Esquife Arranchador*, a satirical biweekly, provided a forum in which a writer might parlay wit and talent into literary notoriety.[30] Editorial opinion in this second effort by Sánchez and García was vehement and original, but cloaked in a satiric code of fictitious names and events. The naval allegory dominated the early issues but after García left,[31] *El Esquife Arranchador* developed a transparent replica of Havana— the "very noble, valorous, loyal and imaginary city of Cayo-puto." Successive issues populated the city with inhabitants of all classes (but with no mention of slaves) including a bureaucracy headed by a superior political chief named D. Chilibrán. Naval sorties against rival publications now formed only one part of *El Esquife's* fare, while officials of "Cayo-puto" who were judged to be in breach of constitutional principles were parodied in "official" minutes, speeches, and letters from "eyewitnesses."

El Tío Bartolo (June 1820–28 November 1821) was the third component of the periodical shock wave of early June 1820. Edited by lawyer José de Aguiar, *El Tío Bartolo* featured conversations between an illiterate rustic, Bartolo, and a parish priest. In every issue, Bartolo would bring an assortment of rumors to the priest for explication. Often the gossip concerned a recent press article or the latest verdict of the censorship junta. In addition to Aguiar's amusing mastery of the rural dialect, *El Tío Bartolo* used real names and titles in the priest's charges of constitutional abuses, immediately creating a sensation. While the format was pleasant gossip, the substance was a detailed public scrutiny of the connections of political power and influence on the island. Aguiar concentrated on the financial bureaucracy headed by Intendant Ramírez; this probably stemmed in part from his disappointment in seeking promotions based upon his father's lengthy service in that branch of the imperial service.[32]

Public reaction to the Imprenta Liberal's offerings was immediate. Subscriptions soared and printer Campe persuaded Aguiar to issue *El Tío Bartolo* as a biweekly.[33] The impact was registered by less pleasant indicators as well. In the third issue of *El Esquife Arranchador* (8 June 1820), Campe categorically denied that he was the editor and decried the maltreatment of one of his employees by someone offended by *El Esquife*'s salvos.[34] Ten days later, *El Indicador* published a public protest by Aguiar, denouncing rumors of a plot to assassinate him and asserting that *El Tío Bartolo* fell within the limits of the free press legislation.[35]

Amidst these controversial *periódicos* came a fourth, *El Argos* (5 June 1820–5 March 1821), edited by the New Granadan physician José Fernández Madrid, in collaboration with José Antonio Miralla, who ceased publishing *La Mosca* shortly thereafter. Fernández Madrid enjoyed a unique perspective, for he had participated in the wars of independence in New Granada and had been president of the republic until overthrown by a royalist counteroffensive. He warned against public or official overreaction to a free press. A review of the Havana press on 1 July 1820[36] linked the current excesses of the press to the previous regime of repression. He cautioned the public not to overreact until time and experience had fashioned a new equilibrium; he sought to disabuse those who equated a free press with public disorder, pointing to England and the United States as examples. Fernández Madrid distinguished between those whose opposition to a free press was based on a personal stake in the former status quo and those who were merely apprehensive in the face of uncertainty. With time and the experience of a free press, he assured his readers, they would learn to treat the periodical press with healthy skepticism.

The moderation of *El Argos* was atypical, for ideological battlelines were already forming. The official printers, Arazoza and Soler, countered the offerings of the Imprenta Liberal by issuing *El Observador Habanero* (15 June 1820–February 1821?). It was printed in the *revista* format, twenty-four to twenty-six pages issued bimonthly for eventual binding into book form. By issuing only twice per month, the editors were, in effect, abstaining from reporting or editorializing on the latest events in Spain and Cuba. Rather, as outlined in the prospectus, *El Observador Habanero* dedicated itself to furthering the constitutional "empire of the laws" by using the press to educate "every class of the State," arguing that "ignorance is always the enemy of reform."[37]

In its emphasis upon education and reform, *El Observador Habanero* acted as the heir apparent of the Patriotic Society.

Indeed, its primary editor, José Agustín Govantes, and most of its contributors—José Agustín Caballero and Félix Varela, for example—were either faculty or students at the San Carlos Seminary and current or prospective society members.[38] Many other members were among the initial ninety subscribers. To a notable extent, *El Observador Habanero* mirrored interest in political economy, featuring lengthy articles on Jovellanos's agrarian reform and Adam Smith's ideas on national development.[39]

For the collaborators of *El Observador Habanero,* political economy entailed an implicit political platform. Their aim was to educate all classes to respect the "invisible hand" guiding Cuban prosperity. Constitutionalism itself was not necessarily a threat, for the new political process might be more sensitive to Cuban aspirations. To subvert the radical possibilities of the constitutional transition, *El Observador Habanero* published articles detailing the ideal qualifications of deputies to the Cortes.[40] Recognizing that the content of the term "constitutionalism" would be partially defined in the public mind through the press, the collaborators of *El Observador Habanero* sought to counter the opinions of *El Esquife Arranchador* and *El Tío Bartolo.*

With publications ranging from Piñeres's *impresos* to *El Tío Bartolo,* the literary environment of the second constitutional period immediately proved to be more electric than its predecessor. This was true in part because writers could draw upon the experience of the first constitutional era. Yet an author's ideology was often difficult to perceive. The embryonic stage of political factions partly accounts for the confusion. Ramiro Guerra y Sánchez, for example, simply assumed that subsequent political options—loyalism, independence, annexationism—were already present.[41] Though there might have been individuals who espoused the positions of independence or annexation, there is little evidence of serious discussion, let alone political action, directed at these alternatives. In 1820, peninsular politics and the promise or peril of constitutionalism seemed to command attention everywhere.

The word "seemed" is appropriate here, because it is difficult to analyze the many public pronouncements in the press; as in the previous constitutional interlude, the issue of constitutionalism itself was not addressed directly. Neither side desired this political issue to filter down to the "population of color" and become a real social issue, nor did they wish to compromise themselves unduly in the event of the restoration of absolutism. Charges of "liberal" or "servile" referred less to theoretical discussions of political ideology than to a confrontation between political "outs" and "ins." Further, the most virulent attacks against "servile" officials of the Restoration years were often shrouded in satire, removing the message in some cases for all but the erudite.

Political uncertainty and a delicate social peace contributed to the illusion of unanimous support for constitutionalism and stimulated the evolution of a set of symbols signifying political loyalties. Reverential references to the French Revolution, for example, indicated a liberal of the most extreme persuasion, an *exaltado*, one who implied that Spain's political transformation had not proceeded far enough. Predictably in the Cuban press, such a position betrayed a peninsular bias, someone without an interest in Cuban sugar prosperity, or one who had languished outside official patronage. More moderate liberals, including the progressive members of the Patriotic Society, emphasized that the French Revolution was not the necessary prototype for Spanish evolution to constitutional liberties, while conservatives pointed to the disastrous social disorder which Napoleon (and by inference, of course, the Constitution of 1812) had brought to the Hispanic world.

Another focus of contention, the Inquisition, allowed authors to react to the extensive reforms initiated by the Cortes in September 1820: "renewed suppression of the Jesuits, reductions of tithes, suppression of ecclesiastical entails, and, most important, suppression of the monastic orders and reduction in the numbers of monasteries of the regular orders."[42] *Exaltados* excoriated the Inquisition as a symbol of the tyranny of privilege and a reminder of the church's support of the Restoration. Moderates applauded the suppression of the Inquisition as an example of a well-conceived reduction of ecclesiastical power. Conservatives studiously avoided direct reference to the Inquisition, preferring to lament the anticlericalism that undermined the church's influence on social peace. Curiously, in Cuba, Bishop Espada's support for the work of the Cortes meant that the religious issue was less divisive than in the peninsula, where it caused the king to withdraw from his "partnership" with the Cortes and begin to conspire for his own restoration.[43]

An even more important shibboleth for the press was "free press" itself. The question of what constituted free press implied debate on the nature of a constitutional society. The problem of libel was, in part, a question of the degree to which the traditional hierarchy was exempt from public criticism. When a member of the prominent Cárdenas family denounced an *impreso* published by the commercial firm of Pluma and Aguilera to protest a broken contract, the censorship board was being asked to decide whether or not the merchants' actions prejudiced the social order.[44] Similarly, in another paper, the controversy hinged on the right of "military citizen" Antonio Pérez la Rosa to criticize publicly the commander of a peninsular battalion.[45] In each case, the essence of the suit lay not in the truth of the charges printed in the press but in the inappropriateness of the targets. Should not an individual's high standing in society exempt him from public scrutiny? Of course, the offended party primarily considered the charges in a personal light. A renewed volume of litigation once again testified to the correlation between a free press and the problem of libel.

Though Cagigal may have been the first victim of the "libels" of a free press—the Havana press is often blamed for exacerbating his declining health and forcing a leave of absence from 22 June to 25 October 1820—the most celebrated confrontation pitted *El Tío Bartolo* against Intendant Ramírez. For five years Ramírez had supervised the important Cuban revenues and acted as patron of Cuban sugar and its institutions (he sponsored the Patriotic Society's efforts to found the Chair of Political Economy). After the reestablishment of constitutionalism, however, he found himself the target of those who had not enjoyed his favor during the Restoration years, especially those merchants (largely peninsular) who resented his efforts to increase revenues by curbing contraband trade.[46] *El Tío Bartolo* led the assault against Ramírez, claiming that the intendant had sold Treasury positions to augment his personal fortune. Ramírez denounced the sixth issue on 3 July 1820,[47] and two days later the Censorship Board, judging it to be injurious and defamatory, ordered its collection.

Legal prosecution of editor Aguiar proved more difficult. On 16 July, Ramírez wrote letters seeking confirmation of a rumor that Aguiar had presented a suit against him in the court of Rafael Lima, and that Lima had admitted the complaint.[48] Ramírez was incredulous because, in compliance with the constitution, he recently (May 1820) had ceded his judicial authority over all matters relating to revenues to Lima, who had made a great show of loyalty to the intendant. Because the two municipal judges who were to try Aguiar on the original charges of libel were occupied with supervising elections, Aguiar had effectively inserted his charges ahead of those of Ramírez, forcing the intendant to wait until Aguiar's suit was settled. In the meantime, Aguiar and other critics could continue their press attacks with impunity.[49]

Ramírez refused to use the press to defend his reputation, and this reluctance seemed to encourage his detractors. The interim superior political chief, Juan María Echeverri, recommended on 14 August 1820 that Ramírez retire to the country on the pretext of his health.[50] The traditional creole historiography, assuming Ramírez's integrity, suggested that wide dissemination of erroneous charges precipitated the intendant's sudden death the following year at the age of forty-four. According to Calcagno,[51] Ramírez was a "true victim of the unruliness of . . . [the] press." It would appear that poor health and the "excesses" of a free press had combined to oust the island's two top officials.

Ramírez's withdrawal did not restore public order. Just three days before, a new scandal had developed out of a confrontation between Aguiar and Ramírez's confidant, Manuel Coimbra, lawyer for the *consulado* and the naval establishment in Havana. Coimbra, named along with Ramírez in the *Tío Bartolo* article, won a verdict of "injurious to his person" against the newspaper. He then used the opportunity for a judicial act of reconciliation (set up by the censorship board as a customary alternative to legal proceedings) to rail against his detractors. In the heat of his own defense (or so his partisans claimed), Coimbra threatened to put a stop to press freedom within the next few months. According to a subsequent investigation,[52] his words caused a violent reaction from a crowd of more than three thousand that overflowed the court and spilled into the street. Coimbra had to be rescued by troops, and Echeverri ordered him held in "protective custody" in the public jail.[53]

El Tío Bartolo's popularity peaked with the Coimbra affair. Ramírez's successor as intendant would later assert that Aguiar's paper propelled "the city and the island to the brink of being lost through the insubordination that it introduced in all the classes."[54] This was also the opinion of Antonio Duarte y Zenea in two letters that he wrote to the censorship board in August 1820.[55] Duarte y Zenea was admittedly hostile to the *exaltado* press, an attitude that stemmed from press attacks on the reputation of his brother and the subsequent difficulty he had in finding a press to print his vindication. Nevertheless, Duarte y Zenea's correspondence included some of the best descriptions of the impact of *El Tío Bartolo*. In a letter of 20 August, he related how he had been forced to wait four days while the Imprenta Tormentaria printed, among other things, six thousand copies of the issue that contained Aguiar's denunciation of Coimbra's threat to the free press. In the interval, he noted that two presses worked day and night under the supervision of shifts of printers, which on one occasion proved to be a "robust slave fettered with chains." At the entrance to the building on the busy Calzada de Guadalupe, all the "notorious" papers of the Imprenta were advertised to passersby. In a second letter four days later, Duarte y Zenea declared that he and other "upright citizens" had been amazed to see the gathering of carriages at Aguiar's door, "the like of which is not seen even at the residence of . . . [Echeverri] or at any other of those subjects of the highest standing." Duarte y Zenea also worried about the impact of six thousand issues of *El Tío Bartolo* upon "ingenuous persons, and others of color." He felt that Echeverri should intervene directly to quash the press abuse that threatened the legitimacy of all authority.[56]

El Tío Bartolo's success soon attracted countermeasures from officialdom and the periodical press. Echeverri took precautions during the elections of 20–22 August—he stationed troops at the voting locations—and Duarte y Zenea noted with some satisfaction in his letter of 24 August that none of those elected to the Cortes or the provincial deputation were "friends or confidants of lawyer Aguiar."[57] By 16 September, a government notary had verified the compliance of the city's five printers[58] with a 27 June order that all printers submit samples of printed items to the press prosecutor, Indalecio Santos Suárez.[59] The periodical press also began to register disaffection at this point. *La Tía Catana Muger del Tío Bartolo* began on 2 August 1820 as a humorous imitation but soon became a rallying point around which prominent citizens could protect themselves from *Bartolo*'s "hydrophobia."[60] *La Tía Catana* went to the occasional *impreso* format early in Septem-

ber but was promptly replaced by *La Galera Constitucional*
(12 September–29 October 1820?), even more strident; it promised to incarcerate *El Esquife Arranchador* and *El Tío Bartolo*
in a reformatory where they would be taught "to respect the
order they are trying to alter."[61] *La Galera Constitucional*
sought to mobilize the "lovers of order" to seek reforms in the
free press legislation, but someone soon took more drastic action: on 3 October 1820, three men attacked Evaristo Sánchez.
He escaped when several passersby and soldiers rushed to his
aid. Sánchez credited their speedy attention to his cries for
help, which included the information that he was the editor of
El Esquife Arranchador.[62]

Even before this attack, Sánchez had become concerned
that many, like Ramírez and Coimbra, masqueraded as loyal
constitutionalists while plotting to undermine press freedom by
arguing for "special status" for the Cuban press. Now Sánchez
proposed a coalition of like-minded publications, a "fleet" of
periodical vessels to voyage together in an armada defending press freedom. In a new feature in *El Esquife Arranchador,*
(4 October 1820) Don Chilibrán convoked the city council of
Cayo-puto, which included *El Tío Bartolo, El Esquife, El Vigía,
El Botiquín, El Liberal,* and *El Patriota.*[63] All present argued
against Don Chilibrán's motion to restrict the "license of the
press." *Bartolo* expressed the consensus, arguing that "this license, this unruliness . . . is the safeguard of civil liberty."

El Esquife Arranchador's reunions of the *flota* press signified a new development in the Cuban press—a coalition of
editors. While their grievances were often personal in origin,
unity lay in their hope that constitutionalism would dislodge
the sugar planters from economic and political hegemony, end
the political favoritism shown the sugarocracy by imperial officials, and terminate the prestige of institutions such as the Patriotic Society, which they associated with their literary rivals.[64]
This ideological position might be characterized as peninsular
because it enjoyed the financial support of the peninsular merchants of Muralla Street[65] and the popular support of Spaniards who were in the national militia or had recently immi-
grated to the island. Yet this position also claimed support from
individuals whose allegiances were not defined by birthplace
but by personal motivations: residents of Havana, for example,
who sought political influence and, in order to stake their con-

stitutional claim to an expanded suffrage, emphasized that they were Spaniards first.

The appearance of *El Navío Arranchador* (November 1820–30 April 1821) amplified the impact of the *flota* press. *El Navío Arranchador* was piloted by Joaquín José García (formerly of *El Indicador Constitucional* and *El Esquife Arranchador*), who expressed editorial solidarity with *El Esquife, El Tío Bartolo,* and *El Botiquín*.[66] *El Navío* sailed from the imaginary city of San Pascasio de Hueso, which was governed by Don Vollerante Pruchinela. Several censorship reverses[67] forced García to develop a new editorial strategy. He replaced key text with blanks, on the pretext that these were documents recovered from a shipwreck and water damage had rendered them partially illegible. This tactic allowed him to portray opposition thought and personalities without the inclusion of explicit references that would trigger the censorship mechanism.

By the end of the first year of a free press, the *flota* press became openly hostile about the failure of constitutionalism to promote significant political change in Cuba. While opponents of the sugar elite scored modest gains in the municipal elections, the sugarocracy controlled the Havana provincial deputation, the deputies to the Cortes, and the good graces of the superior political chief. Censorship still rested in the hands of the elite,[68] producing what *El Esquife*'s editor called a double standard of censorship.[69] Further, the sugarocracy began to appropriate the aura of constitutionalism when Félix Varela initiated his constitutional law course in the San Carlos Seminary on 18 January 1821 with an enrollment of nearly two hundred students.[70] Still, the editors of the *flota* press did not advocate violent change; the constitution should be fulfilled, not imperiled by revolutionary anarchy. García pointedly reminded his readers that one hour of revolution could not be repaired in ten years of sacrifice.[71]

The *flota* press arrived at a more extreme position in late January 1821, when Cagigal and the provincial deputation appointed Francisco Filomeno as an extra judge for Havana, despite the almost unanimous insistence of the Havana municipal council that the provincial deputation lacked constitutional grounds for its action.[72] *El Esquife Arranchador* took up this position, noting that the enabling legislation had specified two individuals for Havana, leaving the provincial deputation with the discretion to appoint judges only in other districts. If the original two judges were deemed insufficient for the volume of litigation, *El Esquife* argued, obedience to the law dictated prior consultation with Spain before adding to their number.[73] For the *flota* press, continually entangled in litigation after unfavorable censorship decisions, the issue of who composed the judiciary was crucial. *El Tío Bartolo, El Botiquín,* and *El Esquife Arranchador* had all suffered multiple censorship reverses, and, along with the recent addition of *El Navío Arranchador,* all awaited judicial verdicts.[74] The appointment of Filomeno clearly sent a message to the press, for Filomeno had publicly expressed his opposition to *El Esquife Arranchador* in the *Diario,* and his admirers had used the same forum to criticize the municipal council and the "public writers" of Havana.[75]

Filomeno's appointment pushed the *flota* press into its most radical stance. Editor Aguiar published an article in *El Esquife* that suggested that Cuban society and its press exhibited two political tendencies: there were "constitutionalists by temperament and cordial adoption, and constitutionalists . . . by royal order." Two issues later, *El Esquife* violated acceptable rhetoric by including the king in this latter group. Aguiar suggested that the citizen who followed constitutional precepts need not recognize or obey any other authority.[76] This statement, that constitutional principles were more important than official edicts, marked the sharpest press challenge to political stability to date. Five days later, *El Navío's* editor went one satiric step further by publishing an account of a revolutionary coup in Cayo-hueso that had resulted in the execution of nineteen officials, including the intendant, the provincial deputation, and the censorship board.[77] The revolution, however, remained satiric fantasy. The editors of the *flota* press seemed unwilling to engage in political plots or desert their imaginary populations. Most importantly, confrontation between the *flota* press and officialdom was temporarily defused by the implementation on 10 March 1821 of new legislation on press freedom.

The press legislation of 22 October 1820 deserves detailed attention.[78] While it affirmed the right of every Spaniard to rush into print without prior censorship (in all matters not relating to the scriptures or Catholic doctrine), its true intent was to rationalize postpublication censorship to a degree that would intimidate potential malefactors. Articles 6 to 25 detailed the categories of press abuse and their penalties. Of the five cate-

gories, the first was "subversive," defined as "publishing principles or doctrines that conspire in a direct way to destroy
or overturn the religion of the state or the current Constitution of the Monarchy." The offense was classified at three levels
(no explicit standard given) with corresponding penalties of
two, four, or six years in prison. The second category was "seditious," which was defined as "when principles or doctrines
are published aimed at exciting rebellion or disturbing public
peace." The gradations and penalties were the same as for
subversion.

A lesser offense might be included under the third category,
"inciting to disobedience," which contained two gradations.
The most serious, when an *impreso* counseled disobedience to
a law or legitimate authority, carried a penalty of one year in
prison. If the *impreso* couched its message in satire, the penalty was only fifty *ducados* or one month in prison. For obscene
impresos, or those contrary to "accepted custom," the penalty
was a fine equivalent to the value of fifteen hundred copies of
the offending item or four months imprisonment. The fifth
category, "libelous," referred to *impresos* that "find fault with
private conduct and stain its honor or reputation." As libel was
undoubtedly the most pressing problem to the legislators, the
penalties were spelled out in more detail, ranging from a sentence of three months in prison and a fine of fifteen hundred
reales to one month and five hundred *reales*, with special mul-
tiplying factors for second and subsequent offenses.

Most important, the new legislation restructured the mechanisms of enforcement. This included new definitions of who
could be held responsible for an *impreso*, who could denounce
it, and who would judge it and determine the penalty. The 1810
legislation had featured a central censorship panel of nine
members in Spain with provincial counterparts comprised of
five members. The authority of the provincial junta extended
only to rating the *impreso*, for sentencing remained the prerogative of the judiciary. The new legislation outlined a substantially different procedure. It sought to clear up the question of authorship or responsibility for censored *impresos*.
Each item submitted for publication had to contain the legal
signature of the author, or editor, or person submitting it to
the printer. The printer, on penalty of fifty *ducados* (or five
hundred if the *impreso* was judged offensive), had to include
his name, address, and the year on every item that his press

printed. If the printer later refused to reveal the identity of the author of an offending item, then the printer assumed responsibility for all penalties assessed. The new law also specified that any Spaniard could denounce an *impreso* as subversive or seditious, while certain officials were authorized to denounce items in all categories except personal injury. The press prosecutor (*fiscal de imprenta*), a lawyer appointed yearly by the provincial deputation, was one such official. Printers were required to remit one copy of everything they printed to the press prosecutor, on penalty of five *ducados* for every omission. Individuals or their legal representatives were still the only ones who could denounce an *impreso* for libel.

The censorship procedure proved the most significant innovation. To assess a denounced *impreso*, an *alcalde constitucional*—a constitutional judge resident in the capital of each province—convoked a panel of *jueces de hecho*, often called *jurados*, or jurors. The juror became the basic unit of censorial supervision and judicial recourse.[79] A juror had to be a citizen, over twenty-five years of age, and a resident of the capital. Jurors were selected by a plurality vote in the constitutional municipal council of the provincial capitals; their number depended upon a formula of tripling the number of municipal council members. Upon receipt of a denunciation, nine jurors, selected by lottery, would convene to decide whether legal proceedings should be initiated. If their decision was affirmative, an order would be issued to prohibit further sale of the issue (the penalty for illegal sale was five hundred times the value of one issue), and proceedings would begin to determine the author or editor of the item. In the case of a charge of subversion, sedition, or inciting to disobedience in the first degree, the person deemed responsible would be imprisoned. For lesser offenses, the accused could arrange a bond to avoid incarceration. In the case of libel there was a brief opportunity (three days if the accused was in town, to a maximum of twenty days if absent) for the accused to be judicially reconciled with his denouncer before the judge.

For the trial itself, a new drawing of twelve jurors (none of the original nine were eligible) was submitted to the defendant, who could refuse up to seven and again reject any of their replacements. There the accused's options ended, and the jury convened to hear evidence. After the presiding judge reviewed the case, the jurors retired to reach a verdict. Conviction required eight out of twelve votes, and in the case of agreement on guilt but not degree, compromise on the lesser charge was mandated. The penalties for various infractions have been noted above. If the verdict was "not guilty," the denouncer had to pay court costs. In either case the procedure was expected to cover the costs of the administration of the legislation. Appeal was allowed only on procedural grounds, and after a guilty verdict, all copies of the *impreso*, or the offending section thereof, had to be collected from subscribers and the press office. A fine equal to one thousand copies of the item would be levied on anyone caught selling the offending item after the judicial verdict had been broadcast in the official press.

The new legislation should have silenced the *flota* press; in fact, it became a severe test for General Nicolás Mahy, a veteran of the wars against France and the new superior political chief (3 March 1821–18 July 1822). Two weeks after assuming office, Mahy was already complaining about the problem that would dominate his correspondence—the extravagance of the Havana press and the failure of the new legislation to curtail it.[80] He located part of the problem in the procedure for selecting jurors. Municipal councils were "creatures of popular whim, only concerned with maintaining their popularity in order to be reelected," and their electoral sessions, by virtue of being open meetings, were subject to outside pressures. He suggested that this was not the appropriate atmosphere for selecting jurors. Further, because "prominent people" had refrained from pursuing appointments as jurors,[81] the majority of those elected were sympathetic to the *flota* press. Many were under the sway of Tomás Gutiérrez de Piñeres because of his defense of local prerogatives against the claims of authority of Mahy and the provincial deputation. Piñeres soon exploited his influence over members of the city council and censorship juries[82] to overshadow the editors of the *flota* press; "piñerista" became the accepted designation of the political opposition to the sugarocracy.

The cleric's ascendency over the censorship process immediately produced partisan verdicts. Mahy charged that papers "incendiary in the extreme" escaped prosecution, while others were denounced and indicted merely on the basis of authorship. Analysis of censorship records confirms the general's assertion: of ten denunciations submitted from March to June by the new press prosecutor, Diego Tanco,[83] only two resulted in indictments and both of these cases awaited the decision of a jury of twelve. Preliminary juries had rejected four charges against *El Esquife* and three against *impresos* by Piñeres.[84] On 18 April 1821 Mariscal de Campo Juan Moscoso, ranking military officer in Cuba, suggested that *piñerista* control over censorship required the suspension of press freedom.[85] While Moscoso tended to view press abuse as a financial strategy to augment subscriptions, he also recognized its potential impact on the lower classes, the "population of color," and the troops stationed on the island.[86]

Moscoso, like many other officials, worried because Piñeres and the *flota* press continued to attack the judiciary, even though the jury procedure in censorship matters reduced the role of judge to presiding official. The legislation of 13 January 1821 complicated matters further by demoting municipal judges (alcaldes) to bureaucrats, while transferring their judicial functions to judges appointed by the provincial deputation under the supervision of the superior political chief.[87] This legislation represented the effort of the Cortes "to rationalize the plethora of magistracies that existed throughout the empire by abolishing all courts of first instance and replacing them with magistrates called jueces de letras."[88] In Cuba, many alcaldes refused to relinquish their jurisdictions,[89] and in this they received support from the *piñerista* press. Piñeres was also reluctant to see judicial authority pass from the municipal level, where he had some leverage, to appointees chosen by the provincial deputation, whose members, as noted earlier, were always prominent members of the Cuban elite. Consequently, he published *Mi opinión sobre jueces de letras* and several *Desengaños*, arguing that the king, his ministers, and any local official who implemented this legislation were in violation of constitutional principles.

Piñeres's charges seem to have been a deliberate test of his influence over the periodical press and the censorship juries. The *piñeristas* went too far when they submitted the legislation for censorship, provoking defections from the *piñerista* press and a crescendo of opposition from the "lovers of order." *El Falucho Vigía* (10 March 1821–10 January 1822?) left the *flota* after only a month, charging that the *piñeristas* were merely posturing as constitutionalists, feigning liberalism by shouting "vivas" to the constitution on street corners, hanging pictures of Spanish generals on their walls, and wearing ribbons on their coat or hat proclaiming "Constitution or Death."[90] About a month later, *El Falucho* introduced a new column, a series of conversations between Blas and Jacinto, "on the corner of Desengaño, city of Reform." The conversations were a parody of *El Tío Bartolo* and featured increasingly vituperative charges against the *piñeristas.*[91]

Another *periódico* to declare war on "los malos escritores" was *El Amigo del Pueblo* (2 April 1821–6 January 1822), founded by the press prosecutor, Diego Tanco![92] Finally, *El Imparcial* (May–28 July 1821?) proudly accepted *piñerista* aspersions of "servility," offering to represent all those who "obey the laws, respect the authorities, and concern themselves actively with the preservation of public order."[93] By early July or August, battle lines had formed in the periodical press: *El Tío Bartolo* and *El Esquife Arranchador* (*El Esquife Constitucional* after 28 July 1821) and *El Indicador Constitucional* were still in the *piñerista* camp, reinforced by *El Impertérrito Constitucional* (formerly *El Botiquín Constitucional*, to at least 1 March 1822) and a newcomer, *La Corbeta Constitucional* (28 June 1821–June? 1822), which blended egalitarian rhetoric with racial slurs against the Cuban elite and the "servile" press.[94] Targeted as members of the "servile" press were *El Falucho Vigía, El Amigo del Pueblo, El Imparcial,* and the *Gaceta de Cayo-Guinchos.*[95]

Official countermeasures, too, were not long in coming. Mahy reversed his early overtures to the peninsular faction—he realized that military discipline was crumbling as the generals and troops who had forced Cagigal to proclaim the constitution became more aggressive in their demands—and he began to use creoles, especially the sugarocracy, as a counterpoise.[96] The excesses of the *piñerista* press also appear to have been a factor in his change of attitude, a change that culminated in mid-1821 with his decision to suspend the Cortes's new tariff legislation. The peninsular bourgeoisie, who dominated the Cortes, were not only interested in Cuban revenues; they also sought control over sugar production and markets. The new tariffs were calculated to provide a protectionist advantage for Spain's struggling industries at the cost of the Cuban producers. Mahy's decision to suspend this legislation struck a blow at the peninsular merchants in Havana, who backed the *piñerista* faction.[97] At the same time, Mahy retaliated against the *piñerista* press; a summary of his correspondence reveals that the general, in a letter of 23 August 1821, repeated charges against *piñerista* control of censorship and detailed remedial action.[98] In addition, Mahy subsidized several publications that met his approval.[99] Mahy's recommendation that José de Arazoza continue as editor of the official *Diario* also formed part of his campaign.[100]

Mahy's campaign against the *piñerista* press brought immediate results. José de Aguiar reported in a letter published in *El Indicador Constitucional* on 14 August that he had suspended publication of *El Tío Bartolo* because it had been hinted to him that the next unfavorable censorship decision would result in imprisonment and that one of Manuel Coimbra's nephews (the same Manuel Coimbra with whom he had been embroiled in the Ramírez controversy) now served as interim commander of Castillo del Morro.[101] Less than a week later, a censorship jury returned a verdict of "libel" against Piñeres for an *impreso* impugning Tomás Romay and the provincial deputation; the cleric was sentenced to one year of detention in a convent.[102] Indeed, from August to the end of 1821, only three of thirteen denounced items escaped indictments, and two of the three also represented victories for the "lovers of order."[103]

Mahy did not limit himself to prosecuting *piñerista* writers; he also tolerated violence against them. He refused to investigate Francisco Ruiz Fernández's charge that Coronel Tomás O'Connelly and eighteen men had sought him out on the night of 13 October to kill him for the continued criticisms of the military hierarchy in *El Impertérrito*.[104] More important, Mahy ignored the extracurricular activities of a police force of sixty men he had established under the command of Domingo Armona to pursue criminals in the environs of Havana; increasingly Armona meted out summary justice in Havana streets. It was more than a coincidence that *El Esquife Arranchador* ceased publication without warning after 19 December 1821, subsequent to filling the last three issues with denunciations of Armona's excesses and Mahy's complicity.[105] Armona would become an increasingly important part of the extralegal campaign against what Mahy saw as "ill-intentioned writers."

The *piñerista* press became much more subdued in the face of Mahy's offensive.[106] Yet the decline of the *piñerista* press was not simply the result of official and extralegal pressure. The independence of Mexico, Central America, and neighboring Santo Domingo also had a sobering effect. Once again, Cuba was reminded of the costs of political innovation, and the press was quick to offer its cautionary counsels. Perhaps the most famous reaction was the *impreso* of José de Arango, *Independencia de la Isla de Cuba*,[107] but even *El Tío Bartolo* featured an impassioned warning about revolution, reaffirming that liberal aspirations were best served by the constitution and by union with Spain. Aguiar decried the renewed equation between "liberal writers" and "revolutionaries" that followed from the events in Mexico; he decided later that month to terminate *El Tío Bartolo*, stating that "things are such that everyone should maintain a profound silence."[108]

The passing of *El Esquife Arranchador* and *El Tío Bartolo* left the field open to more moderate papers like *El Amante de Sí Mismo* (9 January 1822–25 May 1822?). As *El Amante* claimed the mantle of Diego Tanco's *El Amigo del Pueblo*,[109] Tanco's final editorial offered a statement of belief of the new moderate press. Tanco argued that "the best constitution for a people is not the one which offers the best possible advantages for its most complete happiness, but rather the one that is most within its reach." Purely democratic government was not currently possible in the islands of America, tainted as they were by corruption and racial mixture. Tanco outlined the immediate task: gradual reform, education and public schools, and maintenance of the present social peace.[110] His successor's choice of title, *El Amante de Sí Mismo*, and the argument that self-love was an essential principle of natural law, could not have been a more appropriate banner for the new moderate press.

The epilogue to the decline of the *flota* press was written at the end of the second year of press freedom. In March 1822, *El Esquife Arranchador* was resurrected as *El Esquife Constitucional* under new editors[111] in time to witness the defeat of *piñerista* candidates in the municipal elections of March 1822. *El Esquife Constitucional*'s new editors charged that force and bribery had been utilized to ensure candidates acceptable to General Mahy and the creole oligarchy. How much force had been necessary seems uncertain, although Domingo Armona and his cohorts were apparently in high profile.[112]

The election defeat was a bitter blow to the *piñeristas*. Though they had lost elections before—in the fall of 1821 Félix Varela and Leonardo Santos Suárez were elected to the Cortes, and José Antonio Saco, among others, to the provincial deputation—the *piñeristas* could claim that these positions were traditionally the stronghold of the sugarocracy. Now, however, they lost their influence at the municipal level, which included a say in the selection of censorship jurors. Out of frustration *El Esquife Constitucional* dropped its allegorical format and, protected against censors by anagrams, criticized Armona and Mahy directly.[113] It is hardly surprising, then, that Armona and a party of armed men entered the press of Pedro Nolasco Boloña (called the Amigo de la Constitución after the daily of the same name) on the afternoon of 13 April to settle accounts. They thrashed Boloña, struck Juan de Nogerido, contributor to *El Amigo de la Constitución*, menaced several other employees, and smashed presses and trays of type. Armona was reported to have taunted his victims to continue writing if they dared, for he had a "license to kill, . . . [and] plenty of protection to do whatever [he] felt like." Later that day, Boloña, dressed in his uniform of a lieutenant in the suburban volunteer militia, protested to General Mahy but encountered only indifference; Mahy even pretended not to recognize Boloña's insignia.[114]

The Armona affair represented a crucial moment in the evolution of a constitutional free press in Cuba. Would Armona's violations of constitutional liberties be tolerated because they had been directed toward the *piñeristas*? An overview of the reaction to Armona's attack is available in a confidential report submitted to the Spanish minister in London, Luis de Onís, by an informant in Havana, one Moseau.[115] Samples of the periodical press were included to document the seriousness of the situation. The *impresos* ranged from *El Esquife Extraordinario* of 14 April, which broke the story under the title of "Monstruo atentado del Capitán Armona," to a pamphlet of the following day suggesting that this anticonstitutional attack on free press was a symbolic attack on the political legitimacy of constitutionalism.[116] Perhaps the most revealing perspective was contained in "Asombro de un catalán acabado de llegar de la Península, país libre y constitucional en toda la fuerza de la expresión."[117] Dated the day following Armona's raid, this pamphlet expressed the amazement of a "son of Barcelona" at the abuses of constitutional freedoms that he had witnessed in the two weeks since his arrival. He alluded to two previous occasions on which presses had been smashed and editors or printers threatened or attacked. The major distinction between Barcelona and Havana, he argued, was Domingo Armona.

The victims of Armona's raid soon recovered their public voices. Three days after the attack, 16 April, *El Amigo de la Constitución* issued a number from the one operable press in Pedro Nolasco Boloña's establishment. The opening editorial offered a historical perspective on events, emphasizing Armona's actions as just one of a series of affronts to constitutional liberties, which included the Restoration of 1814 and the necessity of forcing Captain General Cagigal to proclaim the constitution in 1820. All these events, the editorial argued, demonstrated that Havana continued to suffer the tyranny of the few because "men do not know how to unite for their own advantage."[118] *Ultima queja al Excmo. Sr. D. Nicolás Mahy,* written by one of the victims, Juan de Nogerido, under the pseudonym "the liberals," also stressed that Armona's outrage was only the latest in a series of incidents that stained Mahy's tenure. Further, Nogerido charged that Mahy had denied Mariscal del Campo Juan Moscoso the consideration that was due him as ranking military officer on the island.

This last charge indicates that the pamphlet, published on 16 April 1822, may have been part of a conspiracy to remove Mahy from office that same evening. Our knowledge of this plot comes from the informant Moseau, who reported that the strategy was to take advantage of the volatile atmosphere of a patriotic songfest, during the celebrations for the second anniversary of the proclamation of the Constitution of 1812, to propose Moscoso as an alternative to Mahy. Mahy apparently caught wind of the conspiracy, for the celebrations were terminated by the arrival of "an armed force" (possibly Armona?). The crowd dispersed, but Moseau warned that effective measures were needed by "your government" or the island might be lost. He suggested that Armona ("a brutal man, without any manners") and his troops were a major cause of the deteriorating situation, for their actions had "more the air of brigands than of police."[119]

Confirmation of Moseau's analysis can also be found in the correspondence of the military commander Juan Moscoso.[120] Moscoso also reviewed the charges against Armona and Mahy, noting that the "people are agitated," provoked by *periódicos* openly critical of Mahy. As the mail from Spain had not arrived for several months, rumors of Mahy's recall had begun to circulate, and Moscoso admitted that he had "heard" his own name mentioned as a possible successor. He did not sound too keen on remaining on the island, and he suggested that future captains general (his usage) be entrusted with their own subordinates to isolate them from the creole elite. Moscoso complained that Cuba was governed "by godfathers and godmothers," whose support had allowed Mahy to ignore the fact that "the people cry out."

Mahy, however, did not alter his course. Intimidation was, if anything, increased after the Armona affair. Juan Nogerido, accused of sedition and subversion for *Ultima queja,* found himself within the week incarcerated in the public jail, despite the free press legislation having expressly forbidden imprisonment of accused authors and editors with common criminals.[121] In court on the morning of the twentieth, Pedro Nolasco Boloña's lawyer, Manuel Bernardo Lorenzano, was menaced by Armona, who came armed with pistols and a sabre.[122] Printer Tiburcio Campe reported that Armona, in passing the doors of the Imprenta Liberal, was heard to remark that he had "taken possession of a half-dozen excellent garrotes to finish off the party."[123]

Mahy weathered the storm of criticism without relaxing his intimidation of the *piñeristas,* although, as a gesture of official integrity, he temporarily suspended Armona,[124] who apparently continued his depredations in an "unofficial" capacity. Meanwhile, Mahy, taking advantage of his control over the censorship juries since the last municipal election, increasingly favored judicial prosecution to supervise the press. On 9 May 1822, *El Esquife Constitucional* reported that one writer had been tricked into giving himself up for imprisonment when he naively thought he was being summoned to a judicial reconciliation with his denouncers. On 25 May, when a jury found Nogerido's *Ultima queja* to be "inciting to disobedience in the second degree," its author had already been languishing in jail for a month. A fellow prisoner complained on 26 May that he had already spent fifty-six days in prison while the charges against him were being formulated.[125] By the end of May, the editors of *El Esquife* awaited sentencing on five charges stemming from infractions during the last two months alone.[126] The last issue of *El Esquife* was published on 29 May 1822.[127]

The Armona affair virtually spelled the end of the *flota* press. The *piñeristas'* demise provided testimony to the resiliency of the sugarocracy, who had, once again with the cooperation of a compliant colonial official, regained political control. Mahy's actions against the *piñeristas* handed the periodical press back to moderate creoles who, in the last eighteen months of the constitutional *trienio*, would turn to a deeper exploration of constitutionalism and other political options.

CHAPTER 4

Constitutional Reprise (II): Creole Constitutionalism, 1822–1823

GENERAL MAHY'S offensive against the *piñeristas* produced a marked moderation in the Cuban press by June 1822 and stimulated wider creole support for constitutionalism, a position previously dominated by the students of the San Carlos Seminary and their progressive educators. Whereas the constitution had appeared a weapon in the hands of the *piñeristas*, it now seemed a blueprint for substantial self-government: all the constitutional institutions—provincial deputation, municipal council, judiciary (and censorship juries)—could now further elite creole interests. The editor of *El Amante de Sí Mismo*, for example, now felt comfortable with the current state of affairs, arguing that only constitutionalism could save the monarchies of Europe.[1] As creoles became accustomed to the role of constitutionalists, however, they watched with some concern as peninsular merchants began to fix their hopes on another restoration of absolute monarchy. The impotence of Spain, underscored when the United States recognized the independence of Spain's mainland colonies in March 1822, only made creoles less willing to accept a political restoration that would redound to the benefit of the defeated troops, commanders, and royalists who flooded the city.[2]

Figure 4-1. Major Cuban Periódicos, 1822–1824

| 1822 | | | | | | 1823 | | | | | | | | | | | | 1824 | | | |
| J | J | A | S | O | N | D | J | F | M | A | M | J | J | A | S | O | N | D | J | F | M | A | M |

Diario de la Habana

Noticioso

Observador   Papel Oficial de Santiago de Cuba
          12   14
Gaceta de Puerto Príncipe

Indicador Constitucional

Correo de Trinidad

Amante de Sí Mismo

Amigo de la Constitución

Gaceta de la Habana

2

        Español Libre
    15   25
       Americano Libre / Revisor Político / Liberal Habanero
         15   28 3   30
         Redactor General
         1   29
           Concordia Cubana
           10   31
             Gaceta (Matanzas)
             Miscelánea
             1   31

KEY
————— Publication data confirmed
- - - - - - - Incomplete publication data

The Cuban stake in continued constitutionalism was the primary theme of the *Gaceta de la Habana* (2 June 1822– April 1823),[3] a triweekly edited by the Díaz de Castro brothers, owners of the Imprenta Fraternal. The editors insisted that the *Gaceta* represented no particular constituency but rather an informal alliance of "lovers of order" who had coalesced around the campaign to defeat *piñerista* candidates in the last municipal election.[4] Only the constitution, claimed the *Gaceta*'s editors, could protect individual rights and prevent the dangerous factionalism now apparent in Mexico and the other independent republics. It was not the constitution, but political opportunism hiding behind the facade of liberalism, that lay at the root of the various crises of the past several years. The editors of the *Gaceta* wanted to avoid political factionalism, particularly over the anti-*piñerista* measures of the recently deceased General Mahy (19 June 1822). They deemed charges of despotism against Mahy irrelevant because "there is no alternative, either we must live as we are living, or, if there should be introduced fatal innovations to seduce the masses and cause them to commit a thousand absurdities and assaults, we must all perish."[5]

An attempted restoration coup in Madrid presented the first challenge to moderate creole constitutionalism. Ferdinand VII's advisors, convinced that popular opinion was now turning against the liberal Cortes, launched a press campaign with the publication of *El Procurador General del Rey* on 22 May 1822. *El Procurador*'s subtitle proclaimed its opposition to constitutionalism: "written at the beginning of the third year of the second captivity of Señor Don Ferdinand VII, legitimate sovereign of Spain, and during the fatal crisis of the frightful persecution of Altar and Throne." Within weeks, open fighting broke out in the streets of Madrid; on 7 July, army and militia units loyal to the Cortes subdued six battalions of the royal guard.[6]

In Havana the arrival of the news of the constitutionalist victory (probably on 29 August 1822) only strengthened the resolve of the moderate press. The narrow brush with political restoration counseled even greater efforts to support the constitutional status quo. One notable contributor to the *Gaceta* that September was José Antonio Saco, Félix Varela's student and replacement in the Philosophy Chair at the Colegio Seminario. Saco, writing under the apt pseudonym "Amigo del Orden," defined himself not only as a constitutional liberal but also as an American who expected to be in charge in his own house.[7] Here was a forthright expression of Cuban self-interest. It coincided with the latest success of the sugarocracy—permission from the Cortes for Cuba to establish its own tariff legislation.[8] Now it seemed that neither independence nor restoration held greater promise than constitutionalism. Loyalty to constitutionalism, then, was born of a peculiar blend of idealism and self-interest: admiration for the theoretical basis of constitutionalism mixed with fear of political innovation, an ironical coincidence of a new assertive "Americanism" and a deepened identification with peninsular politics.[9]

The paradox was not lost on the surviving *piñeristas*. The printer Tiburcio Campe, one of the few veterans of the *piñerista* faction still at liberty,[10] and a collaborator, Manuel Domínguez, founded *El Español Libre* (15 September 1822–25 February 1823) to protest the growing "americanism" of creole constitutionalists. Their first editorial, on 15 September 1822, decried the decline of patriotic support for constitutionalism in Havana and promised to expose those who, under the "new mask of *moderates*," sought to undermine the full intent of the constitution.[11] To illustrate these charges, *El Español Libre* championed the case of José Correa y Bottino.

Army Captain José Correa y Bottino was the son of Diego Correa, whose article "Lo que sufre la Habana," published in *El Amigo de la Constitución* on 27 June 1822, had earned him a ten-year prison sentence. (The article defended an editorial in the *Noticioso* that had criticized the deceased Mahy.) Even the editors of the *Gaceta* felt that the sentence was too extreme, and Correa's son sought vengeance on José Antonio Miralla, the writer who had denounced his father's article.[12] At a ball on the evening of 24 September young Correa y Bottino confronted Miralla; only the intervention of one Rafael Gática prevented violence. When Sebastián Kindelán, interim superior political chief, heard that Correa had threatened Gática, he ordered Correa's arrest and arranged an act of conciliation for the following day. At this event, supervised by Kindelán himself, Correa y Bottino drew his sword and repeatedly stabbed Gática, and then wounded Kindelán.[13]

Such unprecedented violence galvanized the press. *El Español Libre* portrayed Correa y Bottino as a victim of an "american" conspiracy, a man driven to violence by his frustration at seeking justice. In the pages of *El Español Libre* Correa became symbolic of the fate of the truly liberal constitutionalist in a system dominated by "moderates."[14] On the other hand, Correa's actions offered the "lovers of order" a tremendous opportunity to confirm their contention that the real menace to Cuba came from the disintegrating *piñerista* fringe, "about twelve individuals . . . rabid with desire to rule over us, and to bury us among ruins."[15] The censorship juries apparently agreed with the "lovers of order": a quickened tempo of prosecution in October and November resulted in seven indictments in seven cases against a new *piñerista* publication, *El Fiscal del Pueblo* (September–November 1822?), and one each against *El Indicador Constitucional* and *El Amigo de la Constitución.*[16]

In the wake of public reaction against Correa y Bottino, creole moderates pressed their advantage by publishing the triweekly *El Americano Libre* (15 November 1822–28 February 1823). *El Americano Libre's* glowing dedication to the Colegio Seminario ("respected asylum of the sciences . . . mansion of enlightenment . . . illustrious corporation") is significant. Like *El Observador Habanero* and *El Amante de Sí Mismo*, the new *periódico* was in large part a product of the Colegio Seminario. Its director, Evaristo Zenea y Luz, and collaborators like Domingo del Monte and José Antonio Cintra were all students of the course on constitutional law established by Félix Varela in 1821. The prospectus evinced a clear sense of mission: to uphold constitutional liberties, to spur magistrates into compliance with constitutional law, and to offer material for the public instruction of Cuban citizens.[17] *El Americano Libre* promised to overstate its adherence to liberalism in order to dissolve the contentious issue of moderates and *exaltados*,[18] but the content of most issues fell far short of this goal. Despite a reputation as "the most serene and worthy defender of the banner of new political ideas in the island of Cuba,"[19] much of the language of the *periódico* (e.g., "to disseminate enlightenment and knowledge") might have come from members of a previous generation.

Continuities of language and tone in *El Americano Libre* revealed that moderate constitutionalists could not escape fears about what they called "fanaticism."[20] They wished to avoid the conspiracies and revolutions that might turn their "rich american jewel" into a wasteland, and this necessarily meant holding a position that fell short of the *exaltado's* wholehearted embrace of constitutionalism. Nevertheless, they did not seek public order at any cost. Although press factionalism was dangerous, the editors of *El Americano Libre* did not feel that it justified the "measures of terror" taken by Mahy against the *piñeristas*. They advocated freedom of expression "even when there are others with the contrary opinion." Tolerance was a strategy: words, fortified by reason, would prevail when repression might lead to calamity. Their indulgence of dissenting opinion also stemmed from the arrogance of class, education, and youth, which dismissed the possibility of rivalry from their inferiors: "men without principles, without the least literary education." [21] This attitude allowed the editors of *El Americano Libre* to turn a deaf ear to their critics and to concentrate on more substantial issues. The most pressing issue was the upcoming election for deputies to the Cortes.

For the "lovers of order" elections were the Achilles' heel of the constitutional system. Their concern this year (1822) was less the fear of an electoral victory for peninsular candidates than the fear of disruptions by disgruntled parties. The elections began on 1 December with no major incidents reported during the first four days. By 5 December only the parish elections in Santo Cristo remained incomplete. Suddenly one unhappy *piñerista*, Gaspar Rodríguez, struck a creole voter after an argument over who should be eligible to vote. Rodríguez was escorted away, but incensed creole voters, many of whom were also members of the national militia, stayed to discuss the matter. According to Kindelán's sources, the *piñeristas* saw an opportunity to spread rumors of an impending pronouncement of independence, and this alarm caused peninsular members of the militia to rise to arms. A confrontation was avoided only by the astute intervention of several prominent citizens. Meanwhile, members of a predominantly peninsular battalion demanded that Kindelán punish the "uprising" of the creole militia by demobilizing them. A standoff ensued until 7 December, with the peninsular militia occupying sections of the city and creole militia units forming in the suburbs beyond the city walls and sending Kindelán messages that they were willing to act upon his orders. Kindelán feared to prolong the stalemate, for he knew that among the gathering creoles were agents of Simón Bolívar who might use this incident to promote independence. Unwilling for the same reason to use creole troops (for successful military action might be as dangerous as a continued standoff), Kindelán found himself "almost isolated and without coercive power." Reluctantly, he agreed to an un-constitutional investigative commission, and this development, in addition to his threat to muster out the peninsular troops, resolved the confrontation.[22]

In subsequent reports, Kindelán was particularly caustic about the role of the *piñerista* press in this affair. On the day of the confrontation, *El Español Libre*'s editors charged that the elections were legally void because of bribery, fraudulent voters, armed scrutineers, and the distribution of hundreds of lists containing the names of preferred candidates.[23] Similarly, in *El Español Libre*'s issue of the seventh, they argued that Kindelán's management of the crisis indicated disloyalty to the king and the constitution and that only the intervention of peninsular troops had frustrated an independence plot in which the governor was complicit.[24]

Kindelán took several measures to redress the situation. He increased prosecution of problem presses (Tiburcio Campe's Imprenta Liberal and Pedro Nolasco Boloña's *El Amigo de la Constitución*) and by "prudent methods" persuaded other printers not to print anything further relating to this controversy. Kindelán could be more discreet than his predecessor: the Cortes's additional press legislation of 1822 granted greater discretionary power to the censorship juries, particularly in the overseas provinces of Ultramar.[25] In the next several weeks, jurors brought fourteen indictments against *El Amigo de la Constitución* and two against *El Indicador Constitucional* (*El Fiscal del Pueblo* had apparently folded under the barrage of prosecutions the previous month).[26]

Kindelán singled out one *piñerista* for special attention: Juan Nogerido.[27] Nogerido's entanglement with the censorship process increased with the publication of his *Ultima queja*, a denunciation of the Armona affair.[28] He had been a *piñerista* since mid-1821(he had helped to write and distribute Gutiérrez de Piñeres's sixth *Desengaño* of 17 June 1821), but it was the beating he received from Armona that propelled him toward a concerted press campaign, and prison. Between the publication of *Ultima queja* and the militia confrontation of early December, Nogerido's writings had been denounced six times, on every charge from subversion to libel. Only two of the cases had reached resolution, but already he had received sentences totaling twenty-seven months in prison plus costs and fines that undoubtedly would translate into more time served. Yet prison did not stem Nogerido's pen; indeed it seems to have increased his activity and virulence. His serialized "Aviso prudente," his statement on the elections and militia confrontation, prompted four separate denunciations to the censorship juries.[29]

Kindelán's investigation could not prove that Nogerido authored "Aviso prudente," an indication of the subterfuges employed by *piñerista* authors at this stage. Rumors floated about that Nogerido accepted responsibility for literary productions other than his own in exchange for money. It was said that on occasion he recruited another prisoner or even a slave to claim responsibility as author. Once again, these reports were never substantiated. The investigation, however, did uncover an incident involving an article in *El Fiscal del Pueblo*, where the purported author turned out to be Ignacio Witenfeld, an illiterate slave rented out by his free mulatto master to work on construction projects. Witenfeld recognized his signature on the submitted article, but swore that it had been obtained under false pretenses.[30]

Kindelán's strategy of intensified prosecution of the *piñeristas* met with success. *El Español Libre* ceased publication on 25 February 1823. In a telling move, Tiburcio Campe, editor and printer of *El Español Libre*, changed the name of his press from the Imprenta Liberal to the Imprenta de la Amistad.[31] *El Americano Libre* had already dismissed its former rival; after an article in the 3 January issue, its editors felt at liberty to ignore the *piñeristas*, focusing instead on a series of articles about Spanish imperialism in the Americas (the comparison with oriental despotism was a frequent theme in issues 20–29) or on literary productions such as Domingo del Monte's "Noche de luna en la alameda de Paula."[32]

Three days after the passing of *El Español Libre*, *El Americano Libre* announced the successful termination of its task of promoting constitutionalism. Literary activity appealed to its contributors, however, and on 3 March 1823 the printer Antonio María Valdés and other contributors to *El Americano Libre* founded *El Revisor Político y Literario* (3 March–30 August 1823),[33] a *revista* "dedicated to the pleasant and tranquil study of literature." The pages of *El Revisor Político* constituted the most singular demonstration to date of creole intellectual prowess and ideological solidarity. Three generations of creoles were represented—Francisco Arango, the ideologue of the first Cuban sugar boom, Félix Varela, teacher and deputy to the

Cortes, and youthful contributors like José Antonio Saco and Domingo del Monte—but it was the enthusiasm of the newest generation for literary activity that gave the *revista* its tone.[34] *El Revisor Político*'s earnestness was humorously recognized in a letter to the editor. The letter decried the lack of sensationalist items and cautioned the editors to "save their discourses for their class on the Constitution, their harangues for the University, and their meditations for their philosophy exams."[35] In fact, contributors to *El Revisor Político* did not so much ignore politics as discuss it in a very academic manner. José Antonio Cintra, for example, contributed an article on whether a constitutional king had the power to dismiss his own ministers.[36] Yet the confident and even pedantic rhetoric of *El Revisor Político* barely concealed concern that Cuba was enjoying an unnatural interlude of tranquility, that once again the press would be "given over to its own impulses, and man, to his passions."[37] In retrospect we know that this concern was justified, for at that very juncture an independence conspiracy was brewing. It would be the task of a new official to discover it.

General Francisco Dionisio Vives assumed charge of the island of Cuba on 3 May 1823 and declared "the time of illusion has passed; men no longer sacrifice themselves for mere theories."[38] Vives meant the statement as prescriptive rather than descriptive, for he had extraordinary powers to enforce it. His "Instrucciones" gave him free rein to meet any threats to political stability. While the first article enjoined him to uphold the constitutional polity, the second granted him the right to suspend any legislation. He was authorized to expel individuals from the island to reduce factional conflict and to organize a police force to guarantee social order.[39] In the aftermath of Mexican independence, the Cortes saw Cuba as too important to Spain's fortunes to allow it political parity with peninsular provinces. Particularly troublesome was the impact of the free press on Cuba; the "Instrucciones" warned Vives that the deplorable state of the Havana press fully demanded all his consideration and careful attention.[40] While complaints about the press had somewhat abated now (the "Instrucciones" credited the loyalty of the citizenry and the popularity of Mahy), Vives was instructed to make use of the official press "to enlighten . . . public opinion, and to guide those natives to the mark in the naming of juries, making them aware of the unfortunate results that negligence or partiality occasions."[41]

Upon his arrival, Vives found the Havana press relatively subdued despite Tiburcio Campe's release of the first number of a new *periódico* entitled the *Redactor General* (1 May?–29 June 1823?) with the pugnacious banner: "They sustain the law, placed underneath, crowns, mitres, and scepters."[42] The policies of Mahy and Kindelán had achieved a long-term effect on the press. Juan Nogerido, on the day of Vives's arrival, was sentenced to another year in prison for an article printed in *El Amigo de la Constitución* on 23 February 1823.[43] One month later when Vives suspended the Cortes's legislation authorizing the gathering of groups to discuss politics, Vives did not mention the press as one of the factors imperiling Cuban society.[44]

In Vives's efforts to restrain the press, to reduce factionalism between creole and peninsular, to repel interference from dissident America, and to insulate the sugar economy and its enslaved labor from any political repercussions, he reckoned without events in Europe. On 6 July 1823 a French ship of war entered the harbor with an official communiqué from the governor of Martinique confirming that French troops had crossed into Spanish territory on 7 April.[45] Although Vives had not received any official confirmation of this development, it had been known for several weeks that the French, acting on behalf of the conservative monarchs of the Concert of Europe, had invaded Spain to restore Ferdinand VII to absolute power.

With the situation dramatized by the French ship in port, Vives found himself in a position similar to his predecessor's in 1808, when news of the Napoleonic invasion had reached Havana. The political ramifications of this second invasion, however, were not in doubt. Even before news of the French invasion had been confirmed, rumors of the Holy Alliance's plans to restore absolute monarchy endangered moderate constitutionalism as a political option and caused many creoles to consider alternatives to a second restoration. As early as 28 June 1823, Vives noted the proliferation of conspiratorial groups. One of these societies, called the Society of the Sun,[46] was reportedly attracting increasing numbers to the banner of independence. Although Vives disclosed that all or most of the sugarocracy opposed the option of independence, he also complained that these same "sensible men" refused to prosecute the plotters.[47]

Vives did not report that the prospect of restoration had also radicalized the *moderados. El Revisor Político* exuded defiance. The 30 June 1823 issue contained an article by the French author Dominique de Pradt, submitted in translation to the editors as instructive of "our true interests."[48] The article was taken from a chapter of *Paralelo de la Inglaterra y la Rusia* in which the author argued against a rumor that Spain would sell Cuba to the English to erase past debts. De Pradt predicted that such speculation was fruitless because Cuba would soon free itself, or be liberated by the Spanish American republics.

El Revisor Político's publication of this item worried Vives. Although the *periódico*'s editorial line firmly supported constitutionalism, Vives feared that the rumor of an impending exchange of colonial masters had been given greater credibility. Given England's opposition to the slave trade since 1808, this prospect provided the one argument that could swell the ranks of conspirators. To this point, Cuban slave owners and resident slave traders (increasingly Cádiz-based merchants) had successfully defended their vested interests in the continuation of the slave trade: Francisco de Arango had protected the sugarocracy against motions to ban the slave trade in the 1811 Cortes and in the Council of the Indies in 1816. The Spanish had yielded to British pressure in 1817, promising to end the traffic in slaves in 1820, but the revolution of the generals in that year, and Spain's inability to impose her will across the Atlantic, signaled another reprieve. Now, it seemed, only the direct intervention of England could disrupt the bustling extralegal activity that continued with the complicity of officialdom and a revenue-starved Spain.[49]

The international political uncertainties—the French invasion of Spain, the rumors of ceded territories—tested the ideological mettle of the young moderate creoles of *El Revisor Político*. Unwilling to see Cuba in flames, they were, unlike most of their elders, equally opposed to a restoration of royal absolutism. They had taken a stand for constitutionalism: On 1 April 1823, forty-six students and alumni of the class of constitutional law (Domingo del Monte, José de la Luz y Caballero, and Anacleto Bermúdez were numbered among "the industrious and ardent youth of Havana") expressed their firm adherence to the constitution, with a cry of loyalty emanating, they said, from their "impassioned liberalism."[50] They were the voice of the intellectual elite of the San Carlos Seminary, who, having tasted the heady pleasures of literary life, were unwilling to exchange it for the stuffy salons of the Patriotic Society of their fathers.

A dialogue printed in *El Revisor Político* in July diagnosed the rift in creole ranks. Don Servilio eagerly anticipated the restoration of the old regime of order and justice, while Don Constancia expressed amazement that "a sensible man would prefer to be the vassal of a King rather than a citizen of a nation" and would abrogate personal liberties such as freedom of expression. Don Servilio replied that self-preservation had prompted him to swear allegiance to the constitution, and now the same motive explained his pleasure at its imminent derogation: "I used to have more than I have now." Of what value was personal liberty when the corporate privilege of rank more than compensated? Besides, Don Servilio concluded, he had never been refused permission to print anything of public value, including his treatise proving "que el *chocolate quebrante ayuno.*"⁵¹

Don Servilio's position found expression the next month with the publication of *La Concordia Cubana* (10 August 1823–31 January 1824). The editor of this free biweekly, Francisco Javier Troncoso,⁵² stressed human frailty and the interdependence of the human community. He argued that personal liberty was a facade for social irresponsibility. Faced with the lessons of the French Revolution and the newly independent Spanish American republics, Troncoso dedicated *La Concordia* to elaborating Cuba's true best interest—the preservation of property and social peace. *La Concordia* praised the constitution, of course, yet most of its references argued that constitutionalism had never been realized for lack of "unsoiled hands to implement it."⁵³

La Concordia's tacit acceptance of a second restoration of royal absolutism drove the young creoles of *El Revisor Político* to their most adamant embrace of constitutionalism. They denied that man's imperfection was sufficient reason to abandon a moderate liberty based on laws both just and leveling (*niveladora*). These laws conceded rights and imposed obligations, but only prohibited what was necessary to guarantee life and property. When *La Concordia* suggested that Cuba had enjoyed freedom for thirty years now, continued the unsigned editorial in the 13 August issue of *El Revisor Político*, it only proved that Troncoso's concept of liberty was nothing more than freedom of commerce. *El Revisor Político* directly rejected the political compromises that their elders had made in the name of prosperity:

We will not call it liberty to be the patrimony of a king, the plaything of a governor, and the slave of a judge, to be unable to raise our voice to a Count even if he should whip us, or [unable] to read a good book because the Inquisition would not let it pass through customs, or [unable] to be safe in our homes from an order of imprisonment."[54]

Unfortunately for the editors of *El Revisor Político*, their stirring words were swept away by news of the first arrests in the prosecution of a major independence conspiracy. The Soles y Rayos de Bolívar conspiracy, as it has come to be known, had been under Vives's surveillance since early June, when a fortuitous accident put a copy of a projected manifesto into his hands. Large numbers of these pamphlets were being printed at a secret location, and a black pressman, anxious to explain to his sweetheart his unusual absences, furtively brought her a copy as evidence of his legitimate excuse. The girl's owner, a former slave who could read, immediately grasped the import of the pamphlet and showed it to his former owner, who accompanied him to visit Vives.

Vives's first confrontation with the conspirators took place at a meeting of the Havana municipal council at the end of July. At issue was a motion that, should the French invasion of Spain succeed, Cuba would offer asylum to the peninsular constitutionalists and continue the struggle as the final outpost of the Spanish nation. Vives was hard pressed to rally a majority of the municipal council to defeat the proposal. The implication of the vote was not lost on the press. On 31 July 1823, *El Indicador Constitucional* asserted that Vives's role in arranging the electoral outcome had stripped him of his legitimacy as a constitutional authority. "Constitutionalism or death," cried one contributor, invoking the image of Troy. "Before bowing to a fierce and barbarous despotism, let horror, death, and desolation make [Cuba] memorable in the annals of history."[55]

The municipal council's decision forced the conspirators to reject constitutionalism for independence,[56] and Vives mobilized to meet the coming confrontation. He was unsuccessful in his attempt to seed the periodical press as part of his strategy against the conspirators: all printers except Arazoza and Soler refused to accept articles not in agreement with their editorial slant.[57] On 2 August 1823, Vives appointed Alcalde Juan Agustín Ferrety as prosecutor. Investigation revealed that the conspirators' press belonged to José Miguel de Oro,[58] who had been printing a series of pamphlets strongly affirming constitutionalism since the militia confrontation in December.[59] The first arrests were made at 3 : 00 a.m. on the morning of the fourteenth (three days before the conspiracy was to begin), and shortly thereafter two trunks were discovered abandoned in a street outside the city walls. They contained more than five thousand copies of three pamphlets from the "Imprenta de Gobierno Republicano de Cubanacán."[60] One enjoined Cubans to emulate their continental brothers in throwing off the yoke of three hundred years of Spanish rule; another repeated the rumor of an impending sale of the island to England; and the third offered a guarantee of life and property to cooperative Spaniards who realized that Spain was finished as a world power.[61]

The conspiracy was crushed by the evening before it was to have begun: the ringleader of the Society of the Sun, José Francisco Lemus, was captured by a party of men led by the infamous Domingo Armona.[62] In addition to Lemus, a young *habanero* who had been recruited to the cause of independence by Colombian refugees in Philadelphia in 1817, others arrested included the printer Oro, the constitutional magistrate Francisco Garay, the *caraqueño* merchant Juan Jorge Peoli, the Platine writer José Antonio Miralla, and the author of the incendiary article invoking the fate of Troy, Dr. Juan José Hernández.

Denunciations and investigations continued for several months, as Vives took advantage of the conspiracy to make a clean sweep of secret societies on the island.[63] More than six hundred people were indicted, including, for example, the young poet José María Heredia, who at one time belonged to a Matanzas society called Caballeros Racionales.[64] Vives moved masterfully in these lengthy judicial proceedings. Harsh penalties would have disturbed the moderate creoles, while the appearance of justice was necessary to pacify peninsular troops (numbering approximately twenty-five thousand) and adherents of both constitutionalism and reaction. While indictments rooted out conspirators, judicial lenience and official oversights, which allowed some conspirators to escape into exile, reduced the potentially acrimonious aftereffects.[65]

The failed conspiracy reminded Cuban creoles that avoiding political upheaval had been their fundamental concern since the Haitian Revolution. No one knew the effectiveness of this argument better than Francisco de Arango, who issued his influential *Reflexiones de un habanero sobre la independencia de esta isla* in mid-September.[66] Arango was particularly critical of the editors of *El Revisor Político* for their excerpt from Dominique de Pradt because their professed loyalties to constitutionalism paled beside the proindependence message of the text. Arango suggested that holding up Spain's former colonies for Cuban emulation was intellectually dishonest, for a quick survey of the current situation would reveal that these colonies were less emancipated than rebellious, less republican than anarchical fragments of empire now seeking kings, emperors, or dictators to restore social order and economic prosperity. If their example did not disprove that liberty and independence were synonymous, then Arango suggested that the continued prosperity of colonies like Cuba and Canada should convince the wavering. Finally, Arango cited de Pradt's earlier book (1817) on revolutionary America to demonstrate the peculiar perils of revolutionary change in parts of America where populations were heterogeneous.

In the wake of the independence conspiracy, most creoles rallied around Arango's appeal for creole unity, an appeal which translated into a mandate to withdraw from politics and await the outcome of events in Spain. Only the young creoles of the San Carlos Seminary dissented. In a reversal of their actions at the beginning of the year, the editors of *El Revisor Político* terminated their literary *revista* at the end of August and founded *El Liberal Habanero* (probably in September 1823) to denounce the tide of creole resignation.[67] It was a rearguard action, however, for Vives had already won his battle to defuse political factions, prevent political innovation, and prepare the ground for the restoration of Ferdinand VII.[68] Two separate letters dated mid-September to the Cuban deputy Tomás Gener confirm that the danger seemed to have passed. Both praised Vives's role: "The guardian angel of this Island fortunately brought us Vives, for if [the conspiracy] had broken out before his arrival, there would have been no hope for us."[69] Thus it comes as no surprise that Vives reported no resistance when the news of Ferdinand VII's restoration arrived on 8 December 1823.[70]

In the *Diario del Gobierno de la Habana* of the following day, Vives inserted the royal proclamation of 20 October issued from the Real Alcázar in Seville, and added his personal disavowal of the spirit of revolutionary discord that had threatened "the order established over so many centuries of glory for the nation." Now that Ferdinand VII was restored to absolute power, Vives apparently felt more secure about including Cuba within the "nation." With a reminder that "peace and tranquility are what suits an agricultural and commercial country," Vives went about rebuilding the preconstitutional bureaucracy. Among his appointments were Juan Ignacio Rendón (the only judge to merit Vives's confidence to date) and José Franco as press censors.[71]

Once again, the Restoration decimated the Cuban press. With few exceptions—*La Concordia Cubana* lasted until 31 January, the *Gaceta de la Habana* endured for several months—only official or semiofficial publications survived: the *Diario del Gobierno de la Habana*, the *Noticioso Mercantil*, the *Papel Oficial del Gobierno de Santiago de Cuba*, the *Gaceta de Puerto Príncipe*, and the *Correo de Trinidad*. Content in the surviving press, with the exception of the *Noticioso*'s commercial emphasis, parroted the formula that the *Diario* had featured since the 1790s. As happened in the aftermath of the first restoration of Ferdinand VII, strict regulation of content frustrated new competitors for a limited reading public. For five months of declining subscriptions, the Restoration *periódico Miscelánea Curiosa* (1 January 1824–31 May 1824) tried to attract readers with a fare of official and commercial notices spiced with philosophical abstractions (e.g., the act of war, the nature of heroism), biographies of famous thinkers—Juan Luis Vives, Bayle, and Pascal—and moralistic treatments of topics such as suicide. On 31 May, the paper terminated publication with the explanation that "the limits to which it has been necessary to restrict our work, are too narrow for us to have the satisfaction of completely pleasing our subscribers."[72]

In addition to reimposing absolutist standards on journalistic expression, Captain General Vives administered just deserts for several *periodistas* of the second constitutional period. On 23 December 1823, José de Aguiar, editor of *Tío Bartolo*, was imprisoned for one year for his confrontation with Manuel Coimbra.[73] On the other hand, Francisco Javier Troncoso, editor of *La Concordia Cubana*, received the position of treasurer of the Real Casa de Beneficia, and, for his future applications, a glowing recommendation from Vives for his press role in the second constitutional period.[74] Joaquín José

García's past did not catch up with him until May 1825. García, Bergaño's collaborator (1811–14) and editor of *El Navío Arranchador* in the subsequent *trienio*, lost his appointment as official interpreter for several institutions (including the port of Havana) when a jealous competitor exposed his link to *El Navío*.[75]

Although the Restoration meant a return to a restrictive literary environment, it could not erase the experience of the constitutional *trienio*. After the suppression of the *piñerista* threat, a free press had allowed elite creoles to elaborate a political ideology of substantial self-government that did not require political rebellion. As Spain's mainland colonies collapsed into a chaotic patchwork of republics, empires, and dictatorships, Cubans came to appreciate the advantages of a constitutionalism imposed by a disintegrating metropolitan government. Building upon their tentative steps in the first constitutional period, they charted a course of moderate constitutionalism— the forms and rhetoric of constitutionalism manipulated to the benefit of an elite stratum of Cuban society. A progression of *periódicos* revealed their ideological development: the academic treatises of *El Observador Habanero*, the articulation of a creole constitutionalism in the *Gaceta de la Habana* and *El Americano Libre*, and the confident demotion of politics in *El Revisor Político*.

Only when restoration threatened did creole ranks split to reveal a faction more adamant in its embrace of constitutionalism. *El Liberal Habanero* represented the culmination of a process of education and literary experience that brought a new generation of creoles to center stage. From the classrooms of philosophy and constitutional law in the San Carlos Seminary emerged a generation who had studied and expressed themselves in the press with a freedom unknown to Francisco Arango or Félix Varela. José Antonio Saco, Domingo del Monte, José de la Luz, Juan Agustín Govantes, and José Antonio Cintra are only the most notable of a cohort, born around the turn of the century, who came of age in the last year of the constitutional *trienio* and for this reason may be termed the generation of '23. It would be a generation cut down in its literary prime, doomed to a series of political and literary subterfuges that would eventually end in repression and exile.

CHAPTER 5

The "Ever-Faithful Isle,"
1824–1836

THE PEACEFUL restoration of absolutism in December 1823 propelled Cuba towards its reputation as the "ever-faithful isle."[1] While Spain's mainland colonies claimed their independence, Cuba remained committed to the vicissitudes of peninsular politics. Despite Cuban loyalty, however, Spain's hold over the island was tenuous. The Cuban garrison and fortifications were vulnerable to the invasion schemes of European monarchs, leaders of the newly independent Spanish American republics, and exiled Cubans.[2] At this point, the United States stepped in to guarantee Spanish sovereignty. The Monroe Doctrine allowed Spain to retain her remaining colonial possessions in the Americas; indeed, the United States government warned Spain not to cede Cuba and Puerto Rico to another European power. At the same time, President James Monroe pressured the Latin American republics not to interfere.[3]

While the United States fostered international stability for Cuba, Captain General Vives sought internal peace by a skillful accommodation with the creole sugar oligarchy. On 16 January 1824 he recommended a conciliatory approach to the commission investigating the Soles y Rayos conspiracy—he portrayed most of the conspirators as victims of constitutional factionalism in Spain.[4] Grateful for the captain general's leadership and sensitivity, the sugarocracy, which had increasingly sought institutional control over its own destiny since 1790, accepted an extension of Vives's authority. On 25 March 1825, Vives created a military commission to act as a special tribunal in judicial cases affecting state security.[5] On 25 May 1825, in response to the patient lobbying of Vives and others, the Crown approved permanent extraordinary powers for the captains general of Cuba and Puerto Rico—all rights normally delegated to governors under a siege, including summary deportation of individuals, dismissal of officials, and discretionary suspension of all royal orders.[6] Vives's paternal governance muted the immediate impact of this legislation, but it could not disguise the fact that the colonial relationship had been renegotiated in favor of the metropolis. Cuba was no longer the *antemural* of a continental empire; now it was a major part of Spain's revenue and prestige. The captain general's new authority signaled an end to the accommodation between Crown and sugarocracy dating back to the aftermath of the Seven Years' War.

Vives's expanded powers made press abuse within Cuba even more unlikely, but they were no guarantee against the penetration of ideas from beyond the island's shores. The captain general considered the most serious source to be Félix Varela, former professor at the San Carlos Seminary and Cortes deputy. Varela had fled Spain in the face of the vindictiveness of Ferdinand VII; he now resided in Philadelphia, where he published *El Habanero*. Not unexpectedly, *El Habanero* found its way into Cuba, with ninety-two copies of the second issue confiscated in Matanzas alone. More were circulating undetected, and this worried Vives: "All the youths that today are lawyers and graduates have been [Varela's] disciples, well indoctrinated beforehand in the new doctrines."[7]

Vives did not restore the Inquisition,[8] but he elaborated his own measures to prevent the introduction of what he saw as dangerous or inappropriate printed material. In general, Vives sought to improve enforcement of the royal order prohibiting the entrance of papers published by Spaniards in exile. To achieve this purpose and to guard against the "pernicious traffic and the scandalous circulation of unacceptable books," Vives increased customs vigilance and set stiff penalties, including forfeiture of cargo for ships found to be carrying such contraband. He ordered all booksellers to submit an inventory of their stock and to surrender unacceptable books within ten days.[9] In the specific case of Varela, he commissioned one of Varela's "disciples," Juan Agustín Ferrety (prosecutor of the Soles y Rayos conspiracy), to write a lengthy rebuttal to *El Habanero: Apuntaciones sobre El Habanero . . . hecho por un discípulo del mismo Varela.* Ferrety argued that Cuba had enjoyed unprecedented prosperity under the monarchy.[10]

The reestablishment of strict literary standards did not prove as beneficial to members of the Patriotic Society as they might have expected from their experience a decade earlier. Though the Society expressed approval for the Restoration and nominated Vives for the title of Marqués de la Gratitud Habanera,[11] it failed to obtain any economic reward for its political loyalty. Francisco Javier Troncoso and Juan Agustín Govantes complained to the Crown on 30 September 1824 that reorganization of municipal revenues had reduced the Society's income to 10 percent of its former level. Ferdinand VII, however, rejected a plan for supplementary revenues from a proposed sales tax; Juan Agustín Ferrety unsuccessfully appealed the Patriotic Society's case in person in Madrid in March 1827.[12]

Financial problems greatly hampered the Patriotic Society's educational efforts, as became clear in 1828 when Ferdinand VII decreed that parents could no longer send their children to school in the United States because of its republican atmosphere. To be fair, the king had commissioned Francisco Arango to study the educational needs of the island, but apparently did not consult him on the question of schooling in the United States. On 28 May 1828, Arango argued that the decree was unnecessary, for only the rich could afford to send their children abroad and these found their potential inheritances to be a powerful counterpoise to republican ideas. On the other hand, the educational needs of the island posed an acute problem: the lack of education for the middle and poorer classes (those classes always most disposed to revolution, according to Arango) prevented the opportunity of molding them to the interests of the state.[13]

Literary activity was an equally revealing indicator of the cultural fortunes of Restoration Cuba. For writers who saw a correlation between *periódicos* and cultural sophistication, it was disturbing to see the almost complete stagnation of the Cuban press between 1823 and 1828.[14] In 1826 Domingo del Monte, conscious of the prolific production of his exiled friend,

José María Heredia, lamented: "I am wasting myself in vain hopes which I never realize in this sad, handcuffed Virgin of the seas."[15] For del Monte, liberation took the form of an extended trip to Spain, Paris, and the United States. By the end of the decade, foreign places would also stimulate other young creoles: José de la Luz, Felipe Poey, José Antonio Saco, and Leonardo Santos Suárez.

By 1828, however, as the passage of time calmed fears about revolution, racial bloodbath, and invasion from the continent, Vives relaxed his literary surveillance slightly. In the peripheral city of Matanzas, the *Aurora de Matanzas* (2 September 1828–1856), a paper sponsored by the local section of the Patriotic Society, gained a reputation for content. Some of the credit was due its editor, Félix Tanco y Bosmeniel (1797–1871).[16] Though born in Bogotá, Tanco came to Havana at an early age and pursued his studies there. In the last days of constitutionalism in 1823, he was part of an intimate literary gathering, or *tertulia*, that included Domingo del Monte.[17] Tanco was not being immodest when he characterized the *Aurora* as "the least narcotic newspaper being published in the Island."[18]

The *Aurora de Matanzas* presaged the resumption of literary publication in the last three years of Vives's tenure (July 1829–May 1832). Vives approved several *revistas*, in part because prepublication censorship could limit them to specific literary endeavors. The *Anales de Ciencias, Agricultura, Comercio y Artes* (July 1827–June 1830), founded by the peninsular naturalist Ramón de la Sagra, supplied the precedent. The Patriotic Society and Intendant Martínez de Pinillos had brought its editor to Havana to head the Botanical Garden and chair the professorship of botany at that institution.[19] Sagra parlayed the public interest in science (including the new vogue, statistics) and the influence of his patron into a monthly *revista* that ranged from natural history to chemistry. The intendant's letter of support for Sagra's application is of interest, for he complained that Havana boasted few *publicistas* (note new term for a profession that he assumed was distinct from that of writer or litterateur) and that their publications rarely departed from reprinted news or commercial information. Notably, the intendant blamed poor content not on press restrictions but on the "lack of writers who will dedicate their lucubrations to the good of the community."[20] The intendant, Francisco de Arango's successor as lobbyist for the sugarocracy, viewed the

Figure 5-1. Major Cuban Periódicos, 1829–1833

1830 J F M A M J J A S O N D	1831 J F M A M J J A S O N D	1832 J F M A M J J A S O N D	1833 J F M A M J J A S O N D

Diario

Noticioso   /   . . . *y Lucero*

16

Gaceta de Puerto Príncipe

Correo de Trinidad

Noticoso Comercial de Santiago de Cuba

Anales   *Anales de Agricultura*

Diario de Santiago de Cuba

Aurora de Matanzas

La Moda

11

Diario de Matanzas

28

Puntero Literario

2   1

Nuevo Regañón

2   21

Revista Bimestre Cubana

Lucero de la Habana (merged)

1   16

Eco de Villa Clara

3

KEY

————— Publication data confirmed

- - - - - - - - - Incomplete publication data

Anales as the perfect blend of sponsored science and public utility.

Sagra contributed more than a model *revista*. His personality, his unmasked condescension toward the intellectual production (past and present) of Cuban creoles, sparked a creole literary counterattack.[21] Though the image of Sagra basking in the adulation of the resident peninsular population of Havana may have nurtured creole hostility, the specific issue was his denigration of the poetry of the exiled José María Heredia. José Antonio Saco, from his voluntary exile in the United States, responded to Sagra in the pages of the *Mensajero Semanal* (19 August 1828–29 January 1831), which he had co-founded with his mentor, Félix Varela.[22] The intendant finally stopped the escalating series of rejoinders, ostensibly a literary disagreement but one loaded with the political antagonism of creole versus peninsular. Martínez de Pinillos, incensed by Saco's denigration of his Botanical Garden project and its professorial occupant, ordered that Saco's writings be seized at customs.

Sagra's attack on Heredia also stimulated creole writers in Cuba, but they found it impossible to emulate Saco.[23] In exile, Saco could write with complete freedom; operating outside the colonial context, he made no pretense of being a loyal vassal of Ferdinand VII but rather declared himself to be a Cuban patriot. Residents of Cuba had to be more circumspect. *La Moda ó Recreo Semanal del Bello Sexo* (7 November 1829–11 June 1831) provided the outlet for interested creoles. Domingo del Monte and the peninsular José J. Villarino (who had obtained the permission to publish the *revista*) dedicated *La Moda* to the diversion of the female population and featured black and white and color engravings, fold-out sheet music, and a section titled "Moda," which initially was as much a society page as it was a feature on foreign fashion.[24] But the *revista* offered more than entertainment. It became an outlet for creole expression, featuring, for example, José de la Luz's interview with Sir Walter Scott, José María Heredia's travel letters from the United States, and del Monte's poetry, anecdotes, and book reviews. *La Moda* emphasized the correlation between civilization and the press. Now that the periodical press had been established to educate and entertain busy readers, the editors noted that "the mania to write and to read had spread to almost all the classes of society."[25]

La Moda signaled the return to literary pursuits of the generation of '23, and it was not long until a second publication of even greater literary significance appeared: *El Puntero Literario* (2 January 1830–1 May 1830),[26] edited jointly by del Monte and Antonio Bachiller y Morales (1812–1889, student and literary novice), with the collaboration of José Antonio Cintra (1802–1868, lawyer and one of the editors of *El Americano Libre*) and Anacleto Bermúdez (1806–1852, lawyer and signatory of the 1823 manifesto by students of the San Carlos Seminary's class on constitutional law). *El Puntero Literario* formally pointed Cuba in a new literary direction—romanticism.

Creole literati had been aware of the European romanticism of Wordsworth, Byron, and Scott for some time. As early as 1814, an article reprinted in the *Noticioso* had denounced the imaginative excesses of romanticism, while a decade later, del Monte labeled his poetry "romántica" because it flaunted rules he had learned as a youth.[27] *El Puntero Literario*, however, published the first manifesto proclaiming romanticism in Cuba. Indeed, this manifesto preceded the standard literary landmark of Latin American romanticism, the publication in 1832 of *Elvira, o la novia del Plata*, a narrative poem written by the Argentine Esteban Echeverría upon his return from Paris in 1830.[28]

El Puntero Literario's editors found the classic mode of expression, beautiful in its original context, inappropriate for contemporary artistic expression; they sought not to disparage classical literature but rather to find new means of realizing artistic beauty.[29] Nevertheless, their loyalties were never in doubt, for a satirical "edict" in the first issue ordered printers to delete references to gods and semigods and to reject contributions that were not "sprightly, beautiful, variegated, special or at least unaffected," for all else, it was alleged, dulled the imagination.[30] On another occasion, Bachiller y Morales criticized the classicists' use of mythology—which, he said, should not be elevated to the status of a religion, but merely used as a scholarly language to decipher antiquity.[31] *El Puntero Literario*'s editors did not define a program or agenda for the new literary style; rather, they rejected strict adherence to neoclassical canons that concentrated on mythology and adhered to standards of taste and purpose defined in Spain in the first half of the eighteenth century.[32] The romantic emphasis on imagination supported this revolt and freed the poet to shape his subject and his language.[33]

El Puntero Literario's romantic manifesto proved to be popular and controversial,[34] but it did not immediately transform literary taste in Cuba. While few authors clung to neoclassical forms as tenaciously as early contributors to the *Papel Periódico*—thirteen odes on one theme from Horace were published in the year 1791 alone—many Cuban poets had injected enough of their own reality into inherited styles to claim them as their own (for example, the symbolism of Orpheus drinking pineapple juice in Manuel de Zequeira's *A la piña*). *Costumbrismo* also undercut the urgency of a literary revolt against stylistic conventions by introducing the local idiom into Cuban prose.[35] This accommodation, in turn, made it more difficult to expunge past literary habits and cultural heritage. For example, del Monte's admiration for Walter Scott owed as much to his appreciation of *costumbrismo* as it did to the appeal of romanticism.[36] But the romantic appeal of the exotic, rather than the descriptive tradition of *costumbrismo*, appears in del Monte's evocation of the medieval city of Seville under Arab rule.[37] Del Monte's ambivalence is best illustrated by the persistence of classical literary images (such as the lyre for poetic expression) even as he charted a new literary course—"exact descriptions of the human heart."[38]

There were still other reasons for resisting *El Puntero Literario*'s platform. Del Monte's friend Félix Tanco, for example, characterized *El Puntero Literario* as "a kind of abortion of reason gone astray"[39] because he feared that the romantics' criticism of classicism would introduce factionalism into the *bellas artes;* indeed, the allegorical edict in the first issue of *El Puntero Literario* was reminiscent of the *flota* press of the second constitutional period. Tanco recognized that the generation of '23 might be tempted to express rebellion against political authority and cultural consensus through this new literary fashion, a connection later acknowledged by Antonio Bachiller y Morales: "I embraced the new idea [romanticism] with all my heart for the same reason I wanted free trade, opposed monopolies, abhorred guilds."[40] The political edge to Cuban romanticism becomes clear against the background of peninsular literary developments. Though the groundswell of romanticism in both Spain and Cuba corresponded to the decade of the 1830s, the strident anticlassicism of the Cuban devotees was absent in Spain.[41] Cuban romantics were able to conjure up a host of grievances against classicists, and only some of these grievances were literary. Emphasis on creative imagination was particularly appropriate for these young creoles, for imagination could not be shackled by political absolutism or monopolized by elite cultural institutions such as the Patriotic Society.

The political subtext of the clash between romantics and classicists soon materialized into open antagonism. The contest revolved around the Literature Commission of the Education Section of the Patriotic Society. Formed in response to an initiative of del Monte, the Commission was installed on 13 February 1830.[42] Noting the success of *La Moda* and *El Puntero Literario*,[43] the Commission desired its own *revista*, to feature extracts and reviews of publications from Cuba, Spain, and foreign countries.[44] Opposition from within the Patriotic Society, however, shelved the project until May 1831, when a Society member, the Catalan educator Mariano Cubí y Soler, independently published the first issue of the *Revista y Repertorio Bimestre de la Isla de Cuba*. This first issue alluded to the Commission's project, and by a subsequent compromise Cubí y Soler maintained proprietary rights over the renamed *Revista Bimestre Cubana*, while editorial duties fell to the Commission, primarily Domingo del Monte, who apparently set aside his legal career.[45]

The title change to *Revista Bimestre Cubana* signified the Commission's intention: "to imprint a *Cuban* character on its paper."[46] As the *revista* focused primarily on foreign publications, the "Cuban character" was upheld through Cuban collaborators such as Francisco Ruiz, José de la Luz y Caballero, and in the United States, Félix Varela. For the first five issues (from May/June 1831–January/February 1832), the *Revista Bimestre Cubana* reviewed items published in Madrid, Cádiz, Barcelona, Boston, Vienna, Leipzig, Hamburg, and Paris on topics ranging from Latin grammar to the methodology of teaching reading, from poetry to political economy. In its pages the editors offered a list of important works recently published in Europe and America, reflecting a voracious appetite for the intellectual production of the Western world. In the second issue, for example, del Monte offered a short résumé of the latest scientific and literary news from England, France, Italy, Germany, Russia, Spain, and the United States. This cosmopolitan outlook derived in part from del Monte's contacts with Spanish writers, some of whom were in exile in Paris. The emphasis on international as opposed to Cuban or Hispanic letters generated some criticism,[47] but del Monte held firm to his editorial vision. His recent travels had given him an international viewpoint, although he stressed the artist's obligation to portray his own national environment.[48]

The return of José Antonio Saco in early 1832 altered the editorial tone established by del Monte.[49] One of Saco's first efforts was the publication of his *Memoria sobre la vagancia* (written in 1830), an exposé of the "moral infirmities" afflicting Cuban society and preventing its further progress. Saco argued that gambling, lotteries, and other public vices were contributing to idleness and vagrancy and sapping the moral and productive energies of the island. Though he concentrated on a description of the problems, the *Memoria* offered an implicit indictment of officialdom and the Hispanic legacy. Not surprisingly, the Patriotic Society panel, which had awarded the *Memoria* a prize in 1831, recommended certain revisions before publication. Nevertheless, Saco submitted it to censure unaltered, and Captain General Vives approved it as submitted.

The *Memoria* formed the centerpiece of the sixth issue of the *Revista Bimestre Cubana*,[50] an important watershed for the publication. Shortly thereafter, on 7 April 1832, Cubí y Soler ceded title to the *Revista* to the Literature Commission, and Saco assumed editorial and financial responsibility.[51] From this point Saco's politically sensitive articles displaced the literary emphasis of del Monte and other contributors to the first five issues. The *Revista*'s new tone reflected the injection of an exile mentality into the gradualist and coded tactics of criticism utilized by the founders of the Literature Commission. In the next issue, for example, Saco's review of the Reverend Robert Walsh's *Notices of Brazil in 1828 and 1829* not only suggested that Cuba compared unfavorably in many aspects with Brazil, but it also condemned the continued official tolerance of the illegal slave trade.[52] Saco demonstrated the demographic dangers of continued slave importation into Cuba, indicted officials and merchants for their complicity in not facing this potentially explosive situation, and finally suggested free labor and white immigration as alternatives.

Critical acclaim for the *Revista Bimestre Cubana* was enthusiastic. The eminent Spanish poet José María Quintana judged it to be "the best Spanish *periódico* published for a long while."[53] In April 1834, George Ticknor, Harvard professor of modern literature and author of a highly influential history of

Spanish literature, pronounced that "a *review* of such spirit, variety and power, has never been even attempted in Madrid."[54] Ticknor was equally impressed by the display of Cuban literary talent: "Nothing to compare with it has, so far as I am informed, ever been exhibited in any of the Spanish colonies, and even in some respects, nothing like it is to be seen in Spain proper." Others, however, warned that Saco's control of the *Revista* (and Domingo del Monte's return to Matanzas and the practice of law) might mean the end of the publication.[55] Varela cautioned that the *Revista Bimestre Cubana* must be circumspect, for its enemies could use the effrontery of a Cuban paper being "the best paper in all the monarchy" as a powerful argument for its suspension.[56]

The editors and contributors of the *Revista Bimestre Cubana* achieved a second coup even as their publication brought them fame: royal permission to transform the Literature Commission into an autonomous Cuban Academy of Literature, independent of the censures of their literary elders in the Patriotic Society. The Cuban Academy, modeled on a similar academy in Seville, was authorized by the regent, María Cristina, during the interlude following the death of Ferdinand VII on 29 September 1833. Before dying, the king had abrogated the Salic law requiring male succession so that he could pass the crown to his infant daughter Isabel (born November 1830). A dynastic struggle ensued when Ferdinand's younger brother, Carlos, asserted his claim with general support from the ultramonarchist elements of Spain. As the confrontation intensified into civil war, María Cristina enlisted the support of liberals as a counterweight.[57] The approval of the Cuban Academy, then, was an incidental act reflecting María Cristina's accommodation with liberal elements.

On 6 March 1834 (upon receipt of the Royal Charter of 25 December 1833), the Literature Commission reformed itself into the Cuban Academy of Literature. The profile of its twenty-six founding members is revealing; almost all were born within several years of the turn of the century and thus had come of age in the second constitutional period—in short, the generation of '23. With few exceptions, they had received their education in Cuba and identified themselves as Cubans. At least twelve had law degrees and another five had taught or were teaching at the university or the San Carlos Seminary. All the major literary luminaries (with the exception of Antonio

Bachiller y Morales) were included: Domingo del Monte (secretary), José Antonio Saco, José de la Luz, Manuel González del Valle, and Francisco Ruiz.[58]

As some had feared, the literary success of the generation of '23 invited retribution. Resident Spaniards were offended by the deliberately "Cuban" aspect of this literary production and, in some cases, by Saco's open hostility toward the slave trade. More immediately, the Cuban Academy had alienated the hierarchy of the Patriotic Society by not submitting its proposal to the Regency through the Society's director. Their desire for secrecy was understandable—the Society had stymied plans for the *Revista Bimestre Cubana* and had rejected a proposal to establish a chair for the study of literature—but in the long run, ill-advised.[59] When the Cuban Academy published its act of installation in the *Diario de la Habana* on 8 April 1834, the Patriotic Society persuaded Captain General Mariano Ricafort (Vives's successor, 15 May 1832—31 May 1834) to suspend the charter until it could be discussed and approved by the Society.[60] Del Monte reacted angrily with an article in the *Aurora de Matanzas* of 29 April 1834; he indicted those members who could not tolerate intellectual endeavor independent of the Society's vigilance. Their opposition, he claimed, lay in their resentment that the Cuban Academy's founders belonged to "public professions independent of the whim of any high office holder."[61]

Del Monte's article disclosed the frustration of the generation of '23, a frustration made more bitter by the excitement of recent victories. For a brief interlude, the creoles of the *Revista Bimestre Cubana* and the Cuban Academy had probed the expressive boundaries allowed by the colonial order, but now their literary excursions into sensitive issues undermined the mutual accommodation between the sugarocracy and colonial officialdom established under Vives's administration. After a decade of peace and prosperity, the "ever-faithful isle" was about to reap the harvest of its complicity in the extension of the colonial relationship; when the creoles had cooperated with Vives, they had not foreseen Ricafort's replacement, General Tacón.

General Miguel Tacón y Rosique (1775—1855) built his early career in the context of the royalist counteroffensive against Spain's rebellious colonies. Compromised by his service as governor of Málaga and Seville during the second constitutional period, Tacón spent the next decade in prudent obscurity in Málaga. Under the political shift occasioned by the Regency, Tacón's past services were suddenly rewarded by appointments, first to the captain generalcy of Andalusia and then (on 7 March 1834) to the similar position in Cuba.[62] Juan Pérez de la Riva has partially salvaged Tacón's reputation from the abuse of generations of "bourgeois" Cuban historians who depicted Tacón as a "military man of reactionary tendencies, partisan of a rigid discipline, full of hatred and prejudice against those born in the Americas."[63] To paint a more humane portrait, Pérez de la Riva stressed one of the tragic dilemmas of the crumbling Spanish imperium: men who, in Spain, were "progressive liberals" (support of constitutionalism would be a good standard of their political ideas) assumed despotic roles when fortune placed them in command in the Americas. This was especially true of *los ayacuchos*, military men like Tacón who had fought the American insurgents, "forming a Holy Brotherhood of rancor and humiliation."[64]

Creoles like Domingo del Monte could appreciate Tacón's psychological scars,[65] but this did not soften their disappointment when the captain general did not live up to the liberal reputation of the new Spanish government. Tacón refused to implement the Royal Statute of 10 April 1834, which convoked the Cortes but did not restore constitutionalism.[66] Even more serious, especially for the sugarocracy, was Tacón's refusal to honor the unofficial arrangement between sugar producers and officials that dated back to the second Restoration. In direct contradiction of the implied hint of an *anónimo* that counseled "Si vives como Vives, vivirás," Tacón remained both politically and socially beyond creole influence. He surrounded himself with a peninsular clique of wealthy, implacable hispanophiles, including Joaquín Gómez (merchant, mill owner, and known *piñerista* during the second constitutional confrontation), Censor José Antonio Olañeta, and slave traders like Julián Zulueta.[67]

Tacón's antipathy toward the "immorality and other vices" that surrounded him[68] produced a series of urban reforms. He immediately set to creating rural and urban police, to reducing homicides, and to paving streets. These early measures caused many Cubans to defer judgment about the new captain general. Some still hoped that the full import of the Royal Statute might yet be extended to Cuba, and the reserve of *habaneros* in awaiting these developments indicated a discretion bred of past political experience.[69] Blas Osés, one of the prominent progressives, noted "some despotic acts . . . but we had arrived at such a state, that they were almost indispensable."[70]

The issue of press restrictions reversed this brief suspension of judgment. Though the young progressive creoles did not wish to return to the anarchy of the constitutional *trienio*, the moderate press freedoms now enjoyed by their peninsular counterparts seemed essential. They saw press freedom not as a literary luxury but as the very basis on which they hoped to influence the political process. That Tacón would not allow such liberty became clear when Félix Tanco dared to advise the captain general on needed reforms. Tanco's article was published without censorship in the *Aurora de Matanzas* (the appropriate officials were absent from the city and the content was basically a gloss of Saco's already published *Memorial on Vagrancy*); Tacón was immediately enraged.[71] The captain general soon provided more concrete evidence of his attitude toward creole expression: he retained Ricafort's system of press censorship by a trusted military aide. The oppressive literary environment imposed by Tacón had a chilling effect on the generation of '23. By 4 June 1834, a new tone of discouragement entered del Monte's correspondence:

> Since I arrived from New York in 1829 I have not ceased, in the company of my other young, patriotic friends, to promote . . . all that I have judged to be advantageous for the Island, and we have principally employed ourselves in enlightening public opinion, now through the means of the press, now in private conversation, in academic meetings, in the public avenues [*paseos*], in the *tertulia*, in the theaters; but our efforts have been in vain, because the very powerful and absolute system that . . . governs us, has neutralized our peaceful and passive conquests, in the manner of a ferocious beast, which with an imperceptible movement of its brutal tail, destroys the fragile and laborious structure of an industrious insect.[72]

Tacón's attitude towards the press forced del Monte to admit that Cubans were not on equal footing with peninsular Spaniards, that Cubans were "children of colonial despotism."

Creole vulnerability became evident when Tacón exiled José

Antonio Saco on 17 July 1834 for writing the pamphlet *Justa defensa de la Academia Cubana de literatura*. Saco's defense of the Cuban Academy was a measured, legalistic repetition of earlier arguments stressing the royal patent for the academy's independence from the Patriotic Society. While it lacked the fire and eloquence of del Monte's earlier vindication, it clearly projected Saco as the spokesman for the progressive creoles of the academy and the *Revista Bimestre Cubana*. Saco later speculated that, while Tacón might indeed have felt his exile justified, it was designed to placate others: Juan Bernardo O'Gaban, director of the Patriotic Society and the individual most offended by the Cuban Academy controversy, and Intendant Martínez de Pinillos, who still bore Saco ill will for his disagreement with Ramón de la Sagra.[73]

Saco's exile reminded Cuban creoles of the scope of the captain general's authority. Del Monte compared the alarm that greeted Tacón's imperious order to the reaction the previous year to news that cholera had been discovered on the island: "Everyone fears for himself."[74] In this atmosphere, it is not surprising that the *Revista Bimestre Cubana* ceased publication, its final issue undistributed, nor that the academy was given up for lost. Yet for all its drama, Saco's exile was not the act that sealed Cuba's fate.[75] Tacón had several hands yet to play.

Indeed, the full import of Tacón's action did not become clear until the Patriotic Society elections in December 1834, when Tacón, faced with an electoral defeat of the slate championed by himself and Director Juan Bernardo O'Gaban, intervened in contravention of the Society's charter. Francisco de Arango, whose immense prestige championed the opposition slate, and José de la Luz y Caballero had already been elected director and vice-director despite the argument of Secretary Zambrana that Arango's imminent departure for Spain should make him ineligible for the office. Zambrana was expressing the fear of the incumbent faction that, in Arango's absence, the direction of the Patriotic Society would fall to Luz y Caballero, who was viewed as the heir apparent to Saco's mantle of leadership. After the O'Gaban faction won the elections for censor and vice-censor, the crucial election of a secretary became stalemated. The incumbent, Zambrana, received more votes than the challenger—the absent Domingo del Monte—but not the two-thirds majority plus one vote required to return an incumbent. At this point Tacón allowed the suggestion that a simple majority vote would suffice. When Nicolás Santos Suárez argued that the Society's regulations, approved by the Crown, required more than a majority, Tacón created a sensation by answering that he represented the king and thus the point was already decided.[76] It was only after this confrontation that progressive creoles became convinced that Saco's exile had not been merely the result of personal animosities or random chance but in fact mirrored Tacón's attitude to creoles in general.

Tacón's intimidation of the Patriotic Society, or more accurately the faction supporting del Monte's election, only intensified pressures already operating against creole expression. Tacón would not implement the new (and, by contrast to constitutional versions, rather conservative) press legislation of 4 January 1834 until 7 February 1835, five months after he had already established the system of censorship outlined by that legislation.[77] The legislation, which significantly began with an attack on unrestricted press freedom, had an even more repressive effect in Cuba than in Spain because of the supervisory powers it afforded the captain general. Now, all publications had to seek a royal license, granted by the Foreign Ministry upon the advice of Tacón. The legislation empowered Tacón to collect a bond of ten thousand *reales* from each editor as security for any potential fines, to ensure that every publication complied immediately in publishing any official item, to check that no blank spaces were left in issues to suggest censorship, and to see that censors complied with their duties on the pain of penalties equal to those levied on offenders.

By 7 November 1835, Tacón could boast that as the result of his efforts, expressive license had been contained on the island. His censors, he claimed, knew exactly what was appropriate for the Cuban press, and he suggested a perusal of the Havana press as proof that no dangerous item was allowed even if it had previously been published on the peninsula.[78] Prior censorship was the key to his control, and this was rigidly enforced.[79] Not even the Patriotic Society could win approval for a new *periódico* and had to content itself with reviving its *Memorias* in November 1835.[80] In this pervasive atmosphere of official vigilance, where even theater posters had to be approved by the captain general and the word "freedom" was deleted from the opera *Los Puritanos*,[81] only a peninsular Spaniard with good connections could win approval for a literary project. (Mariano

Torrente, for example, received permission to publish a *revista* of excerpts from more than two hundred authors on the subject of political economy.)[82] Repressed by censorship and contained by fear of Tacón's arbitrary powers,[83] the creole literary effusion of the past five years seemed to collapse entirely.

Of course, this bleak literary landscape was partly an illusion. The press silence in Cuba signified only that progressive creoles had shifted their battleground to the peninsula, where their ideas were championed by Saco and other Cuban residents in Madrid (branded by their enemies as the "Club of disloyal *habaneros*"), with an occasional item sent directly from the island for publication in Spain. It was the central irony of this period that the idealistic creoles of the now defunct Cuban Academy had to tie their modest aspirations of reform to the turbulent political vagaries of Spain. These creoles placed their hopes for redress on the reconvened Spanish Cortes, and when elections for Cuban deputies were finally held in May 1836, they managed to elect three deputies of their choice (including Saco as deputy for Santiago de Cuba) over Tacón's concerted opposition.[84]

Tacón feared that the creole press campaign in Spain could result in his recall.[85] On 31 August 1836, the captain general forwarded to Spain evidence of "Club" activities seized from a number of packages that had arrived in the mail from the peninsula.[86] *Páginas cubanas* Nos. 1 and 2, dated Havana, 4 May 1836, was an anonymous denunciation of Tacón's arbitrary measures in the election of deputies. *Cuadro político de la Ysla de Cuba* contrasted the political liberties currently enjoyed by Spain and Cuba, emphasizing that censorship in Cuba extended even to the suppression of peninsular news and *periódicos*.

Carta de un patriota o sea clamor de los cubanos (authored by Saco) reviewed Tacón's arbitrary actions and demonstrated that, in addition to not enjoying the benefits of the Royal Statute of 1834, Cubans could not even count upon the tolerance of the Vives era. At least under Vives, the author argued, there had been tacit agreement between writers and the government; writers had respected their limitations and society had benefited from the establishment of literary and scientific *periódicos*. Now, prospective items had to pass two censors who were lawyers, a military censor who was an aide to the captain general, and in some cases the captain general himself, whose discretionary powers deterred all but the most insipid articles.

Finally, *La Ysla de Cuba tal cual está* (written by Domingo del Monte) reiterated the theme that Cuba had been better off under the Restoration Spain of Ferdinand VII than at present under a "liberal" regime. The pamphlet recounted the effort of loyal *habaneros* since 1833 to keep peninsular Spaniards informed of what was truly happening on the island by contributing to peninsular *periódicos* (*El Eco, La Abeja*). This effort was made all the more desperate now because of the one-sided picture that the Havana press—"those prostituted and enslaved newspapers of the absolutist government"—presented to Spain. In conclusion, the article asserted that notable improvements in urban services and safety were not sufficient to satisfy Cuban aspirations; macadamized streets did not constitute civilization.[87]

Tacón soon faced even more serious press problems in Santiago de Cuba. They began with an article in the *Noticioso Comercial de Santiago de Cuba* on 17 August 1836.[88] This article, entitled "Censura de la censura," espoused expressive freedom. The author argued that while censorship of the periodical press could not produce the havoc of hail in the countryside or pestilence in the cities, it could constrict reason and its concomitant, liberty; he contrasted the expressive freedom writers enjoyed under representative government to the literary tyranny they endured under monarchical despotism.

The significance of "Censura de la Censura," however, went beyond the merits of the author's opinions. The article's appearance heralded a confrontation between Tacón and the newly appointed governor of Santiago de Cuba, Mariscal de Campo Manuel Lorenzo. Their antagonism stemmed as much from peninsular politics as from a clash of personalities. Lorenzo, who took office on 13 June 1836, had been appointed by a new and more radical Spanish government headed by Juan Álvarez Mendizábal, while Tacón owed his nomination to the more moderate Francisco Martínez de la Rosa, responsible for the Royal Statute but now in the opposition.[89] Tacón must have been concerned not only that Lorenzo might be promoted as his replacement, but in the meantime that he might challenge the much-touted "tranquility" for which Tacón claimed full credit.[90] Lorenzo immediately seemed to threaten just such an attitude when, in a letter of 8 August 1836,[91] he reported his difficulty in finding a censor to appoint (the position was unpaid) and his decision to allow the press to continue temporarily without prior censorship.[92] In his attitude toward censorship, as in his immediate rapprochement with the most liberal elements of the *santiaguero* population, Lorenzo revealed himself to be a peninsular liberal without the intransigent anticreole prejudices of the *ayacuchos.*

Perhaps it was Lorenzo's political astuteness[93] that made him aware that he could transfer his peninsular political antagonisms to Cuban soil by allying himself with the traditional *santiaguero* antipathy to Havana. This resentment was rooted deeply in what Santiago de Cuba saw as centuries of imperial neglect. The city, once the launching point for Spain's continental conquests, had atrophied as commerce was routed through Havana. The imperial reaction to the English invasion of 1762—expensive fortifications, commercial freedoms, and the new mail system—had all redounded to the capital's favor, increasing the disparity that already had caused Santiago de Cuba to petition unsuccessfully in 1692, 1725, and 1735 to be removed from Havana's jurisdiction. Again, in 1794, in the context of a royal investigation into the feasibility of dividing the island into two dioceses, petitions argued that to stimulate the prosperity necessary to make the eastern end of the island (Oriente) invulnerable to foreign attack, Santiago de Cuba must also receive a separate secular administration.[94] *Santiaguero* grievances were not redressed, however, for although the island was subsequently split into two dioceses (with Santiago de Cuba as the seat of the archbishopric), all secular authority remained concentrated in Havana.

Two decades later, the intellectual paternalism of the capital provoked the most impassioned controversy to occur between the two cities before 1836. The triggering incident involved a discourse read to the 1817 general meeting of the Patriotic Society by Censor Juan Bernardo O'Gaban, a native of the Oriente.[95] O'Gaban began with a description of the progress of culture and education on the island, which he likened to a "holy confederation" emanating from Havana. He concluded by describing his birthplace—"that inert and abandoned part of our island . . . , [that] sterile spectator of the opulence of Havana." On 11 December 1817, the Patriotic Society adopted the censor's recommendation that it assume responsibility for pressuring Oriente officials into promoting economic societies as the key institution for remedial action. Through the publication of O'Gaban's speech in the *Diario* on 8 January 1818, word of the Patriotic Society's proposal reached Santiago de Cuba. On 9 March 1818, an infuriated municipal council sent the king a response penned by José María Veranés. Veranés argued that Santiago de Cuba did not need enlightenment, but rather the millions of *pesos* flowing into the capital for fortifications, administration, and commerce—in short, he said, "all the Wealth of the rest of the Island that [Havana] has attracted like a sponge."[96]

The censorship controversy between Tacón and Lorenzo in August–September 1836 expressed regional antagonisms made even more bitter by intensified economic inequalities in the intervening decades. According to the census of 1827, the population of the western end of the island was 408,537, in contrast to 131,453 residents in the Oriente. This translated into a growth rate (since the 1817 census) of 27 and 3.6 percent respectively. An even more telling indicator of economic disparity, in an economy primarily based on slave-labor sugar production, was the fact that the slave population in the east had remained constant while in the west it had increased by 56 percent.[97]

For residents of Santiago de Cuba, who in 1836 still enjoyed an accommodation with local colonial officialdom in the Vives mold, Tacón's arbitrary measures, particularly his repeated intervention against the press, revived old hostilities towards interference from the capital. In one short period in October–November 1835 Tacón personally intervened in six issues.[98] Even before Lorenzo became governor, then, Tacón had been involved in a struggle of wills with the *santiaguero* press, without (as he characterized it in a letter of 5 September 1836) "achieving the necessary correction."[99] This frustration undoubtedly influenced Tacón's reaction to the article "Censura de la censura." On 5 September 1836, Tacón informed Lorenzo that he would be personally held responsible for permitting an uncensored press. Tacón pledged to conduct his own search for an appropriate censor, and in the interval ordered that the *santiaguero* press be restricted to the items that the press law defined as not requiring previous censorship. Finally, in an additional letter, also dated 5 September, Tacón informed Lorenzo that he was sending a member of the military commission to arrest the author, editor, and printer of the offending article.[100]

Tacón's impolitic meddling in the affairs of Santiago de Cuba produced a sensation that went far beyond the wounded pride of Lorenzo, who saw himself as an old and loyal soldier impugned by an autocrat without sensitivity to the modest aims of Cubans who wanted to partake of peninsular liberties. Lorenzo revealed for the first time that the article "Censura de la censura" had been reprinted from the peninsular *El Español*, and he argued that it was the patent intolerance of the captain general that had created the problem of finding a citizen willing to take on the responsibility of censorship.[101] More significant were the testimonies collected between 26 and 28 September to document the peace and tranquility of the province and its loyal citizenry's appreciation of Lorenzo's governance. Though such evidence could be coerced by unpopular officials, this was not the tone of the testimonials, which came from members of the municipal council, officials of the ecclesiastical, military, naval, and colonial bureaucracies, several titled citizens, and the British, French, and United States consuls.[102]

The controversy over "Censura de la censura" led directly to the declaration of constitutionalism on the island for the third time. The reaction of Lorenzo and the local populace to Tacón's heavy-handed press censorship played a crucial part in the outcome of events on the afternoon of 29 September, when a ship brought news that a group of army sergeants had invaded the royal palace at La Granja on 12 August 1836 and had forced the regent, María Cristina, to swear allegiance to the Constitution of 1812.[103] How else does one explain Lorenzo's immediate proclamation of the constitution without Tacón's express order, when in letters of 12 and 19 September, showing no hint of antagonism, Lorenzo had reported that he had informed his subordinates of the proconstitutionalist movement in Málaga, and had ordered them to avoid all innovations without the direct command of the captain general?[104] How else does one explain the unanimous endorsement of Lorenzo's actions by an impressive number of authorities resident in Santiago de Cuba at a meeting that evening? The signatories included the interim intendant, several judges, the dean of the cathedral, various military commanders (including José Ruiz de Apodaca, former captain general of Cuba and viceroy of New Spain, now a navy

Figure 5-2. Major Cuban Periódicos, 1836–1837

1836	1837
J F M A M J J A S O N D	J F M A M J J A S O N D

Diario de la Habana

Noticioso y Lucero

Gaceta de Puerto Príncipe

Correo de Trinidad

Noticioso Comercial (SC) / Diario Constitucional / Diario Comercial

                1

Aurora de Matanzas

Eco de Villa Clara

Redactor (SC) / Cubano Oriental / Redactor

           16   18

        Biblioteca Selecta / Recreo Literario

                Libre Imprenta / Eco de Cuba (SC)

            15 1   2

                  Látigo (SC)

            30

                    Pasatiempo Cubano (SC)

              19

                          Miscelánea de Util . . . Recreo

KEY

————— Publication data confirmed

- - - - - - - - Incomplete publication data

commander), members of the municipal council, and other prominent citizens.[105] While Lorenzo may have had some cause to expect that the new political radicalization might propel him into Tacón's position, only the sense of personal affront seems to explain Lorenzo's precipitate action. Similarly, under the protection of the governor's decision (and to some extent, in response to his pressure, which may have overcome creole inertia), many *santiagueros* were willing to exploit this political innovation to redress an old grievance against Havana. Though "illegal," their move had the virtue of appearing to be the compliance of loyal vassals of the Crown, untainted by republican or other political ambitions. Indeed, the "manifesto" supporting the renewal of constitutionalism should not be exaggerated into a radical document at all. Out of the previous two experiments with constitutionalism, the ideology of creole constitutionalism had evolved into a rather conservative alternative to significant political innovation. In Santiago de Cuba, a city always jealous of its local prerogatives and not as subject to fear of slave rebellion or popular discontent as other areas were, constitutionalism seemed a not unwelcome means to greater regional autonomy through limited electoral checks on the power of the captain generalcy.

A pacific transition to the new constitutional order was all that was lacking; this transition, however, was not forthcoming, for Tacón refused to proclaim constitutionalism in Cuba. This decision was not unexpected from someone who, since his first report to the secretary of state, had been recommending that Cuba be denied equal status with Spain.[106] At the same time, Tacón's reports influenced the new holders of power to take action that would reinforce his decision: only days after the sergeants' revolution in Spain, the new government prohibited the extension of constitutionalism to Cuba (even as it authorized election of Cuban deputies to the constitutional Cortes).[107] When this legislation arrived, Tacón issued a communication to Lorenzo (8 October 1836), as well as a circular to the general populace (10 October) demonstrating the illegality of Lorenzo's move and announcing that communications with Santiago de Cuba would be cut off. Four days later, he instituted a naval blockade of the province's ports. The third interlude of constitutionalism and free press in Cuba was thus restricted to the Oriente.[108]

Tacón had only to refuse to implement the constitution to frustrate the hopes of progressive Cuban creoles. Massive social disorder would have been the necessary concomitant of any political or military assault on Tacón's firm purchase on power,[109] and progressive creoles had consistently declined to contemplate this price. Even more adamantly opposed was the sugarocracy, who at this juncture feared a repeat of constitutional excesses more than the more improbable specter of racial conflict. As Pérez de la Riva has noted: "in that moment it was the specter of the priest Gutiérrez de Piñeres rather than Toussaint L'Ouverture which inspired greater fear."[110] The propertied classes' fear of free press may well be imagined, when even José Antonio Saco (in outlining his strategy for exploiting what he thought would be another constitutional period in Cuba) cautioned progressive creole writers ("nuestra familia escritoril") to found a paper to channel public opinion and to argue against the press excesses of the past.[111] Now, of course, his strategy (elaborated in Paris on 8 September 1836, before he learned of the legislation of 20 August) to dominate constitutional institutions like the provincial deputations became totally inappropriate.

Spain's refusal to allow Cuba to participate in the third interval of constitutionalism eroded Lorenzo's support in Santiago de Cuba. Demonstrations by parts of the garrison and by popular elements had already alienated some *santiagueros*.[112] Lorenzo did not command the loyalty of the entire garrison— the Aragonese battalion remained disconcertingly aloof—and the Audiencia, the military governor of Matanzas, and the lieutenant governor of Puerto Príncipe immediately notified Tacón of their loyalties.[113] As a result, Lorenzo was forced to rely increasingly upon his inner circle of advisors. At the center of this group were Lorenzo's brother-in-law, Manuel de Arcaya, commander of the Catalonian battalion, Francisco Muñoz del Monte (cousin of Domingo del Monte and an ardent Cuban who had been politically radicalized by Saco's exile),[114] Porfirio Valiente, and Juan Kindelán. (Pérez de la Riva characterized Valiente and Kindelán as representative of the creole aristocracy.)[115] In response to Tacón's action, Porfirio Valiente and an aide to Lorenzo were dispatched to Spain to plead Lorenzo's case for the constitution, while Muñoz del Monte drafted a memorial to the regent.[116] In his defense, Lorenzo rehearsed his loyal service and unswerving adherence to the constitution, and stressed the faults of Tacón. Although it was true that Tacón had rid the capital of vagrants, Lorenzo argued, he had simultaneously converted Havana into something approaching a prison or a monastery.

The most significant support for constitutionalism, outside of Lorenzo's inner circle and the unwieldy popular support which could be mobilized for public ceremonies, came from the institutions that owed their very existence to the constitution—the free press, the constitutional municipal council, and the provincial deputation. The press was immediately supportive. Printer Loreto Espinal, editor of the *Noticioso Comercial,* was released from prison, where he was being held during the investigation of "Censura de la censura"; he immediately published the *Diario Constitucional,* on 1 October, from his renamed Imprenta Liberal.[117] Francisco Muñoz del Monte became a regular contributor, and his article in the 6 October 1836 issue clearly stated the import of this political transition. "Let us enter into a new era," he admonished his readers, after reviewing measures that had inflicted "silence and genuflections as the strategy to survive."[118] *El Redactor de Santiago de Cuba* (1 January 1833–1848?), the Patriotic Society paper,[119] was equally explicit in praising Lorenzo and the "Spanish people" for restoring "that beloved code in which are found the rights of man, forgotten for a time under the enormous weight of the cruel fetters placed by the obscene hand of rude despotism."[120] A name change for *El Cubano Oriental* (16 October–18 December 1836) signaled Society support for constitutionalism.

Press unanimity almost faltered at mid-month, not because of ideological diversity, but because of the sensitivity of creoles like Espinal to the new peninsular printer Eduardo Gaspar, who had been waiting for a license to begin printing, and who now, with the constitutional innovation, began to publish the *Libre Imprenta* on 15 October 1836. Like his fellow editors, Gaspar viewed the Santiago de Cuba innovation as an extension of peninsular politics, but his status as outsider provoked sniping from Espinal in issues 11, 14, 17, and 18 of the *Diario Constitucional.* The press at this moment was beginning to exhibit some centrifugal pressures as individuals began to lick old wounds or ride old hobbyhorses. (One individual contributed an article to *El Cubano Oriental* on 11 October 1836 which he had been saving since March 1832 for a recurrence of free press.)[121] Gaspar responded to his critics by issuing a more moderate publication, *El Eco de Cuba* (1 November 1836—2 February 1837), to replace the *Libre Imprenta*. In an opening editorial, Gaspar promised that he would preach union within the constitutionalist camp.[122]

The municipal council and provincial deputation also rallied around Lorenzo. The council sent a petition to the Crown on 19 October rejecting the revolutionary label that Tacón had placed on their actions.[123] At the 21 October meeting, one member proposed a general junta of "all military commanders, secular and ecclesiastical authorities, lawyers, doctors, landowners, merchants, and capitalists, to hear the opinion of everyone about the circumstances in which we find ourselves."[124] Not only did the recommendation indicate a new perception of a serious predicament, but it suggested that the municipal council was reluctant to perch alone on the fragile branch of constitutionalism. Lorenzo consented to such a meeting, and on the twenty-third, after hinting at some undefined political transformations due for the western end of the island and reminding the meeting about Tacón's unconscionable deed of holding the Oriente incommunicado, he received the support of those in attendance.[125] On 27 October, Lorenzo was able to forward the provincial deputation's resolution against Tacón's isolation of the Oriente,[126] and, on the eighth of November, he sent a joint petition from the municipal council and provincial deputation requesting that the constitution be allowed to stand despite prohibitions on its transfer to Ultramar.[127]

In the meantime, the *santiaguero* press, buoyed by the addition of two weeklies, *El Látigo* (30 October—December 1836)[128] and *El Pasatiempo Cubano* (19 November—December 1836),[129] continued its support of constitutionalism. At the vanguard was *El Cubano Oriental* with items discussing and defining concepts such as sovereignty, the common good, and the limits of liberty. Each issue had a lead section entitled "Doctrinas políticas"; the following segment is representative of the ideology of the press support for Lorenzo:

The object of Society is the common good: every government is instituted to assure man the enjoyment of his natural rights . . . equality, liberty, security, and property.

Every man is equal by nature and law. . . . Every citizen has the same right to obtain public office; free peoples know no other reason for electoral preference than virtue and talent. The law must protect public liberty as well as individual liberty against the oppression of those who govern.[130]

El Cubano Oriental also recommended certain authors to its readers: Montesquieu ("who is to the science of government, what Lavoisier is to chemistry and Smith, to economics"), Bentham, and Constant. The writings of the ancients were rejected because the U.S. and French revolutions had driven a wedge of experience between contemporary man and the ancients.[131]

Even as the santiaguero press developed its educational role, Tacón marshaled events to undermine constitutionalism in the Oriente. On 18 November, feeling that Lorenzo's support was weakening, Tacón increased pressure by appointing an interim replacement (Juan de Moya) and sending an additional three cavalry battalions to add to the twenty-six thousand infantry and eight cannon massed in Puerto Príncipe as part of his war of nerves with Lorenzo.[132] On 28 November 1836, Lorenzo informed the populace that Tacón had begun a blockade of the harbor, although it was weak and in no way menaced Lorenzo or his communications. The blockade was just another element in the pressure that Tacón was applying now that the pacifying column was on the march toward Santiago de Cuba.[133]

At the same time, Tacón took advantage of mediation offered by John Hardy, the English consul in Santiago de Cuba, who justified his actions on the basis of the volume of trade between Santiago de Cuba and Jamaica, and the substantial amount of English property in the area (of which a large portion of nearby mines belonged to the consul).[134] Hardy, who was already protecting the archbishop, an outspoken opponent of Lorenzo, now became involved in seeking a peaceful resolution to the situation.[135] Through the good graces of the English, the ship Vestal, under the command of Captain William Jones, was dispatched to Santiago de Cuba, and then to Havana with a report for Tacón. On 6 December 1836, Captain Jones returned to Santiago de Cuba with a plan to solve the impasse.[136] Lorenzo initially rejected the offer of safe conduct and the use of the Ves-

tal for whatever destination he might choose. With a column of nearly three thousand men approaching Santiago de Cuba, the die was cast on 17 December 1836, when officials of the León regiment confronted Lorenzo with their unwillingness "to shed Spanish blood." On the following day the pressure was intensified by news that the Bayamo garrison had pronounced for Tacón and arrested the Lorenzo faction. On 22 December 1836, Lorenzo surrendered command of the province.

On the morning of 23 December 1836, the *Vestal* carried away the last vestiges of the third constitutional experiment in Cuba.[137] Because of developments since the second Restoration, this constitutional interlude bore little resemblance to its predecessors. Initiated by rebellion, it was crushed by colonial authority. While a constitutional free press in Santiago de Cuba revealed that creoles still sought economic autonomy and political rights commensurate with Spaniards', creoles could no longer claim rights they had bartered away in their compromise with Vives. Tacón had played his last hand in his vendetta against the Cubans; by denying their right to constitutionalism he forced them to confront their colonial status.

The resolution of the *santiaguero* rebellion, simplified by the legislative exclusion of constitutionalism from the Spanish provinces of Ultramar, denied Cuban pretensions to equality within the Spanish nation. José Antonio Saco, waiting in frustration in Madrid for the Cortes to recognize his credentials as a deputy, clearly perceived the implications in a letter of 27 December to José de la Luz: "We do not have a country," he lamented, "no, we do not have one."[138] On 16 April 1837, the Cortes fulfilled Saco's prognosis by voting 150 to 2 in favor of a special status for Ultramar; in voting 90 to 65 against a motion to seat Saco and his fellow deputies, it also resolved the ambiguity of the preceding year, when Cubans had been denied constitutionalism but allowed to elect deputies to the Cortes.[139] For the first time since the resistance to the Napoleonic invasion, a constitutional government in Spain had publicly proclaimed the colonial status of Cuba. Ironically, the rebellion in Santiago de Cuba—another attempt to satisfy Cuban political aspirations through a complete identification with the peninsula—contributed to the Cortes's decision. Spanish deputies concerned for Cuban revenues argued that once again political liberty in the Americas had led to political instability. On 5 April 1837, when deputy Vicente Sancho predicted that if Cuba were not Spanish, it would necessarily be black, he expressed this view in terms calculated to convince the Cuban sugar oligarchy to accept a special status. The Cortes fully expected the "ever-faithful isle" once more to sacrifice political aspirations to the specter of Haiti.[140]

CHAPTER 6

Conclusion:
Literature and Repression,
1790–1840

THE SUPPRESSION of constitutionalism in Cuba in 1836 clarified the colonial status of the island. The Restoration proceeded smoothly, abetted by the fortuitous departure of most of the conspirators aboard the *Vestal*.[1] The Mail Administration extended its efforts at an intellectual quarantine of the island, opening suspicious packages and searching the luggage of passengers docking in Havana.[2] A note attached to the captain general's report of 30 April 1837 revealed that such vigilance now included private correspondence. Letters for 103 individuals, including Intendant Martínez de Pinillos, Francisco de Arango, and José de la Luz, had been detained. Once again the entire island seemed subject to what Félix Tanco had once termed Tacón's "opiate administration . . . [which] little by little kills a body robust and healthy by nature."[3]

Progressive creoles of the failed academy in Cuba and the "Club of disloyal *habaneros*" in Spain, seeing no immediate alternative to Spanish dominance,[4] sought revenge on Tacón. They contributed to his recall at the end of 1837—the crucial charge was Carlism because the captain general had allowed the archbishop of Cuba to escape extradition to Spain—but

Tacón's removal brought no significant political change or improvement in the literary environment.[5] From his first day in office on 22 April 1838, Lieutenant General Joaquín Ezpeleta demonstrated that his attitude towards the press did not differ significantly from Tacón's "iron hand." He personally supervised the censorship process to disabuse those who had hoped that his administration "would be in notable opposition to that of my predecessor."[6] After rejecting a protest by the Patriotic Society over one of José de Olañeta's censures, Ezpeleta reported that he was once again convinced that only sinister intentions lay behind every attack on censorship: "It is in the interest of my government to sustain censorship as a most salutary check, and to appreciate the prudence and discernment with which censor Olañeta discharges his responsibility."[7]

The persistence of absolutist press standards became a crucial issue for creoles who gathered in Domingo del Monte's Havana house, the center for literary discussions in 1838 in much the same way that Félix Varela's room in the San Carlos Seminary had beckoned the generation of '23 for conversations on philosophy and science.[8] By 1838, however, only a few of the faces remained the same. There were visits from members of del Monte's generation—Francisco Ruiz (now a philosophy professor at the San Carlos Seminary), Manuel González del Valle (a professor at the university), José Antonio Cintra (a lawyer), and occasionally even from Félix Tanco (a mail administrator in Matanzas). Increasingly, however, the *tertulia* displayed a new constellation of Cuban letters. Closest to del Monte were Ramón de Palma (1812–60), José Antonio Echeverría (1815–85), José Zacarías González del Valle (1820–51), and, on occasional visits from Matanzas, José Jacinto Milanés (1814–63). Less intimate with del Monte but still important to the *tertulia* were Cirilo Villaverde (1812–94) and Anselmo Suárez y Romero (1818–78). Finally, there were irregular participants, the most prominent being Antonio Bachiller y Morales (1812–89), José Victoriano Betancourt (1813–75), Manuel Costales y Govantes (1815–66), and José Quintín Suarte y Hernández (1819–88).[9] Unlike del Monte, Luz, and Saco, this generation had never known the stimulus of a free press or the pull of public debate over political issues. They had been nurtured in the protective hothouse of the *tertulia* to be passionate partisans of literature—poetry, drama, essay, and narrative. For this generation—the generation of '38—the prospects for literary life and the periodical press in a repressive environment assumed vital significance.

Richard Madden, English representative in Cuba monitoring Spanish compliance with treaties ending the slave trade, may have reassured Del Monte's *tertulia* with his support of literary activity "for its humanizing effects in all places it matters not where."[10] Indeed, there were encouraging signs that literature might be allowed to flourish. Captain General Ezpeleta apparently did not feel threatened by literary *revistas;* he took no measures against *El Album* (April 1838—March 1839, founded during the last month of Tacón's governance)[11] and allowed additional *revistas.* In July, Dr. Vicente Antonio de Castro, professor of medicine at the University of Havana, received permission to publish *La Cartera Cubana* (July 1838–December 1840), devoted to science, literature, customs, poetry, and miscellaneous items.[12] In an opening editorial entitled "El empresario tomando el café," Castro portrayed his role as a businessman soliciting materials from acquaintances of varying expertise and interests.[13] Less entrepreneurial motives stimulated a second *revista* that same month. Permission to publish *La Siempreviva* (July 1838–1840) was granted to José Quintín Suzarte, who subsequently collaborated with Antonio Bachiller y Morales, Manuel Costales y Govantes, and José Victoriano Betancourt.[14] By July 1838, then, Havana boasted three creole *revistas.* Subscription statistics also spoke well for literary demand. By its June issue, *El Album* had 438 subscribers, while *La Cartera Cubana* counted at least 461 by the following month, and *La Siempreviva* attracted 541 subscribers by the end of the year.[15]

Creole literary activity peaked with the publication in September of *El Plantel* (September 1838–August 1839), originating from the heart of del Monte's *tertulia* and sponsored by the Patriotic Society.[16] Edited by Ramón de Palma and José Antonio Echeverría, *El Plantel* did not depart significantly from the mandate of *La Cartera* or *La Siempreviva*—"useful knowledge," including scientific, literary, and educational items.[17] *El Plantel* was important because of its contributors—they represented the vanguard of creole talent. Here readers could find articles by del Monte on primary education, by José Zacarías González del Valle on economics, by Echeverría on the historians of Cuba, and poetry by Palma and José Jacinto Milanés.

The *revista*'s success was astonishing, for as del Monte noted, *El Plantel* attracted more than one thousand subscribers, "something unheard of in this land."[18]

With the addition of *El Plantel* Cuban literature achieved its "first moment of splendor," but the well-studied literary boom of 1838–39 was short-lived.[19] Probably the key event in its demise was the resignation in December 1838 of directors Palma and Echeverría after a disagreement with the owner and printer of *El Plantel*, R. Oliva. In an apparent breach of the original terms of his agreement with Palma and Echeverría,[20] Oliva tried to persuade them to accept a quarterly profit of six *pesos*. Whether Oliva's actions concealed a motive deeper than cupidity is not certain. Feliciana Menocal has suggested that the printer's arithmetic formed part of a strategy of peninsular Spaniards to sabotage "the best and most Cuban of these *revistas.*"[21] It was more than suspicious that *El Plantel* resumed publication shortly thereafter under the direction of the two most prominent peninsular literary figures in Havana, Mariano Torrente and José María Andueza.[22] Creole/peninsular antagonisms also pervaded a confrontation over a new lithographic press. Del Monte's correspondent in Paris, José Luis Alfonso, had convinced two Frenchmen to emigrate to Havana with their presses and skilled workers. Concerned about the new competition, Mariano Torrente tried to persuade the Frenchmen to merge their operation with the Imprenta Español, arguing that while the new press might enjoy the business of the *habaneros*, the Spaniards would continue to support the Imprenta Español.[23]

The literary momentum of the generation of '38 faltered when plans for another *revista* to replace *El Plantel* never materialized. José Antonio Echeverría intimated that the projected replacement was modeled on the *Revista Bimestre Cubana;* not surprisingly, his enthusiasm was tempered by skepticism that the government would grant the license.[24] José Jacinto Milanés was equally dubious, noting the "agitated circumstances that surround us" and the problems of finding a printer "less obtuse and more philanthropic" than Oliva.[25]

The crisis over *El Plantel*, however, does not reveal the full dimensions of creole frustration, for it was no secret that even four *revistas* could not provide an outlet for some of the best writing of the moment, which addressed the issue of Cuban slavery. Although *La Siempreviva* published an outline of Cirilo

Villaverde's *Cecilia Valdés* in 1839, the first part of this classic novel of Cuban slavery had to be published in New York.[26] Félix Tanco, shortly after finishing *Petrona y Rosalía*, his seminal description of how slavery pervaded even the most common features of everyday life, recognized that his novella could never be published in Cuba and admitted that the only way he could motivate himself to write other "Cuban scenes" was to hope for their eventual publication in the United States.[27] Censorship restrictions of the creole *revistas* also affected Anselmo Suárez y Romero; he confessed that he was inspired to write *Francisco*, the most penetrating novel on Cuban slavery completed in this period, only after del Monte, on behalf of the British abolitionist Richard Madden, commissioned him to write a "novella where the action occurs between blacks and whites."[28] Madden provided Suárez with a decisive element in the creative process—an audience or prospect of publication, something that the *revistas* could not offer.

Whatever their limited scope, the *revistas* were still the visible symbol of creole literary energy. It was a further blow when *El Album's* license expired in March 1839. That same month, noting that *El Plantel* had lost significant numbers of subscribers since the editorial change, del Monte, Palma, and Echeverría offered to buy the *revista's* license from Oliva, but nothing came of the plan.[29] Echeverría, one of the original editors of *El Plantel*, expressed the sudden disillusionment of the generation of '38:

It has left me with a certain sadness, a certain emptiness that I do not know how to fill since I do not have to think about *El Plantel*. My hopes have vanished; it seems as if my literary reputation has died in its prime.[30]

Echeverría should not have taken the collapse of literary activity so personally, for his generation's dilemma was not of its own making; literature's fate in Cuba had been sealed by the interaction of press and politics since 1790. Until fateful peninsular events in 1808 triggered constitutionalism and a free press, the new medium of the periodical press had been harnessed to the progress of sugar prosperity. It became a tool for the *hacendado* interested in international markets or slave cargoes or for the colonial official anxious to document and publicize his measures. Knowledge assumed the status of a "useful" commodity, but colonial restrictions and the growing press monopoly of the Patriotic Society frustrated an open market in ideas. While the periodical press created the potential for a career in letters, content restrictions deprived the medium of the vitality necessary to support this new profession. Writers may have chafed under these restrictions but, faced with their greater interest in sugar prosperity, they had to be satisfied with wresting control of the press from episcopal interference and applying a regimen of consensual self-censorship monitored by the Patriotic Society.

The international reverberations of Napoleon's invasion of Spain changed the function of the periodical press on the island. Free press legislation and the Constitution of 1812 developed out of the peculiar situation of beleaguered Cádiz. Somehow, officials had to implement this legislation in a unique Cuban context. This provided the challenge, the drama, and the danger of the three constitutional interludes. The first, from 1811 to 1814, saw the full discussion of the issues of constitutionalism eclipsed by a series of personal vendettas, often between members of the sugarocracy and those who jealously eyed their fortunes and political influence over colonial officials. Character assassination became a weapon in the struggle to dominate new constitutional institutions, and to control the existing system of wealth and status.

Issues were clearer and stakes higher during the second constitutional period, 1820–1823. Questions of personal or corporate honor no longer dominated the free press. Rather, despite unanimous protestations of loyalty to the Constitution of 1812, debate in the press revealed a growing factionalism over its practical implementation in Cuba. Two positions emerged immediately: minimal political transformation, advanced by a sugar elite had enjoyed unparalleled prosperity from 1815 to 1819; and complete political identification with peninsular developments, promoted by peninsular Spaniards in Cuba and disaffected creoles, and financed by peninsular merchants whose economic influence was growing through profits in the slave trade and in sugar expansion. By 1823, when the sugarocracy regained control over key constitutional institutions like the press tribunals, a third position of moderate constitutionalism gained ascendancy in the press. This position was advanced principally by progressive, predominantly young creoles, who argued that neither restoration nor revolution could

ensure greater creole political autonomy than constitutionalism, without disastrous social dislocation. The moderate press
promoted substantial expressive freedom but decried the excesses already witnessed. In effect, these youthful literati who
came of age in 1823 were proposing a new, expanded consensus of self-censorship that rejected the limitations tolerated by
their elders.

Even progressive creoles with impassioned periodicals, however, could not counteract the ever-present specter of Haiti and
the growing perception of an intimate connection between constitutionalism and conspiracy. The Soles y Rayos de Bolívar
conspiracy of 1823, added to Aponte's uprising of 1812, effectively silenced the adherents of moderate constitutionalism, revealing the contradiction of an elite that desired greater political autonomy under a system of constitutional liberties that,
at the same time, threatened the structure of Cuban society,
skewed as it was by race and class distinctions. Creoles accepted the restoration of royal absolutism in 1823 with emotions ranging from relief to resignation.

After the second Restoration, the generation of '23 redirected
energies unleashed by political and expressive liberties into literary pursuits. It was in this context that the debate over classicism and romanticism assumed importance as a symbolic
controversy masking suppressed political debate. Classicism
implied the safety and sanctity of established norms and conventions while romanticism embodied the exhilarating and lib-
erating tug of expressive individualism. Classicism epitomized
the regimen of Restoration politics while romanticism seemed
to offer an escape into a literary world where talent not privilege
was the key, where imagination was not coerced by external ar-
biters, where the artist could turn his intuitive insights into a
means of understanding and transforming his society.

Literature even seemed to flourish in the final years of the
paternal governance of Captain General Vives (1829–32), the
architect of the tacit pact between a submissive sugar elite and
an aggressive colonial officialdom after the 1823 conspiracy. Yet
even as colonial vigilance relaxed, creoles were tentatively re-
evaluating the bargain that they had struck with the agent of
Ferdinand VII. Faced with British pressure on the slave trade,
the peninsularization of credit and sugar production, the sugarocracy began to investigate strategies to recover prosperity
and influence; the *revistas* of the early 1830s were part of this

cautious exploration of economic and political alternatives. Creole options proved to be very restricted. When Cubans acceded to Vives's extraordinary powers in exchange for peace and prosperity, they did not anticipate General Tacón or the peninsular mood of the 1830s. Tacón (1834–38) immediately perceived the political content of creole literary activity and suppressed its supporting institutions and *revistas*. Then, by refusing to extend renewed constitutionalism to the island in 1836, Spain stripped Cuba of its claim to be part of the "nation." Cuban creoles watched in disbelief as a liberal Spanish Cortes relegated the island to an explicit colonial status.

Cuban writers exacted their revenge by contributing to the successful campaign for Tacón's recall, but their victory was limited—the reinstatement of literary publication from 1838 to 1839. Subsequent officials, however, retained Tacón's system of intransigent censorship. Such aggressive content restrictions deprived the *revistas* of general interest and revenue. It was the recurrent problem of the evolution of the Cuban press: content restrictions affected all but official publications and the occasional paper devoted to commerce. Only during free press had some papers (like *El Tío Bartolo*) begun to probe the potential for periodical readership in Cuba. Consequently, it was still content, not literacy (although literacy was a major concern of government and the Patriotic Society), that described the radius of *periódico* circulation. Concessions granted to creative expression in the press, subsumed with increasing cynicism under the umbrella of "useful knowledge," could only interest a limited readership. Under official restrictions enforced by Tacón and his successors, literary life could support neither editors like *La Cartera Cubana*'s Castro nor those who would dedicate themselves to literary pursuits. Castro admitted that twenty-five individuals had contributed to *La Cartera* "with the most noble disinterest," and in fact many of these contributors had supported the *revistas* with subscriptions.[31] In this sense, the Cuban press had not evolved significantly from the early 1800s. If the language had evolved in fifty years so that "subscriber" no longer referred indiscriminately to the author or purchaser of the literary product, the reality of the press ignored the distinction.

The Cuban writer could not even live in romantic poverty by his craft. His financial plight was nothing new—Domingo del Monte had been forced to abandon literature for law on several occasions, while Félix Tanco was buried away in the Mail Administration office in Matanzas, ever fearful that someone might discover him stealing a moment to write at his desk.[32] Now, however, economic reality confronted the younger writers who had fueled the literary boom of 1838–39. While both Palma and Echeverría had agreed to write for Castro at a rate of ten *pesos* per page after their resignation from *El Plantel* in December 1838,[33] the editor could only offer one *peso* per page six months later to a financially desperate Anselmo Suárez.[34] By 1840, he could not offer any remuneration to his writers at all. Even the dramatist Milanés, who could count on larger revenues from his plays, could not maintain himself through his writing. In mid-1840, Milanés suggested that the "literary career" did not exist in Cuba because writers did not demand enough for their work, allowing actors and printers to grow rich from their creativity. He calculated that his new play, *Poeta en el Corte*, could attract two thousand patrons for two nights at the Tacón theatre, creating a profit of one thousand *pesos*, of which he would ask one-third.[35] Two weeks later, however, Milanés was still trying to sell his play, but now for one hundred *pesos*, or what he calculated would be the minimum expectation of a dramatist in Madrid. He was not in Madrid, of course; and indeed, apart from monetary considerations, his play did not pass publication censorship for another six years.[36]

Milanés's mistake was persisting in his self-image as a citizen of the Spanish "nation" when the Spanish Cortes had already defined Cuba as a colony, a status that included different literary regulations. This double standard was obvious to two Spaniards writing about Cuba for a peninsular audience. Jacinto de Salas y Quiroga characterized the Havana press as "a miserably mercantile medium" because the government did not have enough confidence in its own censorship to allow *periódicos* specializing in areas permitted by law:

> For this reason, political writers do not exist in Cuba; nor [writers] in any other of the areas that relate to the ideas of intellectual progress. Everything is reduced to poetry, narrative, statistics, and history. Poetry without liberty is a day without sun, history without discussion and argument is a darkened beacon. What is statistics without data . . . and narrative without philosophy?[37]

Another *peninsular,* a resident of Havana for nearly a decade, José María Andueza, held the same opinion about the fate of the island's writers—they were "enslaved . . . , oppressed by a discretional censorship contrary to law and the progress of the human spirit." He noted that the press could not even print the "most innocent political opinion" but was largely reduced to copying official edicts and notices from the peninsular press.[38]

Frustrated by the economic limitations of a highly restricted press, the generation of '38 was forced to seek other opportunities. Milanés was fortunate in that del Monte used his influence to secure him an appointment as secretary to the Sabanilla railway project. (Del Monte was already the secretary of the first railroad project to Cárdenas.)[39] Neither José Zacarías González del Valle nor his friend Anselmo Suárez was more fortunate in his literary ambitions. González del Valle admitted that his literary production had brought him "the overwhelming sum of ten pesos."[40] He increasingly devoted himself to teaching law at the university, and "primeras letras" at a school for young girls, reading philosophy or literature in his spare moments and visiting José de la Luz on Thursday evenings and Sunday mornings.[41] Suárez was unsuccessful at finding a position as a schoolmaster until 1842, when he substituted for González del Valle while his friend went to Spain.[42] Palma and Echeverría retired to Matanzas to become schoolmaster and director, respectively, at separate *colegios.*[43] Their opening editorial in *El Plantel,* scarcely eighteen months earlier, took on a malign prophetic note:

> always possessed of the ardent desire to be useful, we do not believe that we can manage to be so by any other means than the one which heaven has placed in our hands, that is, to write: but if a false vocation has dazzled us, we are still young, and we will be able to begin something else of greater profit, if in spite of all our efforts, experience teaches us that we were not born to be public writers.[44]

By 1840 the Cuban Parnassus was in shambles.[45] Although the nadir of creole expression would not come until the aftermath of the Escalera conspiracy in 1844,[46] Cuban literati were dispersed, disheartened, and so diverted by the pressures of earning a livelihood that literature had receded to the status of a neglected avocation.[47] They were trapped in an inherited literary cycle: colonial censorship had channeled literary efforts from politics to literature; but external political events, or perhaps the politicization of literature beyond limits acceptable to colonial authorities, had invited more stringent censorship, depriving literature of its audience appeal and dooming the career of letters. Colonial vigilance over the press was partly responsible for the tradition of literary expression and the achievements of the 1838–39 boom, but it also contained the seeds of destruction. Already deprived of political expression, Cuban creoles now found themselves stripped of the vocation of literature as well.

By 1840 Cuban literati understood the implications of five decades of compromise between expressive ambitions and political constraints. They were heirs to the cumulative impact of so many decisions: the self-censorship of the initial literary generation of the *Papel Periódico;* the self-interested restrictions on a free press placed by the "lovers of order"; the demotion of politics by the progressive creoles of *El Americano Libre* in 1823 after the demise of the *piñerista* press; the acceptance of a second restoration of absolutism and extended authority for the captain general in the aftermath of a narrow escape from the potential dangers of an independence conspiracy. Living under the shadow of the Haitian Revolution, creoles consistently sacrificed political and expressive liberties in exchange for social peace and economic prosperity. By the 1830s, however, Spain was ready to tally up the ledgers of creole concessions. Now there was only irony in the perception of the island as a "new Eden," untouched by the chaotic disintegration of Spain and her former mainland colonies.[48] Creoles had aspired to partake selectively of the tree of knowledge without provoking retribution or the ruin of paradise. Only too late did they realize their nakedness; only too late did literati like Saco and del Monte realize that their fate would be expulsion from the garden.

APPENDIX

Printing in Cuba to 1800

CONSIDERABLE controversy surrounds the circumstances of the first printing press in Havana. The accepted orthodoxy asserts that its owner was the Flemish immigrant Carlos Habré, and that his career spanned the years 1707–27. (Medina, *La imprenta*, pp. ix–xii, reviews this controversy; also see Levi Marrero, *Cuba: Economía y sociedad* [Madrid, 1980], VIII, 219.) Not much more is known about the next press, founded by Francisco José de Paula, although it is probable that the establishment of the University of Havana provided the motivation. Approved by the governor on 4 June 1735, de Paula's press printed its first university thesis the following year. After 1741, however, de Paula disappears from documentary view, and a similar silence surrounds the probable purchaser of the press, Manuel de Aspeitia. Mariano Seguí insisted in a petition in 1812 that his grandfather, Blas de Olivos, had founded the family press in 1760, when no other press existed in the city (Mariano Seguí to Captain General, Havana, 29 July 1812, AGI, Papeles de Cuba, leg. 1862). Indeed, it is quite probable that all the earlier presses had failed, although Seguí was mistaken about the date of foundation, for Marrero has demonstrated that Olivos was already printing by 1756.

Olivos was initially unsuccessful in his bid to publish a gazette and to obtain the title of official printer. Although several authors have cited May 1764 issues of *La Gaceta*, these issues were either premature or exemplary, for neither permission to print the gazette, nor royal privilege, was forthcoming. Medina (*La imprenta*, p. xvi) misinterprets the royal order of 20 January 1777, which states that "neither now nor henceforth would there be any other press in the island but that of the captain generalcy." He sees the royal order as the final frustration of Olivos's hopes, and he buttresses this interpretation by noting the disappearance of Olivos's printing byline. Olivos had not gone out of business but had finally assumed the title of official printer of the captain generalcy.

Olivos's heirs, however, never enjoyed a true monopoly over the printing business of the island. Other presses, such as the Press of the Episcopacy and San Carlos Seminary (founded in 1762 to complement the founding of the Seminary in 1759) were already in existence, and no attempt had been made to close them down. Another printer, Esteban José Boloña, began his career in 1776; he obtained the title of printer for the Royal Navy in 1785. This privilege involved the lucrative contract for printing the many forms designed to monitor personnel, cargoes, and ship maintenance. By 1796, Boloña had become a familiar of the Inquisition and its printer (see testimony of José Severino Boloña, Cádiz, 6 September 1813, AGI, Ultramar, leg. 74).

Pedro Nolasco Palmer, a retired sergeant of the Havana Volunteers, received a printer's license on 20 May 1791 after the personal intervention of Captain General Las Casas. His initial application had been denied on the basis of the legislation, which supposedly granted Seguí a monopoly as government printer. Palmer's next application, made more desperate by the importunities of creditors who had advanced him the money to purchase the press, was successful because of Las Casas's intervention. Las Casas argued that the 20 January 1777 order giving Seguí a monopoly had never been implemented, that Havana was accustomed to several presses, and that Palmer's petition be approved on the basis of past service to the state. Royal approval of Palmer's press stipulated only that Palmer and his heirs should never publish any book or paper (*papel*) without a license, preceded by "the examination, censure, and approval by Persons learned and wise in the subject . . . and trained in the maxims of American political government." (See Marqués de Bajamar to Las Casas, Aranjuez, 20 May 1791, AGI, Papeles de Cuba, leg. 1482; also Las Casas to Porlier, Havana, 18 February 1791, AGI, Santo Domingo, leg. 1256; finally, see documents reprinted in Medina, *La imprenta*, pp. 189–94.)

NOTES

Epigraph

1. *Centón epistolario de Domingo del Monte*, II, in *Anales de la Academia de la Historia* 2 (1920): 344–46, footnote 1.

A Note on Sources

1. Schulman and Miles, "Guide," pp. 69–102, proved helpful in the early stages of research.
2. Typically, *periódicos* are selectively perused and excerpts transcribed to illustrate the investigator's specific interest. Xavier Tavera Alfara, ed., *El nacionalismo en la prensa mexicana del siglo XVIII* (Mexico City, 1963), is representative of the thematic focus; Ruth Wold, *El Diario de México, primer cotidiano de Nueva España* (Madrid, 1970), emphasizes literary content, particularly poetry.
3. Only one overview deviates significantly from this trend: Manuel de la Cruz's *Reseña histórica del movimiento literario en la isla de Cuba (1790–1890)*. This text eschews biographical and publication detail in favor of a literary evaluation of selected works.
4. For a recent overview, see Max Henríquez Ureña's *Panorama histórico de la literatura cubana*. One example may suffice to dem-

onstrate the perils of orienting oneself in this overgrown wilderness of literary detail. Bachiller y Morales's *Apuntes* erroneously listed two *periódicos—La Enciclopedia* and *La Lonja Mercantil*—under the year 1808, and this formed the basis for subsequent repetitions of this error. In 1945, the *Revista Bimestre Cubana* offered an unpublished manuscript of Bachiller y Morales's corrections to his *Apuntes:* Antonio Hernández Travieso's "Un manuscrito inédito de Bachiller y Morales sobre rectificaciones bibliográficas." *La Enciclopedia* now appeared in 1804; *La Lonja* was not mentioned. Nevertheless, nearly two decades later, José Manuel Pérez Cabrera's *Historiografía de Cuba* still listed *La Enciclopedia* as issuing in 1808, presumably on the basis of Bachiller y Morales's original work. To escape this labyrinth of inherited opinion it is necessary to return to the libraries and archives. Only in this fashion, for example, did I encounter a complete run of *La Lonja Mercantil* (12 September–12 December 1800) bound together with other Cuban *periódicos* in the New York Public Library.

Chapter 1. Secularization and Self-Censorship, 1790–1810

1. For a succinct overview of the Cuban transformation, 1763–1838, see Knight, *Slave Society*, pp. 3–24. An imaginative rendering of Havana in the 1790s can be found in Alejo Carpentier, *Explosion in a Cathedral*, trans. by John Sturrock (New York, 1979), pp. 11–14. See also Humboldt, *Ensayo político sobre la Isla de Cuba*, pp. 98–103, for a comparable description of the city a decade later.

2. Mexico City had a population of 130,602 in 1793; Salvador (Bahia), 100,000 in 1800; Lima, 56,627, in 1791. See Richard E. Boyer and Keith Davies, *Urbanization in 19th Century Latin America: Statistics and Sources* (Los Angeles, 1973), pp. 25, 41, 59. In 1790, Philadelphia (including suburbs) was the largest city in the United States with a population of 42,520, followed by New York with 32,328. See Jacob M. Price, "Economic Function and the Growth of American Port Towns in the Eighteenth Century," *Perspectives in American History* 8 (1974): 126. For Havana and the census of 1792, see Ramón de la Sagra, *Historia económico-política y estadística de la isla de Cuba . . .* (Havana, 1831), p. 4.

3. The 1792 census revealed that, for the first time, the "population of color" outnumbered the white population 138,742 to 133,559. As 1790 had marked the first complete year of unlimited slave imports, the full impact of slavery was yet to come. See Thomas,

Cuba, pp. 91–92; also Kiple, *Blacks*, pp. 28–30. For a summary of the development of the Cuban slave trade in the eighteenth century, see Murray, *Odious Commerce*, pp. 3–15.

4. John Robert McNeill, *Atlantic Empires of France and Spain: Louisbourg and Havana, 1700–1763* (Chapel Hill, 1985), pp. 122–30, 162–70; Moreno Fraginals, *Sugarmill*, pp. 15–20. All references, unless otherwise noted, will be from this edition, a translation of *El Ingenio*, published in Havana in 1964. Readers interested in the economic background in more detail should consult the expanded three-volume edition published in Havana in 1978.

5. This section is based upon Kuethe, "Llorones Cubanos," and Knight, "Origins of Wealth." For more detail on the military reorganization, see Kuethe, *Cuba*.

6. Allan J. Kuethe and G. Douglas Inglis, "Absolutism and Enlightened Reform: Charles III, the Establishment of the *Alcabala*, and Commercial Reorganization in Cuba," *Past and Present* 109 (1985): 118–43.

7. Kuethe, "Llorones Cubanos," p. 144.

8. See Appendix, "Printing in Cuba to 1800."

9. Medina, *La imprenta*, pp. xv–xvi, 187–88, includes documents reprinted from the AGI.

10. Seguí to Captain General, Havana, 29 July 1812, AGI, Papeles de Cuba, leg. 1862. No terminal date for the gazette is known, although the printer and historian Antonio José Valdés noted in his history (first published in 1813) that he had perused 1782–83 issues. The last issue specifically cited was number 28, dated 16 May 1783. See Valdés, *Historia*, p. 254.

11. Barrera (1746–1802) was born in Morocco but came to Havana as a child; he later chose a military career.

12. See *CHPP*, II, 382–83, 386, reproducing documents from the *Archivo de General Miranda* (Caracas, 1930), VII, 188–90; also see Guerra y Sánchez, *Manual*, p. 195, for the context of Miranda's stay in Havana.

13. Thompson, "Origin and Development," p. 153; Censer, *Prelude to Power*, pp. 8–11.

14. Censer, ibid., pp. xi–xiii; the editors of the radical press proclaimed a "moral egalitarian *peuple*" who pursued an ideal of popular sovereignty to frustrate the "selfish and self-indulgent *aristocratie*." Censer, p. 4, defines a radical as "one who agreed with the National Assembly's initial commitment to popular sovereignty."

15. *Novísima recopilación*, libro VIII, título xvi, ley 1 (hereafter, *Nov. rec.*, VIII, xvi, 1); for greater detail, see Gómez Aparicio, *Historia;* Schulte, *Spanish Press;* Smith, *The Newspaper*.

16. *Nov. rec.*, VIII, xvi, 23; see Gómez Aparicio, *Historia*, I, 16–27, 39–40; also Schulte, *Spanish Press*, pp. 91–106.
17. Herr, *Eighteenth-Century Revolution*, p. 154. Although Herr was not attempting a history of the periodical press, his book contains analysis superior to that in most standard treatments. For example, he demonstrates that the periodical press was more important than book publishing as a vehicle for new ideas in the decade prior to the French Revolution (p. 163). Herr's use of the press as a source contributes to a vision of eighteenth-century Spain significantly different from that of Jean Sarrailh, *L'Espagne éclairée de la seconde moitié du XVIIIe siècle* (Paris, 1954).
18. Schulte, *Spanish Press*, pp. 107–9.
19. *Nov. rec.*, VIII, xvii, 3.
20. *Correo de Madrid*, Prologue to Tomo III (1788). Nipho founded more than twenty *periódicos* between 1754 and 1791, including the first continental daily on 7 February 1758. See Gómez Aparicio, *Historia*, I, 16–27, 39–40, 50–52; Schulte, *Spanish Press*, pp. 91–109.
21. Herr, *Eighteenth-Century Revolution*, p. 44.
22. Ibid., p. 45.
23. Any vestiges of free press were eradicated after Napoleon's coup of 9 November 1799. See Bellanger et al., *Histoire générale*, I, 403–547.
24. José Moñino (1728–1808).
25. *Nov. rec.*, VIII, xviii, 13; Andrés Muriel, *Historia de Carlos IV*, 6 vols. (Madrid, 1893–94), I, 203–5.
26. Herr, *Eighteenth-Century Revolution*, p. 262.
27. *Nov. rec.*, VIII, xvii, 5; Herr, *Eighteenth-Century Revolution*, p. 262.
28. This perception suggested the periodization of one of the more significant studies of the Spanish press in the eighteenth century: Paul-J. Guinard, *La Presse espagnole de 1737 à 1791* (Paris, 1973), especially pp. 20–22.
29. Pedro Pablo Abarca de Bolea (1718–98).
30. The *Correo de Murcia* (biweekly beginning 1 September 1792), the *Diario Histórico y Político de Sevilla* (1 September 1792), the *Correo Mercantil de España y sus Indias* (Madrid, biweekly, 1 October 1792), and the *Diario de Barcelona* (1 October 1792), all began publication under an improving outlook for the periodical press. For suggestive evidence (if not analysis) of the impact of the 1791 legislation, see Gómez Aparicio, *Historia*, I, 44–53, and Schulte, *Spanish Press*, pp. 111–14. Of particular interest for its reprinted documents is Esteban Molist Pol, *El Diario de Barcelona, 1792–1963* (Madrid, 1964), pp. 7–34.

31. For a discussion of these estimates, see Fahy, "Antislavery Thought," pp. 14.–15.
32. Guerra y Sánchez, *Manual*, pp. 200–204; Moreno Fraginals, *Sugarmill*, pp. 23, 27–28.
33. Las Casas (1745–1807) was captain general from 1790 to 1796.
34. Lampros, "Merchant-Planter," especially pp. 25–56.
35. For approval of the statutes of the Sociedad Patriótica de la Habana, see Royal Cédula to Governor of Havana, Madrid, 15 December 1792, AGI, Papeles de Cuba, *legajo* (hereafter, leg.) 1485.
36. Although *consulados*, economic societies, and the periodical press were all established institutions of the colonial world, their timing and utilization in Cuba reflected the vision of the captain general and his creole collaborators. The *consulado*, for example, was traditionally a bastion of peninsular commercial interests leaning towards monopoly, although Spanish American *consulados* established in the late eighteenth century placed more emphasis on agriculture. In the Cuban case, the *consulado* promised to be an uneasy compromise between peninsular merchants and creole producers (Lampros, "Merchant-Planter," pp. 57–71). In fact, Las Casas's presidency of this institution tipped the advantage in favor of the creole producers. A good example of such unorthodox behavior was the *consulado*'s championing of concessions for an expanded Spanish-Cuban slave trade between 1789 and 1798. See Moreno Fraginals, *Sugarmill*, pp. 19, 23, 47–50.
37. The Patriotic Society, which held its first meeting on 9 January 1793, was also referred to as the Royal Patriotic Society, the Royal Economic Society, and the Economic Society. This confusion, notable in official publications such as the Society's *Memorias* and other official documentation, persisted until the 1840s, when "Economic Society" became the standard term of reference.
38. Lampros, "Merchant-Planter," p. 25, footnote 1, compared with "Catálogo general alfabético de los individuos que componen la Real Sociedad Patriótica de la Havana [*sic*] desde su erección hasta diciembre del 1795," in Ortiz Fernández, *Recopilación*, pp. 115–20.
39. This is an approximate calculation based upon a perusal of the collection of the BNJM.
40. See the 2 September 1794 report of José Agustín Caballero in *APHL*, II, 23.
41. See *CHPP*, II, 178–79. For an analysis of this library's collection by 1828, see my forthcoming study entitled "An Enlightenment in Havana: The Public Library of the Patriotic Society, 1793–1828."
42. Roig de Leuchsenring, *Los periódicos: el Papel periódico de la Havana*, p. 20.

43. CHPP, II, 17, noted that the first *costumbrista* contribution appeared in the ninth issue (19 December 1790) and its topic was gambling.
44. For a representative sample, see Rodríguez, *Artículos.*
45. Report of José Agustín Caballero, 2 September 1794, *APHL*, II, 23.
46. *El Aviso. Papel Periódico de la Habana*, 6 July 1805.
47. Ibid., 8 December 1805.
48. "El Diluvio Universal," by El Tariminauta, *Papel Periódico*, 15 November 1792, pp. 475–78.
49. In addition to Francisco Seguí, the bishop also sent directives to two other major printers in the city: Estevan José Boloña and Pedro Nolasco Palmer. See Appendix for their early careers.
50. For the entire controversy, see documents included in Phelipe Jph. to King, Havana, 30 November 1792, AGI, Santo Domingo, leg. 2236.
51. This section is based upon Sociedad Económica to Captain General, Havana, 2 December 1794, AGI, Santo Domingo, leg. 1564; it includes copies of correspondence with the bishop of Havana.
52. López Sánchez, *Tomás Romay*, p. 25.
53. See Cosme de Trespalacios to King, Madrid, 27 April 1795, AGI, Santo Domingo, leg. 2219.
54. See metropolitan summary of controversy in *expediente* dated Aranjuez, 8 May 1794, AGI, Santo Domingo, leg. 2219.
55. Someruelos's *minuta* of 2 December 1799, AGI, Papeles de Cuba, leg. 1654, acknowledging Francisco de Arango's letter of 26 November.
56. Zequeira (1760–1846), a military officer, gained a reputation as a poet and editor.
57. Medina, *La imprenta*, pp. 120–22, reprints the prospectus as taken from the *Gazeta de México*, X, no. 33. Though Robredo promised articles on commerce and agriculture, data on shipping and prices, and classified ads, the *Aurora* focused on international news.
58. On 6 October 1800, Fernández de Veranés wrote to the captain general appealing for intervention with an unnamed recalcitrant printer; see AGI, Papeles de Cuba, leg. 1620, for this solitary clue to the identity of *La Lonja*'s editor. The New York Public Library contains the prospectus of 2 August 1800, and issues 1–14 (12 September–12 December 1800). Although promising to apply the lessons of "los Económico-políticos" to the Cuban economy, *La Lonja*'s pages were filled with less than stimulating reprints from other sources.
59. Buenaventura Pascual Ferrer (1772–1851), born and buried in Havana, spent much of his bureaucratic career elsewhere. He

studied law at the University of Havana but finding this career blocked by royal legislation limiting the number of new lawyers admitted to practice, he traveled to Spain in 1794 to seek his fortune in royal service. Ferrer returned to the island in June of 1800 en route to Mexico on a government commission, but Spain's war with England postponed the completion of his journey, allowing him to participate in the Havana press. See his résumé submitted by Francisco de Arango on 10 June 1825, in AGI, Ultramar, leg. 138.

60. Medina, *La imprenta*, p. 124.
61. Antonio Robredo and Miguel de Arambarri to Someruelos, Havana, 16 March 1808, AGI, Papeles de Cuba, leg. 1619. Someruelos's supportive attitude toward the press reflected his general sympathy to creole aspirations. For example, Someruelos authorized neutral shipping, largely North American, after the 1801 Treaty of Amiens ended hostilities with the British. He argued that Spain did not have the resources to supply the island. See Guerra y Sánchez, *Manual*, p. 211.
62. Figueroa y Miranda, *Religión y política;* García Pons, *Espada.*
63. For documents relating to the new bishop's appointment and assumption of office, see materials beginning with *1802 Testimonio de las diligencias practicadas sobre la poseción* [sic], AGI, Santo Domingo, leg. 2236.
64. García Pons, *Espada,* pp. 46–47.
65. Richard Herr argues that the divisive social implications of the French Enlightenment were moderated in Spain by the personal prestige of Charles III and the cohesiveness of Spanish Catholicism. The Spanish Enlightenment under Charles III's patronage was chiefly oriented towards "scientific progress, educational reform, economic prosperity and social justice." See Herr, *Eighteenth-Century Revolution,* p. 85.
66. Ibid., p. 42.
67. Arango (1765–1851), cousin of Francisco de Arango, would soon distinguish himself as a "public writer."
68. Quoted in García Pons, *Espada,* p. 47.
69. See *El Aviso,* 30 June 1805, 2 July 1805, 15 August 1805, 18 March 1806, 27 March 1806, and 1 April 1806.
70. See Henríquez Ureña, *Panorama histórico,* I, 95–97.
71. José Agustín Caballero to Someruelos, Havana, 25 May 1807, AGI, Papeles de Cuba, leg. 1620; Someruelos no. 170 to Benito Hermida, Havana, 28 April 1809, AGI, Santo Domingo, leg. 1281, includes copies of all correspondence between the bishop and Someruelos.
72. *Nov. rec.,* VIII, xvi, 41; for the fate of the legislation see Antonio Rumeu de Armas, *Historia de la censura literaria gubernativa*

en España (Madrid, 1940), pp. 111–27. The royal order of 11 November 1806 admitted the failure of the new legislation and restored the *status quo ante.*

73. *Nov. rec.,* VIII, xvi, 32, dated 1802, recognized the insufficiency of the Inquisition but offered no new legislation.

74. Defourneaux, *Inquisición,* pp. 34–35, 46.

75. Documents submitted after the suppression of the Inquisition indicate the agency's activities in Cuba between 19 November 1785 and 14 August 1812. See Joaquín, Archbishop of Cuba, Santiago de Cuba, 16 June 1813, AGI, Santo Domingo, leg. 1551. For the view of the Inquisition's agent in Cuba, see Estevan Manuel de Elosua to King, Havana, 31 January 1824, AGI, Santo Domingo, leg. 2241.

76. The Cuban documentation might be dismissed as exceptional— indeed, Inquisition efforts were often intermittent and dependent upon circumstances and personnel—but it seems to paint a picture similar to events in the peninsula. Defourneaux, *Inquisición,* p. 104, describes the Spanish Inquisition as buffeted by the various political transformations of the reign of Charles IV, and notes that the institution did not recover even after the conservative political reaction of 1800.

77. This phrase, included in a Patriotic Society report, referred to ecclesiastical opposition to the creation of a chair of Spanish grammar at the San Carlos Seminary. See Juan Manuel O'Farril to Eugenio Llaguno, Havana, 25 November 1796, AGI, Santo Domingo, leg. 1490, submitting a report from the Patriotic Society.

78. See José Agustín Caballero's report of 2 September 1794 to the Patriotic Society, *APHL,* II, 21.

79. No other periodical successfully challenged the *Papel Periódico* and the *Aurora* after Ferrer's return to Spain spelled the demise of *El Regañón* on 13 April 1802. It was as if Ferrer's passing had removed the irritation provoking the island's first journalistic pearls. There was no further mention of *El Observador,* Zequeira's series of feature columns in the *Papel Periódico;* indeed, Zequeira resigned as editor in 1802. Antonio Robredo succeeded him (to 1808), leaving the editing of the *Aurora* to Miguel de Arambarri. See Arambarri's deposition in AGI, Papeles de Cuba, leg. 1656, *expediente* certified by Escribano de Gobierno Méndes, 4–5 January 1809. Zequeira unsuccessfully tried to revive a publication dedicated to monitoring both local customs and the periodical press in late 1804, but *El Criticón* apparently failed after eight issues. See Roig de Leuchsenring, *Los escritores,* pp. 61–65; prospectus dated 7 October 1804; nos. 1–8 (16 October–4 December 1804). *La Enciclopedia,* a short-lived weekly issued from Palmer's press in 1804, lamented that the periodical

press was deteriorating into a frivolous pastime. The year 1805 witnessed the brief existence of the *Amigo de los Cubanos*, a biweekly from Santiago de Cuba and the first paper printed outside Havana. *La Miscelánea Literaria* appeared in 1806, but only achieved the fleeting reputation of "the garbage cart." See *APHL*, II, 211–13; also his corrections published by Hernández Travieso, "Un manuscrito," p. 201.

80. Robredo and Arambarri to Someruelos, Havana, 16 March 1808, Papeles de Cuba, leg. 1619.

81. The steady proliferation of the periodical press during the reign of Charles IV was most dramatic in the Indies. It appears that only two *periódicos* existed in the colonies at his accession: the *Gazeta de México*, which was refounded on 14 January 1784 after more than forty years of silence, and traced a sporadic existence back to 1 January 1722; and the *Gazeta de Literatura de México*, first issued in January 1788 (to 22 October 1795). By contrast, the final decade of the eighteenth century witnessed the beginnings of a marked expansion of colonial *periódicos*. The *Diario de Lima*, the first Spanish American daily, began on 1 October 1790 (to 26 September 1793). Several publications in addition to the *Papel Periódico de la Habana* outlived the reign of Charles IV: the *Gazeta de Guatemala* (1797–1816); the *Aurora. Correo Político-económico de la Habana* (3 September 1800–March 1810); and the *Diario de México* (1805–January 1817). Other titles include: the *Mercurio Peruano* (2 January 1791–1795); the *Semanario Crítico* (Lima, 1791); *El Papel Periódico de la Ciudad de Santafé* (Bogotá, 9 February 1791–6 January 1797); the *Primicias de la Cultura de Quito* (5 January–29 March 1792); the *Gazeta de Lima* (4 September 1793–1795; 24 May 1798–1804); *El Regañón de la Habana* (September 1800–27 April 1802); the *Correo Curioso* (Bogotá, 17 February–29 December 1801); the *Telégrafo Mercantil* (Buenos Aires, 1 April 1801–17 October 1802); the *Semanario de Agricultura* (Buenos Aires, 1 September 1802–11 February 1807); *La Minerva Peruana* (8 March 1805–1810); *El Redactor* (Bogotá, 1806–1809); *El Alternativo del Redactor Americano* (Bogotá, 1807–1811).

82. Torre Revello, *El libro*, pp. 165–66, 191. For the case of the Guatemalan *periodista* Simón Bergaño y Villegas, see Antonio González to Someruelos, Guatemala, 24 October 1808, AGI, Papeles de Cuba, leg. 1840. Also see below in chapter 2.

83. This suggests that the crucial variable was not imperial initiative or restrictions, but the relationships among the colonial bureaucracy, the literati, and the elites of the literary capitals. Ambiguous and variable relationships between colonial elites and imperial officialdom have long been recognized as a factor in both the

persistence and the vulnerability of the Spanish empire in America. See, for example, John L. Phelan, "Authority and Flexibility in the Spanish Imperial Bureaucracy," *Administrative Science Quarterly* 5 (June 1960): 47–65; Mark A. Burkholder and D. S. Chandler, *From Impotence to Authority: The Spanish Crown and the American Audiencias, 1687–1808* (Columbia and London, 1977). A recent analysis has isolated this factor as the key to understanding the variety of colonial responses to the peninsular events of 1808: "The political relations between elites participating in politics and the imperial and local governments responding to them were the decisive factors that led to insurrection or loyalty" (Domínguez, *Insurrection*, p. 2).

84. See Lovett, *Napoleon*.

85. Lampros, "Merchant-Planter," pp. 357–64.

86. Kuethe, "El ejército," pp. 47–55, especially p. 48; Guerra y Sánchez, *Manual*, p. 218.

87. See Domínguez, *Insurrection*, p. 105; he notes that "for nineteen of the twenty-one years between 1790 and 1810 Cuba enjoyed trade with all but Spain's enemies. (The exceptions were 1796–97 and 1804–5.)"

88. Kuethe, "El ejército," pp. 52–55.

89. See Las Casas no. 600, Havana, 9 April 1793, AGI, Santo Domingo, leg. 1261.

90. See Juan Vaillant to Las Casas, Santiago de Cuba, 22 December 1790, AGI, Papeles de Cuba, leg. 1434; or Vaillant to Las Casas, 13 November 1795, AGI, Papeles de Cuba, leg. 1435.

91. For example, Kindelán to Someruelos, Santiago de Cuba, 31 March 1806, AGI, Papeles de Cuba, leg. 1540.

92. See Kindelán to Someruelos, Santiago de Cuba, 11 June 1808, AGI, Papeles de Cuba, leg. 1543.

93. Kindelán to Someruelos, Santiago de Cuba, 27 February 1809, AGI, Papeles de Cuba, leg. 1544.

94. Someruelos to Martín de Garay, Havana, 21 November 1809, AGI, Santo Domingo, leg. 1281.

95. Gómez Roubaud to Martín de Garay, Havana, 29 March 1809, AGI, Ultramar, leg. 126. For Gómez Roubaud's clash with Arango over the tobacco monopoly and his general distrust of sugar producers, see Lampros, "Merchant-Planter," pp. 85, 362–73.

96. Suárez de Urbina to Someruelos, Santiago de Cuba, 27 November 1810, AGI, Papeles de Cuba, leg. 1545A, includes a copy.

97. Suárez de Urbina to Someruelos, Santiago de Cuba, 10 December 1810, AGI, Papeles de Cuba, leg. 1545A, contains the issue in question.

98. Humboldt, *Ensayo*, p. 202.

99. Guerra y Sánchez, *Manual*, p. 223.

100. Anna, *Spain*, pp. 51–52.

101. De la Ossa had served as interim editor of *El Regañón* while Ferrer completed his mission to Mexico in 1801.
102. Zequeira and de la Ossa to Someruelos, Havana, 18 January 1810, included in Someruelos's remission of 3 February 1810, AGI, Papeles de Cuba, leg. 1656.
103. Zequeira's notice of retirement in *Gaceta Diaria*, 26 March 1812.
104. Agustín de Ybarra to Someruelos, Havana, 31 January 1809, AGI, Papeles de Cuba, leg. 1656, includes Cervantes's representation and Someruelos's noncommittal *minuta* of 13 February 1809.
105. Domínguez, "Political Participation," pp. 245–46.
106. *APHL*, I, 7, 10–11; Mitjans, *Estudio*, p. 53.
107. *APHL*, II, 11, 23, 36–37. The *Diario de México* boasted only 249 subscribers in July 1810 (down from a high of 687 in 1805) although the number of street sales is unknown and may have partially compensated for this trend. See Erlandson, "The Press of Mexico," p. 20.
108. Stephen Botein, Jack R. Censer, and Harriet Ritvo, "The Periodical Press in Eighteenth-Century English and French Society: A Cross-Cultural Approach," *Comparative Studies in Society and History* 23:3 (1981): 479–80.
109. Ibid., p. 473.
110. See Roberto Agramonte, *José Agustín Caballero y los orígenes de la conciencia cubana* (Havana, 1952), pp. 121–28, for just one example of the connection between oratory and printed items.
111. Miguel de Arambarri, José de Arango y Núñez del Castillo, Francisco de Arango y Parreño, José de Arazoza, Diego de la Barrera, José Agustín Caballero y de la Torre, Tomás Agustín Cervantes y Castro Palomino, Buenaventura Pascual Ferrer, Agustín Ibarra, Domingo Mendoza, José Antonio de la Ossa, Antonio Robredo, Tomás Romay y Chacón, Félix Fernández de Veranés, and Manuel de Zequeira y Arango. Only one individual in this list has not been mentioned in the text or notes thus far: José de Arazoza, printer and editor of the *Diario* in the next decade, was a prominent *costumbrista* after 1807.
112. Of the fifteen individuals cited, several diverge from the pattern on specific biographical details. Diego de la Barrera was born in Morocco in 1746 but came to Havana as a child; José Antonio de la Ossa was born in Venezuela and came to Cuba in 1800. Several would join the Patriotic Society after 1795: Arambarri (1800?); Ferrer (1800); de la Ossa (1801); and Arazoza (1811?). The sample includes five government officials, three ecclesiastics who were also professors, two army officers and one medical doctor.

113. Cervantes to King, Havana, 15 April 1815, AGI, Santo Domingo, leg. 1189. Like his father, he served as *administrador de temporalidades* (supervising the confiscated property of the expelled Jesuit order).
114. Tomás Agustín Cervantes to Juan Bernardo O'Gaban, Havana, 28 January 1809, AGI, Papeles de Cuba, leg. 1656.
115. This view of the Patriotic Society is in notable opposition to that of Shafer, *Economic Societies,* pp. 191–93. Shafer refers to the period 1796–1815 as the "Society Quiescent," but his chronology relies too heavily on the Society's *Memorias* as a source and barometer of activity. The key break in the Patriotic Society's vitality before a resurgence late in the second decade of the nineteenth century would come in 1811 with the proclamation of free press and the end of the Patriotic Society's monopoly over intellectual life and the periodical press.
116. *El Regañón,* 13 April 1802, pp. 205–8. Ferrer's literary talents (*Viaje a la Isla de Cuba* (Madrid, 1796); *Carta de un Havanero* (Madrid, 1797) had earned him Society membership) combined with the insult of finishing seventh in the 1800 elections for Society editor, undoubtedly contributed to the disparaging tone with which he surveyed the Havana literary scene.
117. For examples of the foreign press, see Sebastián Kindelán to Captain General, Santiago de Cuba, 13 January 1806, AGI, Papeles de Cuba, leg. 1540; or Kindelán to Captain General, 27 January 1808, AGI, Papeles de Cuba, leg. 1543.
118. Moreno Fraginals, *Sugarmill,* pp. 51–59.
119. Chadwick, *Secularization,* pp. 38–40. Chadwick emphasizes the impact of the steam press; this is evident in his distinction between "Enlightenment" and "secularization": "Enlightenment was of the few. Secularization is of the many" (p. 9). Nevertheless, scholars have endeavored to measure secularization in the period prior to the steam press. For a review of some efforts, including a discussion of various indices of secularization, see Carolyn C. Lougee, "The Enlightenment and the French Revolution: Some Recent Perspectives," *Eighteenth-Century Studies* 11:1 (1977): 84–102.

Chapter 2. Free Press: Libel and Exoneration, 1811–1814

1. Schulte, *Spanish Press,* p. 130, includes this translation of relevant sections. For the complete text, see Eguizábal, *Apuntes para una historia de la legislación española sobre imprenta desde el año de 1480 al presente,* pp. 82–84.
2. Nettie Lee Benson, "Introduction," p. 4, in *Mexico and the Span-*

ish Cortes, 1810−1822: Eight Essays, ed. Nettie Lee Benson (Austin, 1966).

3. Lovett, *Napoleon,* I, 343−45.

4. The formula specified "one deputy to be elected for each peninsular city that had participated in the last Cortes of 1789, plus one deputy for each peninsular provincial junta and one deputy for each 50,000 peninsular inhabitants, plus one deputy for each 100,000 *white* inhabitants overseas." See Anna, *Spain,* p. 59.

5. Ibid., p. 66.

6. Schulte, *Spanish Press,* pp. 123−30; Gómez Aparicio, *Historia,* pp. 69−75, 79−82.

7. The text was copied from the Cádiz *periódico El Conciso,* once again demonstrating the importance of the periodical press to the island's information network. See BNM, HA 16106. The *Diario* had kept its readers informed about the legislation's progress. When news reached Havana that the Cortes had approved the legislation by a vote of 68 to 32 on 19 October 1810, the *Diario* printed a front-page dialogue in which a father explained the meaning of a free press to his son. See the *Diario,* 29 December 1810, p. 1, reproduced in *CHPP,* I, 19.

8. See Suárez de Urbina no. 199 to Someruelos, Santiago de Cuba, 5 February 1811, AGI, Papeles de Cuba, leg. 1546, responding to Someruelos's cautionary edict of 14 January.

9. Neal, "Freedom," pp. 92−95.

10. Anna, *Spain,* p. 96. He notes that Abascal "persecuted and arrested leading editors, sending them to Spain for trials in which they were always found not guilty. He secretly sponsored a progovernment periodical." For more detail, see Timothy E. Anna, *The Fall of Royal Government in Peru* (Lincoln, 1979), pp. 53−93.

11. Someruelos no. 272 to Nicolás María de Sierra, Havana, 23 February 1811, AGI, Santo Domingo, leg. 1283; ecclesiastical members of the censorship panel were Domingo Mendoza and José Agustín Caballero; other members were José María Sanz, Luis Hidalgo Gato, and Rafael González. See *CHPP,* II, 419. Someruelos's declaration of a free press was printed in the *Diario* of 19 February 1811. See BNM, 16106.

12. *El Lince,* 14 February 1811, p. 4, and 23 March 1811; BNM, HA 9664, contains volume I, nos. 1−109 (8 December 1811), and volume II, Extraordinario no. 159 (1 May 1812).

13. This section is based upon Someruelos no. 316 to Pezuela, Havana, 26 October 1811, AGI, Santo Domingo, leg. 1283, which includes documentation from the censorship board, and nos. 84, 88, and 93 of *El Lince.*

14. The article by "Moribundo" had been published in the *Aditamiento a la Tertulia de la Habana*, 1 August 1811, pp. 50–52.

15. Though Caballero was included in the five appointees to the official censorship board, Someruelos sent a detailed account of *El Lince*'s abuse of the free press, and recommended that Caballero's earlier resignation be accepted. He nominated two substitutes, one of whom, Julián del Barrio (canon of the Havana cathedral), was approved by the Cortes on 9 May 1812. See AGI, Ultramar, leg. 163, dated Cádiz, 9 May 1812. Thus Caballero eventually was removed from the censorship board despite the fact that he enjoyed sufficient literary repute to be nominated in 1811 to the Supreme Censorship Board in Spain. See Caballero to King, Havana, 25 December 181, AGI, Ultramar, leg. 153, citing health reasons for refusing the appointment.

16. Gómez Aparicio, *Historia*, pp. 82–84, referring to the title of an 1811 Cádiz *impreso*.

17. See *minuta* included in a letter of José Agustín Caballero to King, Havana, 25 December 1811 (also *minuta* dated Cádiz, 11 June 1812), AGI, Ultramar, leg. 153.

18. BNM, HA 16354–9, SS. *de la junta censoria interina de esta ciudad*, written by José de Arango on 13 July 1811.

19. Bishop Joseph to [?], Havana, 6 and 8 October 1797, AGI, Santo Domingo, ieg. 1443, suggested Gutiérrez de Piñeres's appointment as episcopal counsel.

20. *Declamación quarta* . . . , included in "Testimonio del expediente obrado a consecuencia del papel infamatorio, calumnioso y subversivo que dió al público el Presbítero Dr. Dn. Tomás Gutiérrez de Piñeres . . . ," AGI, Ultramar, leg. 390.

21. Someruelos was responding to an inquiry from Pezuela based upon accusations contained in a letter from Manuel Martínez de Esparga. Someruelos Reservado no. 8 to Pezuela, Havana, 11 February 1812, AGI, Ultramar, leg. 56; in response to the justice minister's letter of 22 September 1811 (received 23 December 1811).

22. Nearly two-thirds of AGI, Ultramar, leg. 105, relates to the Acosta case.

23. Chaves et al., Reservado, to Someruelos, Puerto Príncipe, 28 March 1812, AGI, Papeles de Cuba, leg. 1623. On 15 October 1814, after the restoration of Ferdinand VII, the Council of State effectively acknowledged Piñeres's accusations about the Audiencia. Judges Mendiola and Robledo were deemed inexperienced and totally under Chaves's sway. The Council recommended a confidential reproof to the regent and additional appointments to dilute his influence. See Consejo de Estado, 15 October 1814, AGI, Ultramar, leg. 56.

24. *Primera defensa de la declamación primera contra el despotismo del poder judicial* (17 January 1812).
25. Audiencia de Puerto Príncipe to [?], Puerto Príncipe, 17 February 1812, AGI, Ultramar, leg. 390.
26. John Tate Lanning, *The Eighteenth-Century Enlightenment in the University of San Carlos de Guatemala* (Ithaca, 1956), pp. 88–89. Collections of Bergaño's Guatemalan writings and the biographical speculations of several editors are available in: Salomón Carrillo Ramírez, *El poeta Villegas. Precursor de la independencia de Centroamérica*, 2d ed. (Guatemala, 1960); Simón Bergaño y Villegas, *Poemas*, prologue by César Brañas, 2d ed. (Guatemala, 1959), based in part on the 1808 edition of *La vacuna . . .* ; David Vela, *Literatura Guatemalteca*, 2d ed. (Guatemala, 1948), pp. 304–16.
27. As mentioned below, the archbishop's accusations, contained in an 8 January 1806 letter to the secretary of justice, would be published by one of Bergaño's journalistic detractors in the *Tertulia de la Habana*, 11 February 1812, pp. 2–6. The poem in question was "Oda acreóntica," published 1 December 1805.
28. Antonio González to Captain General, Guatemala, 24 October 1808, AGI, Papeles de Cuba, leg. 1840; includes González et. al. of same day; transcribed from the original documents by Juan de Dios Ayala on 19 September 1811 in Havana.
29. José Antonio Cameran, surgeon of the Protomedicato and the Royal Jail, 19 May 1809; included in Aguilar to Someruelos, Havana, 25 May 1809, AGI, Papeles de Cuba, leg. 1840.
30. Opinion remitted by Aguilar to Someruelos, Havana, 24 July, 1809, AGI, Papeles de Cuba, leg. 1840; see also Aguilar's communication of 10 February 1810, which includes Bergaño's letter of 20 January. Bergaño was not unknown in Havana; *El Aviso* on 25 January 1807 had published one of his articles from the *Gazeta de Guatemala*. Further, since 30 July 1809 Bergaño had been contributing directly to *El Aviso*, and by 5 October 1809 had already experienced his first censorship reverse. See Roig de Leuchsenring, *Los periódicos: los continuadores*, pp. 100–103.
31. *El Patriota* joined *El Lince*, the *Diario de la Habana*, and *El Mensagero*. Bachiller y Morales claimed that the irregular *El Hablador* had been issued in January 1811 prior to the promulgation of a free press (see *APHL*, II, 117–18). *El Hablador*, however, is more appropriately viewed at this stage as a supplement to *El Mensagero*, an opportunity for Manuel de Zequeira and contributors like Nicolás Ruiz to indulge in more literary pursuits, particularly patriotic poetry and *costumbrismo*.
32. José de Jesús Castillo y Pérez (1786–1851); for fragmentary evi-

dence on Ruiz, see cover copy of Nicolás Ruiz to Captain General [?], Havana, 20 September 1811, AGI, Ultramar, leg. 153, appealing censorship verdict on *El Mensagero*, no. 34.

33. There are also indications that earlier editorial unanimity was breaking down because of Bergaño's desire to use the paper to conduct a defense of his reputation. See *El Patriota*, no. 7, pp. 127–31, "Causes criminales," by Philalethes (Bergaño); also see the *Correo de las Damas*, 27 October 1811, for his account of the editorial split.

34. For García's career at this stage see Kindelán no. 541 to Secretario de Estado y . . . Ultramar, Havana, 8 February 1823, AGI, Santo Domingo, leg. 1295.

35. The prospectus and a complete collection of seventy-five issues are available at the Boston Public Library.

36. Although the *Correo* mentions a precursor of the same title in Cádiz, neither Gómez Aparicio nor Schulte confirms its existence. The legitimate ancestors of the *Correo* were probably the books or collections published for female readers with increasing frequency in the first decade of the nineteenth century. See Roger Poirier, "*Biblioteca Selecta de las Damas*: Its Cultural Significance," *Dieciocho* 7 (1984): 28–41.

37. *Correo*, no. 12, p. 45.

38. In the *Necrología* Bergaño satirically anthropomorphized all the *periódicos* published by the official press. See the *Correo*, 13 July 1811, pp. 143–44. For the *Tertulia*'s reaction, see no. 12, 15 July 1811, pp. 85–95. *CAT*, p. 174, lists Geremías de Gueroca as director, but his one signed (and probably pseudonymous) contribution, sharing a page with an unsigned editorial, does not seem convincing. The largest identifiable contributor was Juan Justo Jiménez, who authored a series decrying public jail conditions.

39. *Tertulia*, no. 15, 5 August 1811, pp. 118–25; the documents were published in vol. II, no. 34, 11 February 1812, pp. 2–6.

40. Rendón to Captain General, Havana, 8 June 1811, AGI, Papeles de Cuba, leg. 1840, including Someruelos's *minuta* of 17 June 1811; Someruelos to Comisario del Santo Oficio, Havana, 22 June 1811, AGI, Papeles de Cuba, leg. 1620; Aguilar to Someruelos, Havana, 13 September 1811, AGI, Papeles de Cuba. leg. 1840, as well as a subsequent letter of 18 September and Someruelos's *minuta* of 20 September 1811. The investigation was still incomplete in early November. See Elosua to Captain General, Havana, 8 November 1811, AGI, Papeles de Cuba, leg. 1620.

41. In this ostensibly anonymous "opinion of a young lady about the public papers of this city," Bergaño sniped at the transitory interest of issues of the *Diario* and *El Lince*, but reserved his

harshest words for the lack of originality of the *Tertulia*. It was almost a declaration of war and might have had something to do with Bergaño's temporary withdrawal from the scene of battle. See the *Correo*, 19 October 1811.

42. Two days later, on 25 November 1811, the *asesor general*, Leonardo del Monte, ordered the recall of all offending issues, and on the following day, a notary went to Palmer's press (now directed by his son Lorenzo) to collect any unsold copies. Someruelos also placed a notice in the *Diario* instructing all subscribers of the *Correo* to return their copies to the government house within three days. See *minutas* of del Monte (25 November 1811) and Someruelos (26 November 1811) in AGI, Papeles de Cuba, leg. 1840. For Palmer's refusal, see Bergaño to Captain General, Havana, 4 November 1812, AGI, Papeles de Cuba, leg. 1826. A year later, Bergaño was correcting the misinterpretation that he had been seeking Someruelos's permission to print no. 67; rather, he pointed out, he had appealed to the captain general to force Palmer to comply with his legal obligation as a printer. Also see Leonardo del Monte to Someruelos, Havana, 17 March 1812, AGI, Papeles de Cuba, leg. 1840.

43. Palacios to Someruelos, Havana, 23 November 1811, AGI, Papeles de Cuba, leg. 1840.

44. Issue no. 67 of the *Correo* was denounced on 4 January 1812 by the bishop's lawyer, Francisco Castañeda, who suggested that Bergaño's writings should be publicly burned. See Junta Censoria to Someruelos, Havana, 4 March 1812, AGI, Papeles de Cuba, leg. 1840.

45. Del Monte to Someruelos, Havana, 17 March 1812, AGI, Papeles de Cuba, leg. 1840.

46. See Figure 2.1, "Major Cuban *Periódicos*, 1811–14," for the month of February 1812. The *Gaceta Diaria*, formerly *El Mensagero*, was the second daily; the triweekly was *El Lince*.

47. This section is based upon *APHL*, III, 268–300, and Hernández Travieso, "Documento inédito," pp. 201–7. The analyst heeds Bachiller y Morales's caution that his year-by-year listing of printed items other than *periódicos* is incomplete. Because the list of items displays only the year of publication, it is impossible to chart publication fluctuations more precisely.

48. *El Patriota Americano*, II, no. 1, pp. 3–13.

49. See *CHPP*, II, 200–208. The following year, Montalvo would be named viceroy of New Granada. See *DBC*, p. 430.

50. *CHPP*, II, 420, reproduces the prospectus; also see pages 419–36, including an index of 91 issues. Harvard University Library contains issues 22–24, 26–27, 29–30, 32–35, 37, 38 extraordinario, and 39–44.

51. *CHPP*, II, 1–9.

52. *Gaceta Diaria,* 26 March 1812, pp. 1–2.
53. Second prospectus for *El Hablador,* 16 February 1812, in BNM, HA 16354–16.
54. Only the editors of the *Semanario* (Manuel Francisco Salinero and the printer Lorenzo Palmer), *La Tertulia* (unknown), *El Censor* (Francisco Sánchez del Pando), and *El Reparón* (unknown, possibly Juan José Valdés) were either definitely not members or evinced an editorial posture that would suggest the same conclusion.
55. See Franco, *Conspiraciones,* pp. 20–31. This book, primarily a collection of documents from the AGI and the Archivo Nacional in Havana, features a valuable introduction by Franco.
56. Three of the 1810 conspirators signed a 20 October 1809 petition appealing Someruelos's restrictions on commerce with the United States. Someruelos defused the projected 7 October 1810 uprising; and the creole conspirators received sentences of eight to ten years in prison, while floggings were administered to complicit slaves. Aponte had been recruited by Luis Francisco Bassave in 1810, and this may provide the only real connection between the two conspiracies. Though he was not prosecuted, Aponte was "retired" from his militia position in the battalion of Pardos and Morenos, in the aftermath of distrust and suspicion. See Franco, *Conspiraciones,* pp. 10–12.
57. William Shaler, a U.S. State Department official in Havana, documented the impact of this debate on Cuban slaveholders in a report of 5 June 1811. On 14 June, Shaler met secretly with José de Arango, who had been named by the Havana municipal council to present its concerns to the Cortes. Shaler and Arango discussed U.S. support for the Cuban slaveholders and the possibility of annexation. See Franco, *Conspiraciones,* pp. 14–15. For Someruelos's actions, see Suárez de Urbina no. 55 to Someruelos, Santiago de Cuba, 25 June 1811, AGI, Papeles de Cuba, leg. 1546, in response to Someruelos's Reservado communication of 31 May 1811.
58. Franco, *Conspiraciones,* pp. 15–17.
59. See Anna, *Spain,* p. 85.
60. Moreno Fraginals, *Sugarmill,* p. 60.
61. See, for example, the *Gaceta Diaria,* 10 April 1812, pp. 1–2.
62. BNM, HA 16354–2, *Continuación del diálogo entre dos amigos* (Havana, 1812).
63. Someruelos nos. 342, 345, and 348, Havana, 11 and 20 February and 5 March 1812, AGI, Santo Domingo, leg. 1284.
64. See Apodaca no. 19 to Pezuela, Havana, 9 June 1812, AGI, Santo Domingo, leg. 1284, seeking arbitration of the censorship panel's grievance against the discretionary legal powers of the *asesor general* in prescribing penalties for their verdicts. Also see his

letter of 12 June 1812 to Pezuela in the same *legajo*, regarding the Audiencia's efforts to streamline censorial procedures in order to expedite sanctions against press offenders.

65. For the text of the constitution, see "Constitución política de la monarquía española (1812)," in *Textos de las constituciones de Cuba (1812–1940)*, ed. Antonio Barreras (Havana, 1940), pp. 3–59.

66. Anna makes the important point that the provincial deputations "were not designed to encourage devolution of power to the provinces overseas but, rather, to serve as an agency for the implementation of central government policies." See Anna, *Spain*, p. 77. The provincial deputation consisted of the superior political chief as president, the intendant, and seven individuals elected for two-year terms.

67. Anna, *Peru*, pp. 83–84.

68. See the *Diario*, 22 July 1812, for official description of celebrations; copy included in AGI, Papeles de Cuba, leg. 1547.

69. See Figure 2.1, "Major Cuban *Periódicos, 1811–14.*"

70. Petition of Arazoza and Soler included in Apodaca no. 356 to Lardizábal y Uribe, Havana, 28 September 1814, AGI, Santo Domingo, leg. 1287.

71. See Seguí's petition to Captain General, Havana, 29 July 1812, AGI, Papeles de Cuba, leg. 1862. The official printer, Mariano Seguí, may have lost favor because of his relationship to Bergaño; sometime before 22 June 1811, Bergaño had been released on bond to Seguí's house. See Someruelos to Comisario del Santo Oficio, Havana, 22 June 1811, AGI, Papeles de Cuba, leg. 1620.

72. Valdés's important *Historia de la isla de Cuba y en especial de la Habana*, the first and only volume of which appeared from his press in 1813, has always been viewed as the first history of the island written from a perspective distinct from that of the elite writers of the Patriotic Society. See *APHL*, II, 133–36.

73. Pérez Cabrera, *Historiografía de Cuba*, p. 145.

74. Gómez Aparicio, *Historia*, pp. 95–102; Schulte, *Spanish Press*, pp. 131–32.

75. This motivation was acknowledged in *El Centinela*, 15 October 1812, pp. 18–19. *CAT*, p. 124, claims that *El Centinela* replaced *El Lince*; however, the first issue of *El Centinela*, 8 October 1812, p. 2, makes it clear that *El Lince* had only ceded its right of publication to *El Centinela*—a procedure that was totally unnecessary under the free press legislation.

76. The *consulado* charged that the secretary-elect of the new constitutional municipal council, Francisco Sánchez del Pando, had used his position as editor of *El Censor Universal* to disparage his political opponents in the *consulado* and preconstitutional

municipal council. See Juan Montalvo and Pedro Juan de Erice no. 232 to Ciriaco González, *secretario interino de la goberna-ción* de Ultramar-Cádiz, Havana, 29 September 1812, AGI, Ultramar, leg. 85; and *Consulado* no. 233 to Carvajal, Havana, 14 October 1812, AGI, Ultramar, leg. 85, which includes transcribed documents from the municipal council. *El Centinela* and *El Censor* would continue to snipe at each other until the eve of the Restoration. For example, see *El Centinela*, 9 September 1813, in reply to *El Censor* no. 229, in BNM, HA 1638–11.

77. Bergaño to Apodaca, Havana, 7 July 1812, AGI, Papeles de Cuba, leg. 1840.
78. Medical reports included in AGI, Papeles de Cuba, leg. 1840.
79. Bergaño to Apodaca, Havana, 12 July 1812, AGI, Papeles de Cuba, leg. 1840. Also in the same *legajo*, Bergaño to Captain General, 20 July 1812; Aguilar to Apodaca, 18 July 1812; Apodaca to Aguilar, 23 July 1812; and Apodaca to Presidente de Guatemala, 1 August 1812.
80. *Diario Cívico*, 12 September 1812, pp. 1–3.
81. Ibid., 19 March 1813, pp. 1–2; also see "Fallecimiento del Señor Jovellanos," in 9 September 1812 issue, pp. 1–4.
82. *Diario Cívico*, 11 November 1812, pp. 2–4.
83. *El Reparón*, 19 November 1812, pp. 3–4; for another example, see critical item by El ciudadano Duarte y Zenea in *La Cena*, 22 September 1812.
84. "Zurra" claimed that Someruelos, before declaring free press, had verbally forbidden the *Diario de la Habana* to publish any item by the "moderate" Bergaño. See supplement to *El Reparón*, 19 November 1812, "Al moderado D. Simón Bergaño y Villegas."
85. Other *periódicos* appeared during the first half of the year, but the dearth of information about them argues that contemporaries were unimpressed. They included *El Consolador* (1 May–16 June 1812); *La Mosca* (June 1812–?); the *Redactor General* (3 July 1812–?). For *El Consolador*, see issue no. 11, 17 July 1812, in AGI, Papeles de Cuba, leg. 1826; for *La Mosca* and *El Redactor*, see notice in the *Gaceta Diaria* no. 193, 26 June 1812, BNM, HA 10743.
86. *CHPP*, I, 53.
87. Santiago de Cuba boasted a *periódico* in early 1811, but *El Eco Cubense* suspended publication in July. See Suárez de Urbina no. 302 to Someruelos, Santiago de Cuba, 18 July 1811, AGI, Papeles de Cuba, leg. 1547. In 1812, however, three titles issued from the press of Matías Alqueza: *El Ramillete* (18 March–9 December 1812); *La Sabatina* (18 November 1812–?); and the *Actas Capitulares de Cuba*, an official publication of the Santiago de Cuba municipal council which ran from 3 December

1812 to November 1813. For detail on the Santiago de Cuba press, see *CHPP.* For the *Diario de Matanzas* (9 January–8 April 1813?), see *CHPP,* I, 126. The most significant provincial publication was *El Espejo de Puerto Príncipe.* Mariano Seguí, displaced as government printer in Havana by Arazoza and Soler, moved to Puerto Príncipe, the seat of the Audiencia, opened a press and published *El Espejo.* The paper immediately established a literary reputation (confirmed by extensive borrowing from its pages by the Havana press) and overshadowed all of its provincial competitors.

88. Prospectus reprinted in *CHPP,* I, 128.

89. Legislation available in Eguizábal, *Apuntes,* pp. 85–90.

90. Del Monte to Apodaca, Havana, 8 April 1813, AGI, Papeles de Cuba, leg. 1840; also Apodaca no. 111 to Antonio Cano Manuel, Secretario de Estado y . . . Gracia y Justicia, Havana, 14 April 1813, AGI, Santo Domingo, leg. 1285.

91. *El Filósofo*'s editor, who only identified himself as "L.A.," outlined his ideology in the first two issues (15 and 22 March 1822).

92. Compare *El Filósofo,* 5 April 1813, pp. 1–4, with the *Diario Cívico,* 11 November 1812, pp. 2–4.

93. The first peninsular satirical publications began to appear in 1812 (*El Tío Tremenda*) and 1813 (*La Pajarera*). See Gómez Aparicio, *Historia,* pp. 110–12. There is no evidence that these publications influenced Bergaño.

94. BNJM has a complete collection. It is possible that *El Esquife* was a reaction to *La Lancha,* a weekly diversion of *La Cena*'s editor and printer, Antonio José Valdés, and a collaborator, Juan Justo Jiménez. Circumstantial evidence includes the naval theme, and the fact that Jiménez had contributed to the *Tertulia,* an earlier literary foe of Bergaño.

95. Documents included in Montalvo, Filomeno, and Boloix to King, Havana, 4 January 1814, AGI, Ultramar, leg. 35. For a more detailed version of the minutes of the Patriotic Society meetings of 11 and 12 December 1813, see those reproduced by Seidel on 18 January 1814, AGI, Papeles de Cuba, leg. 1840.

96. Provincial deputation minutes of 16 December 1813, AGI, Papeles de Cuba, leg. 1840.

97. See minutes of *cabildo ordinario,* 17 December 1813, AGI, Papeles de Cuba, leg. 1840.

98. Del Monte to Apodaca, Havana, 16 December 1813, AGI, Papeles de Cuba, leg. 1840. Apodaca refused to confine the prisoner in the house that contained the press that was the source of his continuing "outrages." To document Bergaño's corrupt influence, Apodaca related that the very night of his incarceration in Cabaña Prison, Bergaño had insinuated himself into the home of the absent commander and had scandalized the commander's

family with his conversation. See Apodaca's *minuta*, 26 December 1813, to del Monte, in same *legajo*.

99. Joseph María Reyna and Ramón Palao to Captain General, Havana, 11 January 1814, AGI, Papeles de Cuba, leg. 1840; also Apodaca to del Monte, 14 January 1814, in same *legajo*.

100. This section is based on the following Havana documents found in AGI, Papeles de Cuba, leg. 1840: Lucas Alvarez to Captain General, 16 January 1814; Apodaca to del Monte, 24 January 1814; Apodaca to del Monte, 25 January 1814; provincial deputation minutes of 27 January 1814 and 29 January 1814; Apodaca to del Monte, 2 February 1814; Apodaca's confidential *minuta* to alcalde of Jesús del Monte, 3 October 1814. Bergaño survived a fall from his hammock in May 1815, living to see himself cleared of all charges and pensioned with back pay. See Captain of Partido of Jesús del Monte to Captain General, 20 May 1815, AGI, Papeles de Cuba, leg. 1840; royal order transmitted to Guatemala on 12 December 1816; José de Bustamante no. 120 to Secretario de Estado y . . . Hacienda, 18 June 1817, AGI, Ultramar, leg. 75.

101. The *Noticioso* was the first morning daily to offer an afternoon supplement. This format gave it an edge on other dailies, especially in reporting commercial news, such as shipping arrivals and departures. *APHL*, II, 118, links the *Noticioso* to the *Semanario Mercantil*, first published by Palmer on 6 March 1811. The *Semanario* went daily on 2 April according to a notice in the *Diario*, 31 March 1811, pp. 3–4. Manuel Francisco Salinero founded the *Noticioso* with the cooperation of the paper's printer. First printed on 12 September 1813, it would survive under several names until its demise as the *Diario de la Marina* shortly after Fidel Castro's rise to power.

102. *El Duende de los Cafées*, reprinted in the *Diario Cívico*, 30 May 1814, p. 3.

103. 24 September 1810–September 1813, or in reality, 29 November 1813. See Anna, *Spain*, p. 117.

104. *Noticioso*, 17–19 May 1814.

105. See Anna, *Spain*, p. 117.

106. *La Cena*, 27 May 1814; also see the *Diario Cívico*, 28 May 1814.

107. *Diario Cívico*, 25 June 1814, p. 4.

108. See the *Diario del Gobierno de la Habana*, 21 July 1814.

109. Also prohibited were dramatic presentations based on texts published during the free press, unless they passed similar censure; the *oficio* is signed Pedro de Macanaz, no date, but surrounding documents would argue Valencia, 4 May 1814. See the *Diario*, 22 July 1814.

110. See Apodaca no. 34, 22 July 1814, AGI, Ultramar, leg. 85, for the captain general's account of events.

111. *El Filósofo*, 22 August 1814, pp. 243–44.

112. *El Espejo*, 27 July 1814, pp. 2–3, AGI, Ultramar, leg. 95.
113. *El Espejo*, a daily since 1 June 1814, continued a subdued existence until 31 October 1816, when Seguí sold his press and left the city.
114. See *La Cena*, 21 April 1814.
115. In *La Cena* on 21 April 1814, for example, Valdés offered a measured comparison of the Spanish and French revolutions. He noted the common wisdom that the French Revolution "will always offer politicians much to learn, and nations, much to avoid." Spaniards, he argued, could avoid the French fate by adhering to their moderate constitutional revolution.
116. See AGI, Santo Domingo, leg. 1637.
117. For *El Café*, see AGI, Santo Domingo, leg. 1637, which includes nos. 31–61; no. 31 contains an index of nos. 1–30.
118. *El Censor Universal*, 27 November 1813, p. 4.
119. For two examples, see Tomás Agustín Cervantes's petition in Juan de Aguilar to Secretario de Estado y . . . Yndias, Havana, 19 April 1815, AGI, Santo Domingo, leg. 1189; petition of José de Arazoza and José de Soler in Apodaca no. 356 to Lardizábal y Uribe, Havana, 28 September 1814, AGI, Santo Domingo, leg. 1287.
120. *Noticioso*, 12 December 1814, p. 1–3.

Chapter 3. Constitutional Reprise (I): The Flota Press Offensive, 1820–1822

1. Anna, *Spain*, pp. 213–20; Comellas Garcí-Llera, *El Trienio constitucional*, pp. 17–25.
2. Cagigal to Duque de San Fernando, Havana, 19 April 1820, AGI, Estado, leg. 12, item 4; includes *Alcance al Diario Extraordinario Constitucional*, dated 17 April 1820. Also see de la Pezuela, *Ensayo histórico*, pp. 473–77; Hernández Travieso, *Varela*.
3. See table in Murray, *Odious Commerce*, p. 18.
4. Moreno Fraginals, *El Ingenio*, II, 133–35. Also see Guerra y Sánchez, *Manual*, pp. 245–53, 262; Lampros, "Merchant-Planter," pp. 417–39.
5. Official publications also started in Santiago de Cuba on 5 April 1819, and Puerto Príncipe on 19 November 1819. For *El Observador de la Isla de Cuba* (Santiago de Cuba) see CHPP, I, 130; for the *Gaceta de Puerto Príncipe*, see ibid., pp. 140–48. The prospectus of the *Gaceta*, originally printed on 8 November 1819, was reprinted approvingly by *El Observador*, 1 December 1819. It was a panegyric to the restricted exploitation of the periodical press. Printer and editor Antonio Guerrero made explicit reference to the calamitous excesses of the first constitutional

period. See issue of *El Observador* in AGI, Papeles de Cuba, leg. 1946.

6. Censorship reverted to preconstitutional forms upon Ferdinand VII's restoration; Captain General Apodaca elaborated new standards for the theater on 28 November 1815. See "Reglamento provisional que deberían observar. . . ," *Diario del Gobierno de la Habana* no. 1981, 2 December 1815, pp. 1–3.
7. Robert Francis Jameson, *Letters from the Havana, during the year 1820*. . . (London, 1821), p. 48.
8. For a general biographical and bibliographical summary, see *DLC*, II, 1073–78. The standard biography is José Ignacio Rodríguez, *Vida del presbítero don Félix Varela* (New York, 1878); many subsequent studies have been summarized with style, if not scholarly notation, in Hernández Travieso, *Varela*, cited above.
9. *Memorias* 26 (28 February 1819): 170–75, contained in AGI, Santo Domingo, leg. 1342.
10. Joseph and Helen McCadden, *Father Varela, Torchbearer from Cuba* (New York, 1969), p. 17.
11. *Memorias* 4 (April 1817): 133–37.
12. Ibid., 12 (31 December 1817): 416.
13. Ibid., 38 (29 February 1820): 394–405.
14. The return to constitutionalism also abolished the Inquisition, although the evidence suggests that this had little impact on Cuba. On 30 June, Bishop Espada remitted the "few papers" of the local office of the Inquisition, noting that there were no outstanding cases or prisoners to complicate the transition. See Espada to Secretario de Estado y . . . Gracia y Justicia, Havana, 30 June 1820, AGI, Santo Domingo, leg. 2237.
15. Jameson, *Letters*, pp. 50–51.
16. Sedano no. 1407 to Cagigal, Puerto Príncipe, 19 May 1820, AGI, Papeles de Cuba, leg. 1940.
17. *APHL*, II, 128; *CHPP*, II, 11, 13, 15, 17, includes an index of fourteen issues to August 1820.
18. BNJM has eight issues to 1 July 1820; also see *APHL*, II, 128; *CHPP*, II, 18–20 for index.
19. Miralla left the Platine region before the outbreak of independence; he spent time in Peru and Spain during the Napoleonic invasion, but left the peninsula after the restoration of despotism. In Havana, he acted as a merchant, principally importing foodstuffs from the United States. In 1819, he won a Patriotic Society prize for his discourse on the importance of white immigration to the island. See José Antonio Miralla, *José Antonio Miralla y sus trabajos*, ed. and comp. Francisco J. Ponte Domínguez (Havana, 1960).

20. *CHPP*, II, 20–23. *La Mosca* only lasted until mid-June, probably due to Miralla's collaboration in *El Argos* after 5 June.
21. Details from *impreso* included in Escudero no. 15 to Secretario de la Gobernación de Ultramar, Santiago de Cuba, 11 July 1820, AGI, Ultramar, leg. 106.
22. See the deliberations of the Junta Preparatoria (1 July 1820), *Diario del Gobierno Constitucional de la Habana* no. 187, 5 July 1820, in Echeverri no. 46 to Antonio Porcel, Havana, 24 July 1820, AGI, Ultramar, leg. 106.
23. Calculating the population of the province of Havana to exceed 245,000, they apportioned four deputies and two alternates to the Spanish Cortes of 1820 and 1821. The procedure was the same for the island's other province, Santiago de Cuba. Typically, the Havana bias of the preparatory junta resulted in an underestimation of the population of the eastern end of the island (Oriente); they allotted one deputy and one substitute on the basis of a projected population of 80,000. See the official correspondence in Escudero no. 15 to Secretario de la Gobernación de Ultramar, Santiago de Cuba, 11 July 1820, AGI, Ultramar, leg. 106. Escudero calculated the population of the Oriente at 158,613.
24. Guerra y Sánchez, *Manual*, p. 260.
25. See materials included in Echeverri no. 46 to Antonio Porcel, Havana, 24 July 1820, AGI, Ultramar, leg. 106.
26. López Sánchez, *Tomás Romay*, pp. 158–70.
27. *El Esquife* suspended publication in 1821 and resumed the following year under new editors (see below).
28. Evaristo Sánchez was one of the major participants in this period of free press; he is an apparent victim of neglect in contemporary literary "histories" like Bachiller y Morales's *APHL*.
29. See *El Indicador*, 13 June 1820, p. 1. For other examples of reprinting strategy, see *El Indicador*'s anticlerical reprints in 10 June 1820, p. 37, and 22 June 1820, p. 87. In addition to the BNJM collection, BNM has nos. 336–462, 1 May–31 August 1821.
30. In addition to sixteen issues in the BNJM collection, see the more substantial series in AGI, Santo Domingo, legs. 1635 and 1636.
31. A falling out ended García's contribution to both *El Esquife Arranchador* and *El Indicador*. In the tenth issue of *El Esquife Arranchador*, Sánchez warned "D. Joaquín" to cease his "contemptible" letters and criticism in the press. Thus García's name should not be linked with *Esquife Arranchador* as is standard in the historiography (even *CAT*, p. 144) but, rather, the rival *El Navío Arranchador*, founded 7 December 1820 (see text follow-

ing in this chapter). This was the publication with which García returned to the high seas of journalism with such disastrous results for his career in public service.

32. See Aguiar to King, Havana, 15 April 1817, AGI, Ultramar, leg. 30.
33. *El Tío Bartolo*, no. 4, no date, p. 16.
34. *El Esquife Arranchador*, no. 3, p. 11.
35. *El Indicador*, 18 June 1820, p. 71.
36. *El Argos*, 1 July 1820, pp. 1–7. The Harvard University Library holds all but four of these thirty-four issues. Fernández Madrid feared that his many occupations would interfere with his literary production. He confessed that he could only devote the time to it that he normally spent at the theater or the bullfights.
37. Prospectus printed in *El Observador Habanero*, 15 June 1820, pp. 1–6. The Library of Congress has a collection of this paper comprising no. 1 (15 June 1820) to vol. II, no. 3 (15 February 1821).
38. Govantes (1796–1844) was a lawyer by 1823 and subsequently a professor.
39. *El Observador Habanero*, no. 6, 31 August 1820; no. 7, 15 September 1820, pp. 1–6.
40. Ibid., no. 2, 30 June 1820.
41. Guerra y Sánchez, *Manual*, p. 258.
42. Anna, *Spain*, p. 232.
43. Ibid., pp. 232–33. For Espada's reaction, see Figueroa y Miranda, *Religión*, pp. 91–127.
44. Antonio Díaz e Ymbrecht to Gefe Superior Interino, Havana, 28 June 1820, AGI, Papeles de Cuba, leg. 1946; verdict unknown.
45. *El Botiquín Constitucional*, no. 32, no date; issued from Palmer's press in early August. Little is known of *El Botiquín* until its name change to *El Impertérrito Constitucional* the following year. For the case of Pérez la Rosa, see Laureano José de Miranda to Gefe Superior Político, 15 November 1820, AGI, Papeles de Cuba, leg. 1946; verdict unknown.
46. Guerra y Sánchez, *Manual*, pp. 261–63.
47. Ramírez to Echeverri, Havana, 3 July 1820, AGI, Ultramar, leg. 133.
48. Letters of Treasury official Francisco Barrutia and Honorary Judge of the Guatemalan Court Manuel Coimbra, dated 17 July 1820, are included in AGI, Ultramar, leg. 133. This same *legajo* contains the best summary of the case from Lima's perspective as he tried in vain as late as 1830 to recover his preconstitutional position as *asesor de la intendencia*; see *expediente* titled only "Habana/ Consejo/ no. 12," which includes materials from 1820 to 1830.
49. This is Ramírez's analysis in a letter dated 22 July 1820 to the

Treasury. See AGI, Ultramar, leg. 44. It was rumored that Lima's father had put up the ten thousand peso bond required to bring the suit to trial. Lima further enraged Ramírez by offering a moratorium to the state's debtors which the intendant feared would jeopardize his ability to pay the troops. See the *expediente* beginning with Ramírez to Echeverri, Havana, 11 July 1820, AGI, Papeles de Cuba, leg. 1959B (includes documents to mid-August).

50. Echeverri Reservado to Antonio Porcel, Havana, 14 August 1820, AGI, Ultramar, leg. 105. See also in the same *legajo*, Echeverri no. 46 to [?], Havana, 10 September 1820, for an update with new examples of press "excess" from *El Tío Bartolo* (nos. 16, 17, 18).

51. *DBC*, p. 536.

52. See report by Antonio Ponce de León y Maroto and Lorenzo Ybarra, dated 28 August 1820, included in Cagigal no. 167 to Antonio Porcel, Havana, 22 December 1820, AGI, Ultramar, leg. 86.

53. Coimbra was eventually cleared for his unconstitutional statement; the Tribunal ruled that his threat was the product of a "momentary madness" and patently impossible to execute. When finally released from the Castillo de la Fuerza, Coimbra found that the commander of the navy had taken advantage of his incarceration to replace him. In vain Coimbra argued that his dismissal violated constitutional procedures, and his appeal faltered even as he saw new press assaults on his reputation (for example, *El Esquife Arranchador*, 9 September 1820, p. 43).

54. Arambarri to Treasury, Havana, 11 December 1823, AGI, Ultramar, leg. 44.

55. Laureano José de Miranda to Echeverri, Havana, 23 September 1820, AGI, Papeles de Cuba, leg. 1946, includes Duarte y Zenea's letters of 20 and 24 August.

56. Duarte y Zenea had good reason to worry about the efficacy of official supervision over the press. The censorship board threatened to suspend activities in August if the provincial deputation did not promptly authorize expense reimbursements. See Ymbrecht to [Echeverri], Havana, 25 August 1820, AGI, Papeles de Cuba, leg. 1946; contains minutes of 16 August meeting.

57. Duarte y Zenea's analysis appears correct. The deputies to the Cortes for 1820 and 1821 were Lieutenant General José de Zayas and Magistrate José Benítez for Havana; Antonio Modesto del Valle (Puerto Príncipe); and Juan Bernardo O'Gaban (Santiago de Cuba). See Figueroa y Miranda, *Religión*, pp. 97–98. O'Gaban's shameless defense of slavery, *Observaciones sobre la suerte de los negros . . .* , is usually cited as the epitome of sugarocracy ideology (see Moreno Fraginals, *Sugarmill*, p. 58). Provincial deputation members comprised Juan Ignacio Rendón (Havana), Indalecio Santos Suárez (Santa Clara), Juan Montalvo

(Matanzas), Francisco del Calvo (Bejucal), Bernardo Gayol (San Antonio Abad), and Pío de Lara (Trinidad); Tomás Romay remained in the position of secretary.

58. Lorenzo Palmer, Tiburcio Campe, Desiderio Herrera, José de Arazoza, and José Severino Boloña.

59. Santos Suárez to Echeverri, Havana, 3 August 1820, AGI, Papeles de Cuba, leg. 1941; also see *expediente* beginning with Echeverri's 4 August 1820 order.

60. Prospectus dated 2 August; nine undated issues from the Imprenta Liberal.

61. La *Galera Constitucional*, no. 2, pp. 5–8.

62. *El Esquife Arranchador*, 7 October 1820, pp. 73–74.

63. Ibid., 4 October 1820. I have encountered no details on *El Vigía* except the fact that Echeverri no. 85, Havana, 13 October 1820, remitted nos. 1–3 to the peninsula. See AGI, Santo Domingo, leg. 1291. *El Liberal* is the *Diario Liberal y de Variedades de la Habana*, which was published from late 1820 under the following motto: "Force ensures the State; custom [*las costumbres*] civilizes it; laws improve it." See APHL, II, 127. I encountered a random issue (no. 23, 26 November 1820, AGI, Papeles de Cuba, leg. 1946), containing a lengthy editorial on European politics and a protest by J. T. G. regarding illegal elections at the university. *El Patriota* was not a *periódico*, but an *impreso*, or brief series of *impresos*, by *El Patriota Religiosa*. One issue was included as an illustration of the excesses of the Havana press in Echeverri Reservado to Antonio Porcel, Havana, 14 August 1820, AGI, Ultramar, leg. 105.

64. *El Esquife Arranchador*, 31 January 1821, p. 200.

65. The exact composition of his group is not clear even in Lampros's study of merchants and planters: "Opposing [the planters] was a merchant group with strong commercial ties to the Spanish peninsula." See Lampros, "Merchant-Planter," p. 316.

66. *El Navío Arranchador*, no. 9 [4 January 1821?], p. 36.

67. Miranda to Cagigal, Havana, 9 January 1821, Papeles de Cuba, leg. 1946.

68. In early November, the Cortes confirmed the Supreme Censorship Board's nominations for the province of Havana: Juan Bernardo O'Gaban and José Eduardo Fernández (convent chaplain) as ecclesiastical representatives; Tomás Romay, Wenceslao Villa-Urrutia (brother-in-law of Ramírez and, like him, a peninsular sympathetic to the sugarocracy), and Andrés de Jauregui as secular censors.

69. *El Esquife Arranchador*, 11 November 1820, pp. 113–15.

70. Hernández Travieso, *Varela*, pp. 194–97. For Varela's opening address, see *El Observador Habanero*, vol. II, no. 1, 15 January 1821, pp. 1–6.

71. *El Navío Arranchador*, no. 9 [4 January 1821?], pp. 33–35.
72. See *El Esquife Arranchador*, 27 January 1821, pp. 195–96, for report of appointment on the 23d; also *El Navío*, 8 February 1821, p. 74.
73. *El Esquife Arranchador*, 31 January 1821, pp. 197–99.
74. See numerous reports of the Censorship Board in AGI, Papeles de Cuba, leg. 1946.
75. *El Esquife Arranchador*, 31 January 1821, p. 200.
76. Ibid., 31 January 1821, p. 201–2; 10 February 1821, pp. 209–12.
77. A shaken Don Pruchinela addressed his rebellious constituency: "What more do you want? Perhaps my own life to content your desires?" See *El Navío Arranchador*, 15 February 1821.
78. See legislation in Eguizábal, *Apuntes*, pp. 98–111. Mahy published the new press regulations in the *Diario*, 10 March 1821. See Juan Ignacio Rendón to Mahy, Havana, 12 March 1821, AGI, Papeles de Cuba, leg. 1978.
79. No longer was there any debate about the competent judge to correspond to an individual's corporate identification. Article 74 stated that press abuse invalidated corporate privilege; clerics and military men, for example, now had to submit to the universal procedure.
80. Mahy no. 5 to Ramón Gil de la Quadra, Havana, 17 March 1821, AGI, Santo Domingo, leg. 1292. Mahy was plagued by poor health and died on 19 July of the following year. On 18 July 1822, he was replaced on an interim basis by Sebastián Kindelán, who governed until the arrival of General Vives on 3 March 1823.
81. In Mahy's description it is unclear whether these upright citizens had not attended the meeting itself, or had merely refused nomination. See Mahy no. 746 to Secretario de Estado y . . . Ultramar, Havana, 15 April 1821, AGI, Santo Domingo, leg. 1337.
82. See Pedro de Osés y Herrera to [Mahy?], Havana, 10 October 1821, AGI, Ultramar, leg. 106.
83. Tanco had just returned to the island in 1819 after a lengthy exile occasioned by his service in the government of Joseph Bonaparte. On 24 March 1821, *El Tío Bartolo* expressed concern over the appointment of Tanco, not only for his known opposition to press criticism of authority, but because the very position in a Cuban context was calculated to prosecute "liberals."
84. My calculations based on *APHL*, II, 386–393. Bachiller y Morales summarized records from the Havana municipal council that were incomplete with regard to the final verdict on items indicted. For more detail on two acquittals, see the cases of Genaro Guen in five letters from Rendón to Mahy, Havana, 2–14 July 1921, AGI, Papeles de Cuba, leg. 1978. Guen's articles appeared in issues 86 and 87 of *Esquife* (9 and 13 June 1821).
85. Comisión de la Gobernación de Ultramar, Palacios, 24 July 1821,

AGI, Ultramar, leg. 35; includes summary of Moscoso's letter of 18 April 1821.

86. Juan Moscoso Reservado to Secretario de Estado y . . . Guerra, Havana, 28 May 1821, AGI, Santo Domingo, leg. 1338.

87. For an informative summary of issues, see dialogue printed in *El Sábelo Todo o el Robespierre Habanero*, 26 April 1821, pp. 3–4. *El Sábelo*, whose title was copied from a Madrid *periódico*, ran from 5 April 1821 to at least 1 July 1821, and was primarily concerned with internal politics of the national militia. AGI, Santo Domingo, leg. 1635, contains ten issues.

88. Anna, *Spain*, p. 94.

89. Audiencia, Puerto Príncipe, 4 May 1821, AGI, Ultramar, leg. 98, for the case of Puerto Príncipe. Also see Guerra y Sánchez, *Manual*, p. 258.

90. *El Falucho Vigía*, 12 April 1821, pp. 2–4. *El Falucho* sailed out of Cayo-guindos under the command of Honorato Inexorable to do battle with a "multitude of servile pirates." AGI, Santo Domingo, leg. 1636, contains thirty-seven of sixty-six issues to 10 January 1822.

91. The fourth conversation is contained in issue no. 17, 22 May, suggesting that the first of this series appeared on 12 May 1821.

92. *CHPP*, I, 158, 178; my reading of BNJM issues suggests that Tanco's method was less invective than example, probably because of his peculiar conflict of interest. Reference to "los malos escritores" is from issue no. 73, 6 January 1822, p. 290.

93. *El Imparcial*, 28 July 1821, pp. 7–8. The BNM contains issues 2, 3, 6, and 20 of this paper, which probably began in late May.

94. *La Corbeta Constitucional*, 28 June 1821, pp. 1–4.

95. Battle lines based on *El Impertérrito*, 2 August 1821, included in Mahy no. 71, 6 August 1821, in AGI, Ultramar, leg. 106, and confirmed by the 30 September 1821 issue. See also *CHPP*, I, 141; *La Corbeta*, no. 1, 28 June, 1821, pp. 1–4. From the opposing perspective, *El Falucho* saw Piñeres's influence in issues of *El Esquife Arranchador* and *El Impertérrito*. See *El Falucho*, 7 June 1821 and 24 June 1821. The *Gaceta de Cayo-Guinchos* abhorred the "detestable" excesses of "Dr. Tomás Níperes" and *El Tío Bartolo*. See the *Gaceta*, 10 September 1821, in BNM, HA 16329:9. *Impertérrito* also included *El Navío Arranchador* in its list of "servile" *periódicos*, perhaps because García had ceased to publish it in April.

96. Guerra y Sánchez, *Manual*, pp. 269–70.

97. Mahy's decision to suspend this legislation guaranteed him a favorable review in the history books of the Cuban creoles. See *El Revisor Político*, 1823, quoted in *DBC*, p. 401; Moreno Fraginals, *El Ingenio*, II, 133–35; and Guerra y Sánchez, *Manual*, pp. 262–70.

98. Anonymous summary dated Palacios, 24 January 1822, AGI, Santo Domingo, leg. 1338. This document, a résumé of Mahy's eleven letters on the subject of the press between 19 April and 26 September 1821, was prepared by the Ministry of Ultramar as evidence for the Cortes's deliberation over an additional law to the press legislation. Consequently content focused on press disorder rather than Mahy's remedial actions, and does not provide details on Mahy's letter of 23 August.

99. Publications are unnamed, but documents indicate that Mahy had already drawn 350 *pesos* from the Treasury for this purpose. See Mahy Reservado no. 10 to Secretario de Ultramar, Havana, 8 September 1821, AGI, Ultramar, leg. 106. The expenditure was approved in Madrid on 4 December 1821.

100. Mahy no. 162 to [?], Havana, 12 September 1821, AGI, Santo Domingo, leg. 1292.

101. *El Indicador*, 14 August 1821, in BNM, HA 12005. Suspension of *El Tío Bartolo* was temporary. Publication resumed by November 1821. The termination of *El Navío Arranchador* at this juncture might also be connected to official pressures.

102. López Sánchez, *Tomás Romay*, pp. 174–80. It is unclear whether Piñeres ever served his sentence—a successful appeal, and then the intervention of Romay in 1823, may have suspended the sentence. There is no doubt, however, about the cleric's retreat from literary activity.

103. My calculations are based upon *APHL*, II, 394–96; the records for 1821 end abruptly in late November.

104. Francisco Ruiz Fernández to Mahy, Havana, 5 December 1821, AGI, Papeles de Cuba, leg. 2003, contains Mahy's marginal note of 24 December 1821.

105. *El Esquife Arranchador* nos. 134–36, 13–19 December 1821.

106. This was the judgment of an anonymous official in Madrid who reviewed Mahy's correspondence on the press from 19 April to 2 September 1821 (Ministry of Ultramar summary, Palacios, 24 January 1822, AGI, Santo Domingo, leg. 1338).

107. AGI, Santo Domingo, leg. 1635, contains reprint of this 11 October 1821 article by the Imprenta Liberal (Santiago de Cuba).

108. *El Tío Bartolo*, 7 November 1821, pp. 435–36; 28 November 1821, pp. 495–98.

109. See the new editor's prospectus in *El Amigo del Pueblo*, 4 January 1822, pp. 286–89.

110. Ibid., 6 January 1822, pp. 290–92.

111. Under the revised title *El Esquife Constitucional*, the publication reappeared 2 March–29 May 1822 (see AGI, Santo Domingo, leg. 1636). *El Esquife Constitucional*, 20 March 1822, p. 4, admitted the editorial change, but provided no clue to the identity of the new editor(s). The printer Pedro Nolasco Boloña

may have been involved, but this speculation is based upon subsequent events (see text following in this chapter).

112. Ibid., 23 March 1822, pp. 3–4.

113. Ibid., pp. 1–3.

114. This is a composite scenario based largely on a manifesto compiled by the victims of Armona's raid and published nearly two weeks later. See *El Esquife Arranchador*, 27 April 1822.

115. Onís no. 349 to Secretario de Estado, London, July 1822, AGI, Estado, leg. 17, *expediente* 136; contains report which Onís had received from a confidential agent in Havana. It was not the first report from this source, for Onís mentioned earlier remissions in nos. 257 and 322 in appealing for continued financial payments for his informant. The signature on the report, written in French and dated 25 April 1822, appears to be "Moseau." The report was not mailed immediately, for it included *impresos* dated to 8 May.

116. *El Esquife Extraordinario*, 14 April 1822, p. 1–2: "La libertad de imprenta está protegida por las Cortes," an *impreso* by "La vindicta público ofendida."

117. Circumstantial evidence indicates that it must have been included in some *periódico* from the press of José Boloña.

118. *El Amigo de la Constitución* no. 225, pp. 1–2.

119. See Onís no. 349 to Secretario de Estado, London, July 1822, AGI, Estado, leg. 17, *expediente* 136.

120. Three letters of Juan Moscoso to Joseph Geta, Havana, 21 April, 25 April, and 15 May 1822, AGI, Santo Domingo, leg. 1339.

121. *El Impertérrito Constitucional*, no. 3, no date, pp. 1–2; issue 1 is dated 14 April, so issue 3 of this biweekly should be dated 21 April 1822.

122. *El Esquife Constitucional*, 27 April 1822, pp. 3–4, remitted by Lorenzano.

123. This charge against Armona was voiced in an undated *impreso* included in Moseau's report, cited above. As it was addressed to Señor Redactor and printed by P. N. Boloña's press, it was probably an inclusion in either *El Esquife Constitucional* of 17 April or 8 May, or *El Amigo de la Constitución* of 16 April.

124. DBC, pp. 73–74; no date of suspension is given. An article in *El Esquife Constitucional*, 26 May 1822, pp. 2–3 refers to Armona as "ex-comisionado."

125. Ignacio González Balbontín was the author of "La conversación entre los negritos Francisco y María," printed in an 1822 issue of *El Esquife Extraordinario*. The conversation used slave dialect to obscure slightly another direct denunciation of Armona and Mahy. Verdict of jury was printed in the *Gaceta de la Habana*, 2 June 1822, p. 3. *El Esquife Constitucional*, 26 May 1822, pp. 2–3, outlines complaint of Juan de Aguilar.

126. APHL, II, 398–401. One contributor, Ignacio Félix del Junco,

eventually received a six-year sentence for an article published in the *Esquife* on 23 March 1822. See Francisco Filomeno to Sebastián Kindelán, Havana, 9 November 1822, AGI, Papeles de Cuba, leg. 1978.
127. AGI, Santo Domingo, leg. 1636, contains this issue.

Chapter 4. Constitutional Reprise (II): Creole Constitutionalism, 1822–1823

1. *El Amante de Sí Mismo*, 12 May 1822, p. 133–35. *El Amante* also offered the cheerful prognosis that, after the initial confusion of revolutionary upheaval, "liberal" revolutions promoted philosophical studies, while "servile" revolutions generally corrupted *belles lettres* (23 May 1822, p. 150).
2. Guerra y Sánchez, *Manual*, pp. 270–72.
3. "Discurso preliminar," *Gaceta de la Habana*, 2 June 1822, p. 1. AGI, Santo Domingo, leg. 1636, contains nos. 1–6, 12–65 (29 October 1822).
4. Ibid., 2 July 1822, p. 4.
5. Ibid., 11 June 1822, pp. 1–3. The "lovers of order" disposed of the problems of Armona and O'Connelly by arguing that the charges of the *piñerista* press had not been proven, thereby ignoring the fact that neither case had been investigated.
6. Translated quote in Schulte, *Spanish Press*, p. 143.
7. See the *Gaceta*, 15 September 1822, p. 4, for Saco's "confession of faith." His first article on 1 September 1822 was a rather pedantic treatise on citizenship, a crucial point in the context of new representational bodies based on limited suffrage; also see the *Gaceta*, 1 September 1822, p. 3.
8. Moreno Fraginals, *El Ingenio*, II, 135, referring to legislation of 8 January 1822.
9. Annexationism did not present a serious political alternative in the fall of 1822. Too much has been made of the mission of Bernabé Sánchez to the United States in September 1822. The United States' cabinet rejected Sánchez's proposal of annexation for fear of British retaliation. Joel Poinsett's evaluation of Sánchez to President Monroe undermines the significance of Sánchez's negotiations: "a silly fellow, without education, without judgment and unauthorized" (quoted in Thomas, *Cuba*, p. 99). Considerably more sentiment for annexationism existed in the United States than in Cuba in the fall of 1822.
10. The Díaz de Castro brothers "exposed" this group in an editorial in the *Gaceta*, 11 October 1822, pp. 1–2. Those listed included Campe and Domínguez, Ruiz Fernández (*El Amigo de la Constitución*), Juan Nogerido (formerly of *El Esquife Constitucional*,

now in prison but contributing to *El Amigo*), and one ex-cleric Armenteros (now publishing *El Fiscal del Pueblo*).

11. See *CHPP*, II, 411, for transcription of editorial. Traditional historians have depicted *El Español Libre* as the "intractable opponent of whatever was beneficial for the liberty of our country." See *CHPP*, II, 408. Campe's reputation has suffered from the fact that the first and subsequent literary histories of the island have uncritically accepted the opinions of his creole critics. For example, Bachiller y Morales's charge that *El Español Libre* was Cuba's equivalent of the peninsular *El Zurriago*, Spain's most "exaltado" paper of the *trienio*, is a gross exaggeration (*APHL*, II, 134). For *Zurriago*, see Gómez Aparicio, *Historia*, pp. 147–50.

12. *Gaceta de la Habana*, 11 July 1822, p. 2.

13. See ibid., 1 October 1822, pp. 1–3, for a fairly dispassionate chronology. Dates are my estimates. Correa y Bottino's actions may have stemmed partly from his own frustrations in seeking legal exoneration of his family's reputation. He tried unsuccessfully to denounce an article in the 15 August *Gaceta*; a jury voted 8 to 1 against his case on 27 August. For the verdict, see the *Gaceta*, 10 September 1822, p. 4.

14. For maximum effect, editor Campe suggested that moderation was only a cover for machinations in behalf of Cuban independence. See Diego Tanco's critique of *El Español Libre*, no. 8, in the *Gaceta*, 8 October 1822, pp. 2–4.

15. *Gaceta de la Habana*, 29 September 1822, pp. 1–2.

16. Calculations based on *APHL*, II, 406–9. Meanwhile, the *piñeristas* could gain no satisfaction from the censorship juries; for example, both denunciations against the *Gaceta de la Habana* were dismissed. The *Gaceta*, 11 October 1822, listed *El Fiscal* as a *piñerista* survivor and claimed that its editor was "ex-cleric Armenteros."

17. Prospectus for *El Americano Libre* included in BNJM collection, p. 1.

18. Ibid., p. 2.

19. *CHPP*, II, 408.

20. *El Americano Libre*, 15 November 1822, pp. 1–3. Also see the prospectus, pp. 2–3.

21. *El Americano Libre*, 15 November 1822, pp. 2–3; also 17 November 1822, pp. 1–3; 20 November 1822, pp. 1–3, replying to *El Amigo de la Constitución*, no. 433; 24 November 1822, pp. 1–5, for a review of the Havana press.

22. Kindelán no. 502 to Secretario de Estado y . . . Ultramar, Havana, 15 December 1822, AGI, Ultramar, leg. 111; also Guerra y Sánchez, *Manual*, pp. 281–83.

23. Kindelán no. 507 to Secretario de Estado y . . . Ultramar, Ha-

vana, 15 December 1822, AGI, Santo Domingo, leg. 1294. Kindelán included, among other evidence, issues 35–38 of *El Español Libre.* See also *El Español Libre,* 5 December 1822, pp. 1–7; only the charges of the list differed from *piñerista* denunciations of irregularities in the previous municipal elections.

24. *El Español Libre,* 7 December 1822, pp. 1–6.
25. For the royal order of 16 February 1822, I have used the text as published in *El Observador de la Isla de Cuba,* 16 August 1822, pp. 1–4. The Cortes added penalties for articles written in satirical or allegorical style—an article could be judged seditious, for example, if the jurors decided, "according to their conscience," that anagrams, allegories, or other literary devices masked a more serious intent. Another revision specified that the penalty for "libelous writings" would be doubled in the overseas provinces (Ultramar). Finally, the legislation implicitly confirmed Mahy's poor estimation of elected municipal councils: it granted authority to the provincial deputations to select two-thirds of the censorship jurors.
26. *APHL,* II, 409–11. Once again, the *Gaceta de la Habana* was the only denounced *periódico* to escape indictment.
27. The investigation was ordered by a resolution of the provincial deputation on 14 December as ammunition for a representation to the Cortes, finally sent in Kindelán no. 551 to Secretario de Estado y . . . Ultramar, Havana, 13 March 1823, AGI, Ultramar, leg. 87.
28. Francisco Filomeno to Captain General, Havana, 15 May 1822, AGI, Papeles de Cuba, leg. 1978.
29. "Aviso prudente" ran in *El Amigo de la Constitución,* 7–9 December 1822.
30. See documents sent from the court of Francisco Filomeno to the provincial deputation on 8 February 1823 in Kindelán no. 551 to Estado, Havana, 13 March 1823, AGI, Ultramar, leg. 87.
31. *CHPP,* I, 178.
32. *El Americano Libre,* 19 January 1823, pp. 6–8.
33. The New York Public Library has all seventy-one issues to 30 August 1823, and an index.
34. In one article, Domingo del Monte argued that literature was superior to philosophy and science because it made ideas palpable and therefore had the capacity to move men to action. See *El Revisor Político,* 4 September 1823, pp. 1–3.
35. Ibid., 7 March 1823, "Lamentos de un subscriptor," pp. 3–6.
36. Ibid., 4 July 1823, pp. 1–5.
37. Ibid., 16 April 1823, p. 4.
38. Vives no. 4 to Secretario de Ultramar, Havana, 10 May 1823, AGI, Ultramar, leg. 111, contains the *impreso* of this address to the Cuban people.

39. "Instrucciones" signed by Vadillo on 2 December 1822 (including a lengthy section of Vives's comments dated Madrid, 22 November 1822), in AGI, Ultramar, leg. 111.
40. Article 6 of the "Instrucciones."
41. Article 7 of the "Instrucciones." In addition, Article 8 enjoined Vives to use the official press as a reliable alternative to official mail communications between the peninsula and Cuba.
42. AGI, Periódicos, Caja 1, no. 5/4, contains issues 48 (17 June) and 60 (29 June) of the *Redactor General,* issued from Campe's Imprenta de la Amistad.
43. See Filomeno to Vives, Havana, 6 May 1823, AGI, Papeles de Cuba, leg. 2101.
44. Vives feared that these discussion groups, authorized by the legislation of 18 December 1822, could provide an alternative to the press for the airing of political ideas. See Vives no. 49 to Secretario de Estado y . . . Ultramar, Havana, 12 June 1823, AGI, Ultramar, leg. 87.
45. Vives no. 63 to Secretario de Estado y . . . Ultramar, Havana, 7 July 1823, AGI, Ultramar, leg. 88. The governor of Martinique sought a treaty to conserve commercial relations, but Vives offered only to protect French life and property on the island.
46. Pezuela states that Vives faced four masonic societies, although only the Society of the Sun was willing to risk traumatic political change and the possibility of racial conflagration. He suggested that this position reflected their recruitment of "outsiders" from the dissident Americas, and creoles who either desired independence or merely hoped to profit from political turmoil. See Pezuela, *Ensayo,* p. 514.
47. Vives's report of 7 July 1823 contains a summary of the above information from a previous remission dated 28 June 1823. See Vives no. 63 to Estado, Havana, AGI, Ultramar, leg. 88.
48. *El Revisor Político,* 30 June 1823.
49. For a summary of Cuban efforts to protect the slave trade in an increasingly hostile international atmosphere, see Thomas, *Cuba,* pp. 91–105.
50. Representation reprinted in Morales y Morales, *Iniciadores,* pp. 56–57.
51. *El Revisor Político,* 31 July 1823, pp. 4–6.
52. Troncoso, a peninsular merchant resident in Havana since 1806, had become "native" in attitude by 1822. He was accepted into the Patriotic Society in 1821, and his petition for honors dated 5 May 1825 included endorsements from officials and prominent members of the sugarocracy. See Vives no. 164 to Secretario de Estado y . . . Gracia y Justicia, Havana, 5 May 1825, AGI, Ultramar, leg. 89.
53. See *CHPP,* II, 163.

54. *El Revisor Político,* 13 August 1823, pp. 1–4.
55. *El Indicador Constitucional,* 31 July 1823. Quoted from *Defensa que produjo El Dr. D. Juan José Hernández* . . . , printed by Antonio María Valdés's Imprenta de la Universidad y del Comercio, AGI, Santo Domingo, leg. 1295. This pamphlet was Hernández's defense against the denunciation on 12 August of one of his articles for being seditious and for inciting disobedience. On 22 September, a jury acquitted Hernández, and he was released from prison. See Rendón to Vives, Havana, 22 September 1823, AGI, Papeles de Cuba, leg. 2101.
56. Guerra y Sánchez, *Manual,* pp. 278–79, views the Soles y Rayos conspiracy as a plot by Colombia and Mexico to deprive Spain of revenue and of a base for renewed military expeditions. This view exaggerates this dimension and ignores the chronology of creole disaffection. The conspirators were not merely "outsiders" acting for external motivations; many creole conspirators had been gradually radicalized to the point where they too would risk independence as a solution.
57. Vives was particularly critical of the *Gaceta de la Habana*'s support for the *exaltados* in the municipal council. See Vives no. 5 to Secretario de Estado y . . . Justicia, Havana, 16 December 1823, AGI, Santo Domingo, leg. 1295.
58. AGI, Ultramar, leg. 164, contains Ferrety's testimony dated 20 January 1825.
59. See AGI, Santo Domingo, leg. 1636, for three samples: *Los justos sentimientos de un habanero fiel; Ataque a la Inquisición;* and *Iturbide en los infiernos.*
60. Vives no. 78 to Secretario de Estado y . . . Ultramar, Havana, 1 September 1823, AGI, Ultramar, leg. 113.
61. Pamphlets included in Vives no. 77 to Secretario de Estado y . . . Ultramar, Havana, 14 August 1823, AGI, Ultramar, leg. 113.
62. Morales y Morales, *Iniciadores,* p. 34.
63. See Zaragoza, *Insurrecciones,* I, 399.
64. Heredia (1803–39) had returned to practice law in Matanzas after graduating at the age of twenty on 9 June 1823. He had been influenced by Dr. Juan José Hernández to join the Society; but in a celebrated letter that he wrote to the district prosecutor before going into hiding, Heredia stated that he had withdrawn his membership over a year earlier: "Overheated theories of social perfection may have made me fall into error, but my soul is not stained with bloody schemes, nor is it susceptible to them." See letter quoted in Morales y Morales, *Iniciadores,* p. 3; *DBC,* pp. 339–40.
65. Zaragoza, *Insurrecciones,* I, 398–99. Lemus was sent to Seville, where he escaped and made his way back to America. Others like

Peoli and José Teurbe Colón were allowed to escape from prison to exile in Mexico. Heredia was not discovered in his hiding place in a sugar mill outside Matanzas, where he stayed until leaving for exile in Boston in November 1823.

66. The manuscript was dated 12 September 1823. See *BAN* 47 (1948): 123–39.

67. For *El Liberal,* see *CHPP,* I, 412, 418. For *La Concordia's* campaign for peace and prosperity, see ibid., pp. 165, 167.

68. Though Vives was ever vigilant to portray his situation as untenable (he was seeking extraordinary powers), his summary of events dated 16 December 1823 states that he had won the cooperation of landowners, the nobility, and some of the commercial classes even before the conspiracy was crushed. See Vives no. 5 to Secretario de Estado y . . . Justicia, Havana, 16 December 1823, AGI, Santo Domingo, leg. 1295.

69. O'Reilly to Gener, Havana, 14 September 1823, AGI, Ultramar, leg. 158; see also Brigadier Vicente Folch to Gener, Havana, 13 September 1823, in same *legajo.*

70. Vives to Secretario de Estado, Havana, 15 December 1823, AHN, Estado, leg. 6367–2. Vives seemed slightly amazed and gratified by the positive response of "all the classes." See Vives no. 1, Havana, 15 December 1823, AGI, Santo Domingo, leg. 1295.

71. *Diario,* 11 December 1823.

72. *Miscelánea Curiosa,* 31 May 1824, p. 1. BNJM has a complete collection of this paper, which admirably demonstrates Restoration limits.

73. Vives [no number] to Captain General, Havana, 23 December 1823, AGI, Papeles de Cuba, leg. 2007.

74. Vives no. 164 to Secretario de Estado y . . . Gracia y Justicia, Havana, 5 May 1825, AGI, Ultramar, leg. 89, included with documents in Troncoso's résumé.

75. Vives [no number] to Secretario de Estado y . . . Hacienda, Havana, 8 March 1825, AGI, Santo Domingo, leg. 1298, includes the testimony of Luis Payne, official interpreter for the captain generalcy, about García's press role. Eleven issues of *El Navío* were included as evidence. By May 1825, García's appointment had been suspended and his "bad conduct" was still being adduced as the reason for denying him positions in 1833. See Secretario del Despacho de Fomento to Secretario de Justicia, [Madrid], 28 May 1833, AHN, Ultramar, leg. 1611.

Chapter 5. The "Ever-Faithful Isle," 1824–1836

1. On 18 March 1824, a grateful Ferdinand VII dispatched titles of "Siempre Fidelísima" and "Siempre Fiel" to the city of Havana

and the island of Cuba, respectively. These titles, dated Palacio, 18 March 1824, are included in AGI, Ultramar, leg. 77.

2. For more detail on Vives's solutions to this problem, see Roberts, "Revival," pp. 14–49.

3. See Thomas, *Cuba*, pp. 103–5; Guerra y Sánchez, *Manual*, pp. 291–99.

4. For Vives's recommendations, see AGI, Ultramar, leg. 114, included as an introduction to the *fiscal*'s summary dated 18 January 1824. For his summary of the postconstitutional transition, see Vives no. 40 to Secretario de Estado y . . . Justicia, Havana, 23 January 1824, AGI, Ultramar, leg. 89.

5. See Llaverías y Martínez, *Comisión.*

6. Zaragoza, *Insurrecciones*, I, 406–7. For a discussion of these extraordinary powers, see 13 July 1825, deliberations of the Council of Indies, AGI, Ultramar, leg. 4.

7. Vives no. 133 to Secretario de Estado y . . . Justicia, Havana, 26 January 1825, AGI, Santo Domingo, leg. 1299.

8. Vives no. 49 to Secretario de Estado y . . . Justicia, Havana, 26 March 1824, AGI, Santo Domingo, leg. 1556.

9. AHN, Estado, leg. 6367–2, section 93. All the above measures were published in the *Diario de la Habana*, 16 April 1826. For an inventory of all ten Havana booksellers, see AGI, Papeles de Cuba, leg. 2129A.

10. *Apuntaciones* is a random enclosure in AGI, Santo Domingo, leg. 1298. The captain general revealed his strategy in Vives [no number] to Secretario del Consejo de Indias, Havana, 20 October 1825, AGI, Santo Domingo, leg. 1299.

11. *CHPP*, I, 345.

12. Ferrety to King, Madrid, 23 March 1827, AGI, Santo Domingo, leg. 1557, includes report of 30 September 1824.

13. Arango to Secretario de Estado y . . . Justicia, Guines, 24 May 1828, AGI, Santo Domingo, leg. 1570.

14. The *Noticioso Comercial* (Santiago de Cuba), 3 March 1829, p. 3, states that "the number of newspapers that a country publishes . . . is the thermometer of the degree of culture a people radiates." The *Noticioso Comercial* began publishing on 9 May 1826 in a format that imitated its namesake in Havana. Santiago de Cuba was the only center outside Havana that successfully supported two papers.

15. Karras, "Literary Life," p. 77; translated quote is from Domingo del Monte to Heredia, Havana, 12 August 1826, *CEDM*, I, 23. Karras provides a good discussion of the bibliography on Domingo del Monte as an introduction to his interesting, if speculative, "biographical novel."

16. Tanco was the brother of Diego Tanco, press prosecutor and editor of *El Amigo del Pueblo* in 1821.

17. Del Monte's collection of Tanco's letters from 26 October 1823 to 27 November 1843 forms volume VII of *CEDM*.
18. Félix Tanco to Domingo del Monte, Matanzas, 10 April 1829, *CEDM*, VII, 41–42.
19. See Guerra y Sánchez, *Manual*, pp. 327–29. Six months after the demise of the *Anales*, Sagra returned to a more crowded periodical scene with the *Anales de agricultura e industria rural* (January–December 1831). See *APHL*, II, 139.
20. See Martínez de Pinillos no. 1068 to Secretario de Estado, Havana, 24 July 1827, reprinted in *CHPP*, I, 255, 257.
21. The creoles' antipathy to Sagra stemmed from a plagiarized article he had dedicated to their edification. See Hernández Travieso, *Varela*, p. 202.
22. Sagra directed his initial critique against two reviews of Heredia's poetry published in the *Mensajero*, one written by the Spanish poet Alberto Lista, and the other by the editors of the proscribed *Ocios*, an émigré publication of Spaniards in London. See Saco, *Colección*, I, 230–33.
23. This was the assessment of Félix Tanco to Domingo del Monte, Matanzas, 10 April 1829, *CEDM*, VII, 41–42.
24. *La Moda* emulated European publications of this genre. Del Monte requested Felipe Poey in Paris to subscribe to several, including *La Mode*. See Felipe Poey to Domingo del Monte, Paris, 12 December 1829, *CEDM*, I, 43.
25. *La Moda*, I, [i–ii]. An editorial dispute caused del Monte to withdraw after 12 June 1830. See *CHPP*, II, 39.
26. BNJM has all sixteen issues; the Boston Public Library has nos. 1–2, 5, 8–13, 15–16.
27. Félix Tanco agreed that the poet's only obligation was to "sensitivity and good taste." See F. Tanco to del Monte, Havana, 30 April 1824, *CEDM*, VII, 17.
28. See Brushwood, *Genteel Barbarism*, pp. 3–4.
29. *El Puntero Literario*, 2 January 1830, p. 4, entitled "Romanticismo," responding to an article critical of romanticism in the *Aurora de Matanzas* on 12 November 1829.
30. Ibid., 2 January 1830, pp. 1–2.
31. Ibid., 27 March 1830, pp. 3–4.
32. *DLC*, II, 658–60.
33. Del Monte, for example, employed the romance ballad style to write about the *monteros*, the free yeomen of rural Cuba. See Karras, "Literary Life," p. 134.
34. The manifesto was reprinted by other Cuban *periódicos*. See, for example, the *Gaceta Cubana* (Santiago de Cuba), 12 March 1830, pp. 2–3, in AGI, Papeles de Cuba, leg. 2015. *El Puntero Literario* continued to fuel the fire with more articles, including a series translated from the French—*Ensayo sobre los clásicos*

y románticos. This article by M. Desmarais ran in issues 13–17, 3–24 April 1830.

35. *PHLC*, pp. 148–51.

36. This is clear in del Monte's article eulogizing Gaspar Jovellanos as someone whose evocation of "costumbres antiguas," if developed, could have earned him a reputation as Spain's Walter Scott. See *La Moda*, 7 November 1829, pp. 6–8; 30 January 1830, pp. 201–7.

37. Ibid., 3 April 1820, pp. 341–43. Of course it also reflected del Monte's recent visit to that city, where Moorish influence was still palpable. The first section of *La Moda* also featured excerpts on the same subject by Washington Irving.

38. Ibid., 27 February 1830, p. 272, juxtaposed to the issue of 8 May 1830, pp. 411–12.

39. Félix Tanco to Domingo del Monte, Matanzas, 7 March 1830, *CEDM*, VII, 46–47.

40. Quoted without reference in *PHLC*, p. 208.

41. For Spanish romanticism see Remak, "West European Romanticism," p. 290.

42. The Literature Commission featured the same personnel as the Education Section: del Monte, Blas Osés, Manuel González del Valle, José Policarpo Valdés, and the fifteen-year-old Venezuelan José Antonio Echeverría. See Karras, "Literary Life," pp. 128–29.

43. See *El Puntero Literario*, 27 February 1830, p. 4.

44. See prospectus presented by Blas Osés and Anastasio Carrillo, in Adrian del Valle, "*La Revista Bimestre Cubana* en su primera época," *Revista Bimestre Cubana* 27 (1931): 329.

45. This at least was José Luis Alfonso's interpretation of the letter from del Monte dated 15 December 1831; see Alfonso to del Monte, Lazareto de Malta, 27 July 1832, *CEDM*, I, in *AAH* 2 (1920): 115–19.

46. See del Monte's report of the Commission's work in 1831 in *Revista Bimestre Cubana* 2 (September/October 1831): 273–78.

47. *El Nuevo Regañón de la Habana* (2 November 1830–21 February 1832) criticized the *Revista Bimestre Cubana* for not including books published in Cuba or Spain in its regular list of recently published titles. *El Regañón* was refounded by Buenaventura Pascual Ferrer's son, Antonio Carlos, but the father soon resumed control, with additional help from Francisco Javier Troncoso. See *DLC*, II, 674.

48. Karras, "Literary Life," pp. 180–83.

49. We know that Saco had intended to return the previous fall, for "the useless ones in New York" attached great importance to the *Revista*. See Tomás Gener to Domingo del Monte, New York, 12 August 1831, *CEDM*, I, in *AAH* 2 (1920): 76–77.

50. *Revista Bimestre Cubana* 6 (March/April? 1832): 19–65.

51. Saco's ascendancy rested not only on his literary reputation but also on the backing of Varela and Gener. See Varela to Luz y Caballero, New York, 1 June 1822, in de la Luz y Caballero, *Vida íntima*, II, 130–31; hereafter *Vida íntima*. Gener's approval of Saco's editorship is implied in his letter of 12 August 1831, cited above in note 49. Gener's concept of activism in May 1832 was a "constellation of upright lawyers, native sons, informed, enthusiastic and patriotic." See Gener to Domingo del Monte, New York, 11 May 1832, *CEDM*, I, in *AAH* 2 (1920): 106–7.
52. *Revista Bimestre Cubana* 7 (30 June 1832): 173–231.
53. *APHL*, II, 144, quoting from Domingo del Monte's report of the Literature Commission for 1832.
54. George Ticknor to Domingo del Monte, Boston, 24 April 1834, *CEDM*, II, in *AAH* 2 (1920): 330–31.
55. Tomás Quintero to Domingo del Monte, Madrid, 26 August 1833, *CEDM*, II, in *AAH* 2 (1920): 313–14: "it makes me fear that the *Revista* will die because of the character of Saco, and because of your dedicating yourself from here on in to the law."
56. Félix Varela to Luz y Caballero (c. 1834), *Vida íntima*, II, 159–61.
57. For the basic narrative surrounding the Cuban Academy, see Guerra y Sánchez, *Manual*, pp. 322–39; for the Spanish background, see Raymond Carr, *Spain, 1809–1975*, 2d ed. (Oxford, 1982), pp. 150–54.
58. The organizational data for the Cuban Academy is available in Saco, *Colección*, III, 6–10; biographical information is taken primarily from *DBC* and *DLC*.
59. Karras, "Literary Life," pp. 206–7.
60. The minutes of the Society meeting of 15 April 1834 are reprinted in Saco, *Colección*, III, 15–23. Significantly, only twenty-four members were present (compared to 112 who would vote at the general meeting in December of the same year), and only one of these, Juan Justo Reyes, the Andalusian professor and "turncoat," had had anything to do with the academy.
61. See reprint of article in *CEDM*, II, in *AAH* 2 (1920): 336–39, footnote 1.
62. Tacón y Rosique, *Correspondencia*, p. 15. An excellent introduction by Pérez de la Riva can be found on pages 13–96.
63. Guerra y Sánchez, *Manual*, pp. 343–44. For another example, see Santiago Saiz de la Mora, "Consideraciones sobre el gobierno del general Tacón en Cuba," *Revista Bimestre Cubana* 52 (1943): 293–303, 384–457.
64. *Correspondencia*, p. 17, includes Ricafort, Ezpeleta, Valdés, and Pezuela, among this group of "routed military men, liberal conspirators in their country, reactionary tyrants in Cuba."
65. Del Monte to Tomás Gener, Matanzas, 3 August 1834, reprinted in Morales y Morales, *Iniciadores*, pp. 208–9, footnote 1; a sec-

ond passage from this letter is contained in footnote 2, pp. 206–7. For another example of creole recognition of psychological damage, see Anastasio Orozco y Arango to Domingo del Monte, Puerto Príncipe, 8 March 1835, *CEDM*, II, in *AAH* 3 (1921): 177–81.

66. For the text, see Barreras, *Textos de las constituciones*, pp. 60–66. The statute established a new structure for the Cortes, however, by guaranteeing a separate body for royal appointees from the nobility and clergy (Estamento de Próceres), in addition to a chamber for elected representatives (Estamento de Procuradores). Legislation would henceforth require the approval of both *estamer tos* as well as the signature of the monarch. For the historical context, see Marichal, *Spain*, pp. 60–61.

67. Zaragoza, *Insurrecciones*, I, 459.

68. Tacón no. 1 to Secretario de Estado, Havana, 30 June 1834, AGI, Papeles de Cuba, leg. 2350A.

69. José G. del Castillo to Andrés de Arango, [Havana?], 7 July 1834, reprinted in Morales y Morales, *Iniciadores*, pp. 218–19, footnote 1.

70. Blas Osés to Domingo del Monte, Havana, 16 July 1834, *CEDM*, II, in *AAH* 3 (1921): 127–28.

71. Domingo del Monte feared that as a result of the investigation ordered by Tacón, Tanco would lose his income as an official of the mail administration in Matanzas. Domingo del Monte to Tomás Gener, Matanzas, 3 August 1834, reprinted in Morales y Morales, *Iniciadores*, pp. 206–7, footnote 2; and another part on pp. 208–9, footnote 1.

72. Domingo del Monte to Tomás Gener, Havana, 4 June 1834, *CEDM*, II, in *AAH* 2 (1920): 344–46, footnote 1.

73. Saco, *Colección*, III, 65–67.

74. Del Monte to Gener, Matanzas, 3 August 1834, cited above; also see Francisco Ruiz to Domingo del Monte, Havana, 21 July 1834, *CEDM*, II, in *AAH* 3 (1921): 128–29. The fear also crystallized the opposition of those who had been initially ambivalent to Tacón. See, for example, José G. del Castillo to Andrés de Arango, 22 July 1834, reprinted in Morales y Morales, *Iniciadores*, p. 209, footnote 1.

75. This incident may not deserve all the attention it has received. For example, Guerra y Sánchez stated that Saco's exile confirmed Cuba's colonial status and initiated the escalating spiral of violence that secured Spain's dominance until the end of the century (Guerra y Sánchez, *Manual*, pp. 334–39).

76. See description of meeting in José Luis Alfonso to Domingo del Monte, Havana, 16 December 1834, *CEDM*, II, in *AAH* 3 (1921): 164–65; also Agustín Bozalongo to Domingo del Monte, Havana, 18 December 1834, pp. 165–66. The case of Bozalongo is of in-

terest, for he apparently switched allegiance between the 15 April 1834 vote against the academy (his name is included in the minutes published by Saco) and his letter to del Monte after the voting in December.

77. For the legislation of 4 January (amplified on 1 June) 1834, see Eguizábal, *Apuntes para una historia,* pp. 243–60. In accordance with this unimplemented legislation, Censor Olañeta submitted a report on 17 January outlining his activities during the previous four months. He revealed no more serious problems than an article which had been submitted for the readers' "intellectual emancipation," an inference which had caused him to reject the article. See José Antonio de Olañeta to Tacón, Havana, 17 January 1835, in *BAN* 37 (1938): 539–43.

78. Tacón no. 142 to Secretario de Estado y . . . Interior, Havana, 7 November 1835, AGI, Papeles de Cuba, leg. 2350A, acknowledging official appointments of José Antonio Olañeta and Juan Ignacio Rendón as *censores regios.* Tacón's reference to the Havana press—the *Diario de la Habana* and the *Noticioso y Lucero*—would have been equally true for their provincial counterparts: the *Noticioso Comercial, El Redactor de Santiago de Cuba,* the *Gaceta de Puerto Príncipe,* the *Correo de Trinidad,* the *Aurora de Matanzas, El Eco de Villa Clara,* and *El Fénix de Sancti-Spíritus.*

79. See the captain general's prosecution of the Junta Superior de Medicina y Cirugía for an unauthorized item in the *Diario* of 25 April 1835 (Tacón [no number] to Secretario de Estado y . . . Interior, Havana, 31 July 1835, AHN, Ultramar, leg. 4, *expediente* no. 7). Tacón charged that the junta's publication had challenged Olañeta's authority, a judgment subsequently upheld by peninsular authorities (see attached opinions).

80. *Memorias de la Real Sociedad Patriótica,* November 1835, pp. 5–7.

81. Mitjans, *Estudio,* p. 117.

82. The *Revista General de la Economía Política* was more like a condensed library on this theme than a *revista.* It was issued in three volumes in August, October, and December 1835; see BNM, 1/51008. Torrente, who had begun his project of writing texts on the topic of political economy under the ministerial protection of Luis López Ballesteros, was given the position of customs treasurer in Havana both as a reward and as economic support for his further writings and study. See his résumé in Intendant Conde de Villanueva no. 5213 to Secretario de Estado y . . . Hacienda, Havana, 28 November 1833, AGI, Ultramar, leg. 81.

83. For an example of paranoia, see Ramón de Palma to Domingo del Monte, Havana, 18 March 1835, warning him not to keep any compromising papers (*CEDM,* II, in *AAH* 3 [1921]: 316).

84. For Tacón's measures to subvert the elections, see footnote in *Correspondencia*, pp. 23–34; for the role of one of Luz y Caballero's students, Juan Bautista Sagarra, in Saco's election, see Luz y Caballero to Saco, Havana, 30 May 1836, *Vida íntima*, I, 207–16. In this congratulatory letter, Luz y Caballero informed Saco of the mandate of Nicolás Escobedo, Domingo del Monte, and "all the good thinkers" to represent all Cubans and not alienate moderates by being more of a litterateur than a patriot. The session for which they were elected was almost over and all three were reelected in July 1836. See Guerra y Sánchez, *Manual*, pp. 369–72.
85. See, for example, Tacón Reservado no. 12 to Ministerio de Interior, Havana, 31 January 1836, *Correspondencia*, pp. 211–13.
86. Tacón Reservado no. 15 to Secretario de Estado y . . . Gobierno, Havana, 31 August 1836, AHN, Ultramar, leg. 4462.
87. All pamphlets included in Tacón Reservado no. 15, Havana, 31 August 1836, AHN, Ultramar, leg. 4462. An attached *minuta* titled "La sección no. 18 Ysla de Cuba/ Gobierno 1837" approved of Tacón's vigilance over the mails and cited enabling legislation.
88. The article is transcribed in "Testimonio del expediente formado para acreditar el buen estado de paz," AGI, Ultramar, leg. 112.
89. Provincial rebellions toppled the Martínez de la Rosa government in July 1835. The appointment of Mendizábal was designed to placate the provincial radicals, and indeed this government instituted a series of far-reaching ecclesiastical reforms in the period September 1835–May 1836. See Marichal, *Spain*, pp. 65–70.
90. *Correspondencia*, p. 58.
91. Included in "Testimonio," AGI, Ultramar, leg. 112.
92. Licenciado Antonio Asencio was absent from the city on the day "Censura de la censura" was published. See Hilario de Cisneros Saco to Tacón, Santiago de Cuba, 23 February 1837, AGI, Papeles de Cuba, leg. 2222A, where the censor defends his innocence on the basis of a lengthy illness requiring a retreat to the countryside.
93. Pérez de la Riva dismissed Lorenzo as "a typical Spanish soldier, who from pronouncement to pronouncement had arrived at Mariscal de Campo." See *Correspondencia*, p. 58. Ironically, Lorenzo's consistent liberalism, however opportunistic, seems to have offended Pérez de la Riva more than Tacón's duplicity.
94. See, for example, Ysidro Joseph de Limonta, Royal Lieutenant in Santiago de Cuba, to Eugenio Llaguno, Santiago de Cuba, 26 August 1794, AGI, Santo Domingo, leg. 2236. This *legajo* also contains other like-minded representations from Santiago de Cuba in response to the royal order of 18 December 1793.
95. O'Gaban's *discurso*, printed in the *Diario de la Habana*, 8 Janu-

ary 1818, pp. 1–2, is included in "Expediente para promover la cultura y educación en la parte oriental de la Ysla de Cuba," to be found in AGI, Ultramar, leg. 34. This *expediente* was prepared by the Patriotic Society in the wake of the controversy provoked by O'Gaban's speech.

96. "Expediente para promover. . . ," AGI, Ultramar, leg. 34, includes Veranés's representation of 28 February 1818, as well as the 18 March 1818 letters of Captain General José Cienfuegos and Intendant Ramírez, president and director respectively of the Society, admonishing the governor and intendant of Santiago de Cuba, and the archbishop, to support the Society's project. Madrid reviewed the disputes and decided to ease the situation by filing it away. The captain general was informed that he must forbid in the future any periodical articles that might offend "corporations or individuals." See Consejo to [Captain General], Madrid, 15 March 1819, AGI, Ultramar, leg. 3.

97. See discussion in *Correspondencia*, p. 56. As the disparity would increase substantially by the 1841 census, we can presume accelerated divergence between 1827 and 1836.

98. Lorenzo no. 10 to Secretario de Estado y . . . Gobierno, Santiago de Cuba, 20 October 1836, AGI, Ultramar, leg. 89. Issues involved were nos. 519–22 (29 October–3 November 1835) of *El Redactor de Santiago de Cuba*, and nos. 57–58 (27–28 October 1835) of the *Noticioso Comercial*.

99. See the first of two letters of Tacón to Lorenzo, both dated 5 September 1836, included in "Testimonio," AGI, Ultramar, leg. 112.

100. Ibid.

101. Though the letter containing these charges was not forwarded until 20 October, Lorenzo makes it clear that he began to collect documents and write the exposition by 24 September. See Lorenzo no. 10 to Estado, Santiago de Cuba, 20 October 1836, AGI, Ultramar, leg. 89.

102. See "Testimonio," AGI, Ultramar, leg. 112.

103. The news was contained in a Seville daily of 18 August, which printed the regent's order of 13 August as conveyed in the *Gaceta Extraordinario de Madrid* of 15 August 1836. The sergeants' actions concluded a series of provincial rebellions expressing dissatisfaction with the highly restrictive elections of July 1836. According to Marichal, just as the propertied classes were becoming accustomed to the limited parliamentary government decreed by the Royal Statute of 1834, disenfranchised city dwellers and members of the national militia sought a more radical alternative (*Spain*, p. 75).

104. Lorenzo to Tacón, Santiago de Cuba, 12 September 1836, and another letter of 19 September, included in AGI, Ultramar, leg.

90. Tacón Reservado no. 17 to Secretario de Estado y . . . Gobierno, Havana, 18 October 1836, in the same *legajo*, includes a copy of the report sent the same day to the War Ministry.

105. This document, supported by twenty-three signatories and "many other notable and distinguished persons," was included in Tacón Reservado no. 17 to Estado, Havana, 18 October 1836, AGI, Ultramar, leg. 90.

106. Tacón no. 1 to Estado, Havana, 30 June 1834, AGI, Papeles de Cuba, leg. 2350A. Tacón and his inner circle of advisors increasingly approved measures to differentiate Cuba from the peninsula. For example, Tacón convened his confidants at his home on 22 February 1836 to suspend the legislation of 21 November 1835 redefining municipal councils and establishing provincial deputations. See Tacón no. 187 to Secretario de Estado y . . . Gobierno, Havana, 5 March 1836, AGI, Ultramar, leg. 90. On 2 May 1836, this group met again and accepted a report which allowed reforms of the municipal council but suppressed provincial deputations, for fear of chaos that could arise during "representative" elections. See Tacón no. 202 to Secretario de Estado y . . . Gobierno, Havana, 4 May 1836, *Correspondencia*, pp. 229–30.

107. The call for elections for the constituent congress of 1836–37 was published on 13 August 1836. More than a year of sessions began on 24 October 1836. Marichal (*Spain,* pp. 91–92) estimates that this body "approved a good portion of the most important legislation of nineteenth-century Spain."

108. Tacón Reservado no. 17 to Estado, Havana, 18 October 1836, AGI, Ultramar, leg. 90; includes his measures of 10 and 14 October 1836. The Ministry of War, in reviewing this communication, admitted that it could not aid Tacón, making extraordinary powers the only possible solution. Thus we see the ironic result: a rebellion against arbitrary power only increased imperial support for arbitrary actions.

109. Even before Lorenzo's rebellion, Tacón enjoyed significant support from the peninsular and mercantile sector for suppressing any political contagion arising out of the rumored mutinies in the peninsular provinces. See petition of 28 September, signed by more than one thousand supporters in the *Diario de la Habana,* 4 October 1836, pp. 1–2, in AGI, Periódicos, Caja 1, No 5/1.

110. *Correspondencia,* p. 51.

111. *El Tío Bartolo* and *El Esquife Arranchador* were specifically mentioned as prototypes to be avoided. Saco to [Luz y Caballero], Paris, 8 September 1836, *Vida íntima,* II, 209–12.

112. See *Correspondencia,* p. 161.

113. Their letters are included in Tacón no. 17 to Estado, Havana,

18 October 1836, AGI, Ultramar, leg. 90. The military governor of Matanzas might have been predisposed to disobey Lorenzo because of the latter's earlier edict prohibiting political innovations without Tacón's express order. Puerto Príncipe was a more complicated case, for only under the former constitutional boundaries was it included within the jurisdiction of Santiago de Cuba.

114. Muñoz del Monte's trajectory is apparent in two letters to Domingo del Monte. His ambition to write patriotic poetry is expressed in a letter regarding *Rimas Americanas.* See Francisco Muñoz del Monte to Domingo del Monte, Santiago de Cuba, 26 December 1833, *CEDM,* II, in *AAH* 2 (1929): 321–25. His sentiments for political liberty (though not independence, as some historians have stated) are apparent in his letter dated Santiago de Cuba, 23 October 1834, *CEDM,* II, in *AAH* 3 (1921): 147–48.

115. Juan Kindelán was the son of Sebastián Kindelán, who had served as governor of Santiago de Cuba and interim superior political chief between Mahy and Vives. He had been Santiago de Cuba's choice for deputy to the Cortes in the year preceding Saco's election of May 1836.

116. This petition was included in Lorenzo no. 10 to Estado, Santiago de Cuba, 20 October 1836, AGI, Ultramar, leg. 89. The charges were repeated with less detail about Lorenzo's offended honor in Lorenzo [no number] to Secretario de Estado y . . . Gobierno, Santiago de Cuba, 23 October 1836, AHN, Ultramar, leg. 3365.

117. Hilario de Cisneros Saco to Moya, Santiago de Cuba, 14 February 1837, AGI, Papeles de Cuba, leg. 2194. By the third issue (3 October 1836) the *Diario Constitucional* was fully in support of Lorenzo, and published his militia call-up of 2 October.

118. *Diario Constitucional,* 6 October 1836, pp. 1–3.

119. See Juan B. Sagarra's report as secretary of the Patriotic Society, dated Santiago de Cuba, 5 October 1833, included in AGI, Santo Domingo, leg. 1306.

120. *El Redactor de Santiago de Cuba,* 2 October 1836, pp. 1–2.

121. See *El Cubano Oriental,* 16 October 1836, p. 3.

122. See *El Eco de Cuba,* 1 November 1836, p. 1. Moderation might have also been a product of his first brush with constitutional censorship, for his article "Corroborante de la libertad," in issue 1 of the *Libre Imprenta,* was absolved of the charge of libel against the clergy only on a technicality. See the report of the *juez de hecho,* Francisco Muñoz del Monte, in the *Diario Constitucional,* 21 October 1836.

123. *El Cubano Oriental,* 22 October 1836, pp. 13–14.

124. See minutes printed in *El Cubano Oriental,* 3 November 1836, p. 37.

125. See his response, "Habitantes de la Provincia de Cuba," in *El Cubano Oriental*, 26 October 1836, pp. 21–22.
126. Lorenzo no. 15 to Secretario de Estado y . . . Gobierno, Santiago de Cuba, 27 October 1836, AHN, Ultramar, leg. 3365.
127. Lorenzo [no number] to Secretario de Estado y . . . Gobierno, Santiago de Cuba, 8 November 1836, AHN, Ultramar, leg. 3365.
128. Little is known about *El Látigo*, which began its weekly appearances on 30 October, stressing adherence to legal standards of the constitution. In a review in the *Diario Constitucional* (12 November 1836, p. 4), "El Amigo de la verdad" claimed that Licenciado José Antonio Pérez was the sole editor of *El Látigo*.
129. In addition to *El Eco de Cuba*, Gaspar published a Sunday supplement entitled *El Pasatiempo Cubano*, beginning 19 November 1836, dedicated to the advancement of the arts and sciences and the propagation of constitutional doctrine. See *CHPP*, I, 320–21.
130. *El Cubano Oriental* no. 2, 18 October 1836, p. 5.
131. The editor (probably Manuel María Pérez) explicitly left Rousseau off this list because he rejected the premise of a spontaneous social pact as the basis of law. Rather, the editor of *El Cubano Oriental* argued, law's immutable existence had to be discovered in the nature of things. See ibid., 1 November 1836, pp. 23–24, "Conversación sobre derecho público, entre un rústico y un hombre educado."
132. Tacón no. 279 to Secretario de Estado y . . . Gobierno de Ultramar, Havana, 18 November 1836, AHN, Ultramar, leg. 3365; also Tacón no. 291 to same, 18 December 1836, in same *legajo*, noting that Lorenzo had rejected Moya's authority.
133. *Correspondencia*, p. 63. Perhaps this atmosphere of a test of wills, rather than a potential civil war, explains why, as late as 30 November 1836, the *santiaguero* press exhibited few signs of trepidation.
134. See AGI, Estado, leg. 1, folio 31, for translated copy of John Hardy to Viscount Palmerston, Santiago de Cuba, 25 December 1836. For more extensive narrative of the denouement, see *Correspondencia*, pp. 62–64.
135. Guerra y Sánchez, *Manual*, pp. 378–79.
136. Tacón no. 29 to Secretario de Estado y Gobierno de Ultramar, Havana, 4 December 1836, AHN, Ultramar, leg. 3365, outlines his plan for Jones.
137. On board were Lorenzo, Arcaya, Muñoz del Monte, Kindelán, and others.
138. José Antonio Saco to José de la Luz, Madrid, 27 December 1836, *Vida íntima*, II, 214–15.
139. For the elections in late 1836 see Guerra y Sánchez, *Manual*, pp. 380–81.

140. *Correspondencia,* pp. 68–69. Tacón's official reports as captain general were an important influence on the Spanish deputies.

Chapter 6. Conclusion: Literature and Repression, 1790–1840

1. Others, like the printer Loreto Espinal, also fled the island (Cisneros Saco to Moya, Santiago de Cuba, 14 February 1837, AGI, Papeles de Cuba, leg. 2194). Only a few unfortunate individuals—the printer Eduardo Gaspar and soldiers from the Catalonian regiment, for example—were judicially processed and expelled from Cuba. See *BAN* 35 (1936): 54–57, for a list (created in Madrid on 4 March 1839) of all those individuals processed and expelled from the island by Tacón. *El Redactor del Santiago de Cuba* shed its temporary identity as *El Cubano Oriental.* As the organ of the Patriotic Society and the only remaining newspaper in Santiago de Cuba, it was not unexpected when the governor persuaded the Patriotic Society to issue the paper as the official daily of the city. See *CHPP,* I, 309–11.
2. Tacón no. 373 to Secretario de Estado y . . . Ultramar, Havana, 30 April 1837, AHN, Ultramar, leg. 4462.
3. Félix Tanco to Domingo del Monte, Matanzas, 9 August 1836, *CEDM,* VII, 71–72.
4. Creoles like Francisco de Arango remained firmly committed to union with Spain, and this position attracted the major spokesmen of the next literary generation as well: José de la Luz, Domingo del Monte, and José Antonio Saco. Even José María Heredia and Gaspar Betancourt Cisneros, ardent supporters of independence in the 1820s, now shared this perspective. See Guerra y Sánchez, *Manual,* pp. 398–99.
5. For more detail see Pérez de la Riva's introduction to *Correspondencia,* pp. 70–80. Tacón also alienated Intendant Martínez de Pinillos, now ennobled with the title of conde de Villanueva. The captain general's initial concessions—the exile of Saco in particular—had given way to outright challenges such as the cancellation of the privileges of a steamship company in which the intendant was a major stockholder (*Correspondencia,* pp. 85–89). The conde de Villanueva, whose long management of Cuban revenues had made him a force in international finance, now added his well-modulated voice to those who maintained that Tacón's actions could prejudice the loyalty of the "ever-faithful isle." See, for example, his masterful letter of 10 February 1838, where he subtly indicts Tacón for preventing the circulation of the peninsular press in Cuba and for opening private mail: Villanueva to Secretario de Estado y . . . Hacienda, Havana, 10 February 1838, AHN, Ultramar, leg. 3361.

6. Ezpeleta no. 26 to Secretario de Estado y . . . Justicia, Havana, 31 May 1838, AHN, Ultramar, leg. 1621. Ezpeleta (1786–1863) had been born in Cuba during the governance of his father, José de Ezpeleta (1785–89).

7. Ezpeleta to Secretario de Estado y . . . Ultramar, Havana, 2 July 1838, *BAN* 10 (March–April 1911): 78–79. Ezpeleta lamented that his vigilance over the foreign press was less effective. In one recent mail ship, for example, *impresos* had constituted thirteen out of fourteen bundles (Ezpeleta no. 3 to Secretario de Estado y . . . Ultramar, Havana, 31 August 1838, AHN, Ultramar, leg. 8). Havana now sported cafés where foreign papers were made available to customers, and a newspaper reading room had been established recently in the city for the same purpose. See Ezpeleta no. 27 to Secretario de Estado y . . . Justicia, Havana, 19 June 1838, AHN, Ultramar, leg. 1621.

8. For Varela's era, see Hernández Travieso, *Varela*, p. 129.

9. Less important figures included Francisco de Paula Orgaz (1815–73), Rafael Matamoros (1813–74), Leopoldo Turla (1818–77), Ramón Zambrana Valdés (1817–66), Ramón Piña (1819–61), and José Silverio Jorrín (1816–97).

10. R. R. Madden to Domingo del Monte, [Havana?], 2 July 1838, *CEDM*, III, in *AAH* 6 (1924): 213–14. Madden recounted his successful efforts at setting up a literary institution in Jamaica at a time, he said, when slavery in one of its worst manifestations still existed.

11. Founded by Luis Caso y Sola, *El Album* featured original literary contributions from the generation of '38. The Library of Congress has the complete collection.

12. These were the headings of the *revista*'s five sections. Castro had unsuccessfully applied for permission to publish a *periódico, El Instructor Habanero,* devoted to literature and science. Censor Olañeta advised Ezpeleta to reject the application, and the subsequent permission for *La Cartera Cubana* suggests their preference for the *revista* format, which allowed more complete and less arduous supervision (*CHPP,* II, 86). For a subject index, see Feliciana Menocal, "Indice general de la Cartera Cubana," *BNJM* 4 (1962): 48–71.

13. *La Cartera Cubana* 1 (July 1838): 5–8.

14. For Suzarte's application, see *CHPP,* II, 79. Only the names of Suzarte's collaborators appear in volume III. The Library of Congress has the complete collection.

15. *El Album* 3 (June 1838): 127–28; *La Cartera* 1 (July 1838): 391–97 (the list is incomplete and some subscribers took multiple copies); *La Siempreviva*'s subscription list was published over the entire year. All three *revistas* surpassed the 300 subscriptions necessary to cover production costs, according to an

estimate of costs by editor Castro in *La Cartera* 4 (January 1840): 5–8. Admittedly, there was substantial overlap in the names of those who subscribed to these *revistas*.

16. *El Plantel* 1 (September 1838): 3–4. For an index of materials, see Feliciana Menocal, "Indice general de *El Plantel*," *BNJM* 3 (1961): 158–72. The Boston Public Library has all but the first of ten issues.

17. See prospectus in *CHPP*, II, 55.

18. Domingo del Monte to José Luis Alfonso, Havana, 10 February 1839, *RBN* 4 (1910): 93–94.

19. *PHLC*, p. 243. Individual works, authors, and genres from this literary outpouring have attracted an extensive bibliography: for an overview, see *PHLC*, pp. 198–234; for individuals and publications, see *DLC*.

20. See their letter of resignation published in the *Diario de la Habana*, 28 December 1838, in *CHPP*, II, 60. Unfortunately, the letter offers no details.

21. Feliciana Menocal, *Indices analíticos* (Havana, 1964), p. 18. Menocal does not document this assertion in the introduction to her valuable index, but circumstantial evidence supports her argument (see text following in this chapter).

22. Creole/peninsular tensions had surfaced the previous year when the printing of Andueza's romantic novel delayed the publication of the *Aguinaldo Habanero*, a collection of poetry and prose edited by Ramón de Palma and José Antonio Echeverría. See José Antonio Echeverría to Domingo del Monte, Havana, 13 January 1837, *CEDM*, III, in *AAH* 5 (1923): 162–63. *PHLC*, p. 200, notes that this was the first novel in book form to be published in Cuba.

23. A. Moreau de Jonnès to Domingo del Monte, Havana, 15 January 1839, *CEDM*, IV, 4–5. The Frenchman refused, not only because of his loyalties to the Cuban creoles who had supported his move, but because he feared that Torrente and Costa merely wanted a painless apprenticeship in his techniques.

24. José Antonio Echeverría to Domingo del Monte, Havana, 31 December 1838, *CEDM*, III, in *AAH* 4 (1922): 300–302.

25. José Jacinto Milanés to Domingo del Monte, Matanzas, 28 February 1839, *CEDM*, IV, 33–34.

26. The publication history of Villaverde's *Cecilia Valdés* is complex. Two introductory excerpts appeared in *La Siempreviva* in 1839 and eight chapters were published in New York in 1839. It was not until 1882, however, that Villaverde revised and expanded the novel into its much acclaimed version. See Farinas, "Dos Versiones," pp. 142–48.

27. Tanco to del Monte, Matanzas, 20 August 1838, *CEDM*, VII, 112–14.

28. Suárez to del Monte, Ingenio Surinam, 15 March 1838, *CEDM*, IV, 38–39. Suárez y Romero, *Francisco*, contains a valuable introduction by Eduardo Casteñeda, pp. 9–25. The novel first appeared as *Francisco. Novela Cubana (las escenas pasan antes de 1838)* (New York, 1880).

29. Domingo del Monte to José Luis Alfonso, Havana, 27 March 1839, *RBN* 4 (1910): 97–98. *El Plantel* failed in August 1839.

30. José Antonio Echeverría to Domingo del Monte, Havana, 31 December 1838, *CEDM*, III, in *AAH* 6 (1924): 300–302.

31. *La Cartera Cubana* 4 (January 1840): 5–8. Editor Castro estimated that of five hundred subscriptions that a Cuban *revista* might attract, only one hundred of these were obtained without coercion. He admitted that as of January 1840, *La Cartera* counted only two hundred subscribers, significantly below the three hundred needed to defray costs. Also see José V. Betancourt, "Seguros literarios," *La Siempreviva* 3 (March 1839): 52–55, for a lighthearted analysis of the economics of literary life in Cuba. Betancourt suggested that editors take out insurance to cover potential losses. Of course, he did not speculate as to what the premiums might be for such a high-risk area as Cuba.

32. F. Tanco to Domingo del Monte, Matanzas, 31 May 1838, *CEDM*, VII, 103–4.

33. José Antonio Echeverría to Domingo del Monte, 18 January 1839, *CEDM*, IV, 8–10.

34. José Zacarías González del Valle to Anselmo Suárez, Havana, 25 June 1839, in González del Valle, *Vida literaria*, pp. 134–36; hereafter, *Vida literaria*.

35. José Jacinto Milanés to Domingo del Monte, Matanzas, 19 August 1840, *CEDM*, IV, 173–74. The Tacón theater opened 15 April 1838 and seated 2,287 patrons (*PHLC*, p. 204).

36. José Jacinto Milanés to Domingo del Monte, Matanzas, 3 September 1840, *CEDM*, IV, 177–78; also see Rine Leal, *Breve historia del teatro cubano* (Havana, 1980), pp. 37–40.

37. Salas y Quiroga, *Viajes*, p. 126. Salas y Quiroga (1813–49) had previously traveled in the Americas in 1831–32, founded a *periódico* in Madrid in 1837, and would publish his travel journals upon his return to Madrid in 1840.

38. Andueza, *Isla*, pp. 104–5.

39. Milanés officially received his appointment in March 1840. See José Jacinto Milanés to Domingo del Monte, Matanzas, 24 March 1840, *CEDM*, IV, 133–34.

40. José Zacarías González del Valle to Anselmo Suárez, 3 January 1840, *Vida literaria*, pp. 172–76.

41. José Zacarías González del Valle to Anselmo Suárez, 25 November 1839, ibid., pp. 154–61; his description of his weekly routine continues in his letter of 9 December 1839, pp. 168–71.

42. Francisco Calcagno, "Vida, pasión y gloria de Anselmo Suárez y Romero," appendix to Suárez y Romero, *Francisco*, p. 206. Calcagno's article was the preface to a 1947 edition of the novel.

43. Ramón de Palma to Domingo del Monte, Matanzas, 9 March 1840, *CEDM*, IV, 127–29. Echeverría offered Milanés a part-time teaching job at his *colegio*, but Milanés never accepted because of a subsequent misunderstanding between the two men. See José Jacinto Milanés to Domingo del Monte, Matanzas, 7 January 1840, ibid., 115.

44. *El Plantel* 1 (September 1838): 3–4.

45. Literary activity did not cease entirely. *La Cartera Cubana* continued until December 1840, and Antonio Bachiller y Morales, in collaboration with the peninsular poet and land surveyor Ildefonso Vivanco, published the *Repertorio de Conocimientos Útiles* from 1 November 1840 to 25 April 1841. The *Repertorio*, however, soon failed for familiar reasons. In the final editorial, the editors blamed content restrictions for their financial woes: 204 subscribers were providing only 51 pesos of the 111 needed to print 500 copies. See the *Repertorio*, 25 April 1841, pp. 205–6 (the Boston Public Library has the complete collection). Two larger circulation newspapers, *La Prensa* (1 July 1841–29 May 1870) and the *Faro Industrial* (November 1841–31 August 1851) provided space for the beginnings of the *costumbrista* explosion of 1844–78 (*PHLC*, pp. 234–35), but their editors were restrained by what one later termed "myopic censorship." See the editorial reminiscence by José García de Arboleya in *La Prensa*, 18 May 1862, transcribed in *CHPP*, I, 313–14. Not only did the range of literary endeavor narrow, but active contributors like Bachiller y Morales, Villaverde, and Gaspar Betancourt Cisneros could not compensate for the voices that had fallen silent.

46. The best recent study concludes that the Escalera conspiracy "was almost certainly a major conspiracy of the people of color, led by the free element among them, known about but not supported by certain liberal creoles, verbally but not materially encouraged by British officials, and blown out of proportion intentionally and irrationally by the Spanish authorities and creole planters." See Robert Louis Paquette, "The Conspiracy of La Escalera: Colonial Society and Politics in Cuba in the Age of Revolution" (Ph.D. diss., University of Rochester, 1982), p. 294. The conspiracy took a tremendous toll on Cuban literary life. The government executed Gabriel de la Concepción Valdés (1809–44), the mulatto poet known as Plácido, whose testimony implicated many prominent creoles associated with del Monte. José de la Luz returned home from Europe and was placed under house arrest. Fearing a similar fate, Domingo del Monte remained in Europe in exile.

47. See José Antonio Echeverría to Domingo del Monte, Matanzas, 18 July 1840, *CEDM,* IV, 167–68. Also Palma to del Monte, Matanzas, 9 March 1840, ibid., 127–29.
48. *Circular que dirige El Exmo. e Yllmo. Sor. Don Juan José Díaz de Espada y Landa* . . . , 31 July 1824, AGI, Ultramar, leg. 375.

BIBLIOGRAPHY

Archival Sources

Archivo General de Indias (Seville). Sección V: Gobierno, Audiencia de
  Santo Domingo, legajos 1189, 1261, 1281, 1283, 1284, 1285,
  1287, 1291, 1292, 1294, 1295, 1298, 1299, 1306, 1337, 1338,
  1339, 1342, 1443, 1490, 1551, 1556, 1557, 1564, 1570, 1635,
  1636, 1637, 2219, 2236, 2237, 2241.
Archivo General de Indias. Sección IX: Estado, legajos 1.31, 12.4,
  17.92, 17.136.
Archivo General de Indias. Sección X: Ultramar, legajos 3, 4, 30, 34,
  35, 44, 56, 75, 77, 81, 85, 86, 87, 88, 89, 90, 95, 105, 106, 111,
  112, 113, 126, 133, 153, 158, 163, 164, 375, 390.
Archivo General de Indias. Sección XI: Papeles de Cuba, legajos 1434,
  1435, 1485, 1540, 1543, 1544, 1545A, 1546, 1547, 1619, 1620,
  1623, 1654, 1656, 1826, 1840, 1862, 1940, 1941, 1946, 1959B,
  1978, 2003, 2007, 2101, 2129A, 2135, 2194, 2222A, 2350A.
Archivo Histórico Nacional (Madrid). Estado, legajo 6367-2.
Archivo Histórico Nacional. Ultramar, legajos 4.7, 8, 1611, 1621, 3361,
  3365, 4462.

Newspapers and Revistas

The following is a list of important *periódicos* cited in the text. For additional information consult Teresita Batista Villareal et al., *Catálogo*

de publicaciones periódicas cubanas de los siglos XVIII y XIX (Havana, 1965), and Steven M. Charno, *Latin American Newspapers in United States Libraries* (Austin, 1968). All *periódicos* unless otherwise indicated emanated from Havana.

El Album, 1838–39.
El Amante de Sí Mismo, 1822.
El Americano Libre, 1822–23.
El Amigo de la Constitución, 1821–23.
El Amigo del Pueblo, 1821–22.
Anales de Ciencias, Agricultura, Comercio y Artes, 1827–31.
El Argos, 1820–21.
Aurora. Correo Político-económico de la Habana, 1800–1810.
Aurora de Matanzas (Matanzas), 1828?–56?
El Botiquín Constitucional, 1820–22.
El Café del Comercio, 1814.
La Cartera Cubana, 1838–40.
La Cena, 1812–14.
El Censor Universal, 1811?–14.
El Centinela en la Habana, 1812–14.
La Concordia Cubana, 1823–24.
La Corbeta Constitucional, 1821–22.
Correo de las Damas, 1811.
Correo de Trinidad (Trinidad), 1820–69.
El Cubano Oriental (Santiago de Cuba), 1836.
Diario Cívico, 1812–14.
Diario Constitucional (Santiago de Cuba), 1836.
Diario de Matanzas (Matanzas), 1829–31.
El Español Libre, 1822–23.
El Espejo de Puerto Príncipe (Puerto Príncipe), 1812–16.
El Esquife, 1813–14.
El Esquife Arranchador, 1820–22?
El Falucho Vigía, 1821–22.
El Filósofo Verdadero, 1813–14.
El Fiscal del Pueblo, 1822.
El Frayle, 1812.
Gaceta de la Habana, 1822–23.
Gaceta de Puerto Príncipe (Puerto Príncipe), 1819–48.
La Galera Constitucional, 1820.
El Indicador Constitucional, 1820–23.
El Látigo de Cuba (Santiago de Cuba), 1836.
El Liberal Habanero, 1823.
Libre Imprenta (Santiago de Cuba), 1836–37.
El Lince, 1811–12.
La Lira de Apolo, 1820.

La Lonja Mercantil de la Habana, 1800.
El Mensagero Político Económico-literario de la Habana, 1809–12.
Miscelánea Curiosa, 1824.
La Moda ó Recreo Semanal del Bello Sexo, 1829–31.
La Mosca, 1820.
El Mosquito, 1820.
El Navío Arranchador, 1820–21.
Noticioso, 1813–44.
Noticioso Comercial de Santiago de Cuba (Santiago de Cuba), 1826–37.
El Observador Habanero, 1820–22.
Papel Periódico de la Habana, 1790–1854.
El Pasatiempo Cubano (Santiago de Cuba), 1836.
El Patriota Americano, 1811–12.
La Perinola, 1812.
El Plantel, 1838–39.
El Puntero Literario, 1830.
El Redactor de Santiago de Cuba (Santiago de Cuba), 1833–44.
El Regañón de la Habana 1800–1802.
El Reparón, 1812–13.
El Revisor Político y Literario, 1823.
Revista Bimestre Cubana, 1831–34.
El Sábelo Todo ó el Robespierre Habanero, 1821.
La Siempreviva, 1838–39.
Tertulia de las Damas, 1811–12.
La Tía Catana Muger del Tío Bartolo, 1820–21.
El Tío Bartolo, 1820–21.

Pamphlets

Arango, José de. *Independencia de la isla de Cuba.* Havana, 1821.
———. *SS. de la junta censoria interina de esta ciudad.* Havana, 1811.
Arango y Parreño, Francisco. *Reflexiones de un habanero sobre la independencia de esta isla.* Havana, 1823.
Bergaño y Villegas, Simón. *El Desengaño, ó sea despedida de la corte y elogio de la vida del campo.* Havana, 1814.
Continuación del diálogo entre dos amigos. Havana, 1812.
Cuadro Político de la Ysla de Cuba. Burdeos, [1836?].
Ferrety, Juan Agustín. *Apuntaciones sobre El Habanero . . . hecho por un discípulo del mismo Varela.* Havana, 1825.
Gutiérrez de Piñeres, Tomás. *Declamación primera contra el despotismo del poder judicial.* Havana, 1811.
———. *Mi opinión sobre jueces de hecho.* Havana, 1821.
———. *Sobre elecciones parroquiales.* Havana, 1821.

Manifiesto contra el autor de la Ylustración contenciosa. Puerto Príncipe, [1813?].

Monte y Aponte, Domingo del. *La Ysla de Cuba tal cual está.* New York, 1836.

Nogerido, Juan de. *Ultima queja al Excmo. Sr. D. Nicolás Mahy.* Havana, 1822.

Proclama patriótico-civil. Puerto Príncipe, [1813?].

Saco, José Antonio. *Carta de un patriota o sea el clamor de los cubanos.* Madrid, [1836?].

————. *Justa defensa de la Academia Cubana de Literatura.* New Orleans, 1834.

————. *Paralelo entre la isla de Cuba y algunos colonias inglesas.* Madrid, 1837.

Selected Secondary Works

Andueza, J. M. de. *Isla de Cuba pintoresca, histórica, política, literaria, mercantil e industrial.* Madrid, 1841.

Anna, Timothy E. *Spain and the Loss of America.* Lincoln, Neb., 1983

Bachiller y Morales, Antonio. *Apuntes para la historia de las letras y de la instrucción pública en la isla de Cuba.* 3 vols. Havana, 1936–37.

Batista Villareal, Teresita, et al. *Catálogo de publicaciones periódicas cubanas de los siglos XVIII y XIX.* Havana, 1965.

Bellanger, Claude, et al. *Histoire générale de la presse française.* 5 vols. Paris, 1969.

Brushwood, John S. *Genteel Barbarism. Experiments in Analysis of Nineteenth-Century Spanish-American Novels.* Lincoln, Neb., 1981.

Calcagno, Francisco. *Diccionario biográfico cubano.* New York, 1878.

Censer, Jack Richard. *Prelude to Power: The Parisian Radical Press, 1789–1791.* Baltimore, 1976.

Centón epistolario de Domingo del Monte. Edited by Domingo Figarola-Caneda. 7 vols. Havana, 1923–57.

Chadwick, Owen. *The Secularization of the European Mind in the Nineteenth Century.* Cambridge, 1975.

Charno, Steven. *Latin American Newspapers in United States Libraries.* Austin, Tex., 1968.

Comellas García-Llera, José Luis. *El Trienio constitucional.* Madrid, 1963.

Comisión Nacional de UNESCO. *El Regañón y El Nuevo Regañón.* Havana, 1965.

Cruz, Manuel de la. *Obras de Manuel de la Cruz.* Vol. 3, *Literatura Cubana. Reseña histórica del movimiento literario en la isla de Cuba (1790–1890).* Madrid, 1924–26.

Defourneaux, Marcelin. *Inquisición y censura de libros en la España del siglo XVIII.* Translated by J. Ignacio Tellechea Idigora. Madrid, 1973.

Domínguez, Jorge I. *Insurrection or Loyalty: The Breakdown of the Spanish American Empire.* Cambridge, Mass., 1980.

———. "Political Participation and the Social Mobilization Hypothesis: Chile, Mexico, Venezuela and Cuba, 1800–1825." *Journal of Interdisciplinary History* 5:2 (1974): 237–66.

Eguizábal, José Eugenio de. *Apuntes para una historia de la legislación española sobre imprenta desde el año de 1480 al presente.* Madrid, 1879.

Erlandson, Erling Halvard. "The Press of Mexico with Special Consideration of Economic Factors." Ph.D. diss., Northwestern University, 1963.

Fahy, Joseph Augustine. "The Antislavery Thought of José Agustín Caballero, Juan José Díaz de Espada, and Félix Varela, in Cuba, 1791–1823." Th.D. diss., Harvard University, 1983.

Farinas, Lucila. "Las dos versiones de *Cecilia Valdés*: evolución temático-literaria." Ph.D. diss., New York University, 1979.

Figueroa, Esperanza. "Inicios del periodismo en Cuba." *Revista Bimestre Cubana* 49 (1942): 39–68.

Figueroa y Miranda, Miguel. *Religión y política en la Cuba del siglo XIX: El Obispo Espada visto a luz de los archivos Romanos, 1802–1832.* Miami, 1975.

Franco, José Luciano. *Las conspiraciones de 1810 y 1812.* Havana, 1977.

García Pons, César. *El Obispo Espada.* Havana, 1951.

Gómez Aparicio, Pedro. *Historia del periodismo español.* 2 vols. Madrid, 1967.

González del Valle, José Zacarías. *La vida literaria en Cuba (1836–1840).* Edited by Francisco González del Valle. Havana, 1938.

González Palencia, Angel. *Estudio histórico sobre censura gubernativa en España.* 3 vols. Madrid, 1941.

Guerra y Sánchez, Ramiro. *Manual de historia de Cuba.* 2d ed. Havana, 1964.

Henríquez Ureña, Max. *Panorama histórico de la literatura cubana.* 2 vols. Mexico, 1963.

Hernández Travieso, Antonio. "Un manuscrito inédito de Bachiller y Morales sobre rectificaciones bibliográficas." *Revista Bimestre Cubana* 56 (1945): 193–226.

———. *El Padre Varela.* 2d ed. Miami, 1984.

Herr, Richard. *The Eighteenth-Century Revolution in Spain.* Princeton, 1958.

Humboldt, Alejandro de. *Ensayo político sobre la Isla de Cuba.* Introduction by Fernando Ortiz. Havana, 1960.

Instituto de Literatura y Lingüística de la Academia de Ciencias de Cuba. *Diccionario biográfico cubano*. 2 vols. Havana, 1980, 1984.

———. *Perfil histórico de las letras cubanas desde los orígenes hasta 1898*. Havana, 1983.

Karras, Bill James. "The Literary Life of Domingo Delmonte y Aponte." Ph.D. diss., University of Colorado, 1969.

Kiple, Kenneth I. *Blacks in Colonial Cuba, 1774–1889*. Gainesville, Fla., 1976.

Knight, Franklin W. "Origins of Wealth and the Sugar Revolution in Cuba, 1750–1850." *Hispanic American Historical Review* 57: 2 (1972): 231–53.

———. *Slave Society in Cuba during the Nineteenth Century*. Madison, Wis., 1970.

Kuethe, Allan J. *Cuba, 1753–1815: Crown, Military, and Society*. Knoxville, Tenn., 1986.

———. "El ejército criollo y la fidelidad cubana durante la época del libertador." *Revista de Occidente* 30–31 (1983): 47–55.

———. "Los Llorones Cubanos: The Socio-military Basis of Commercial Privilege in the American Trade under Charles IV." In *The North American Role in the Spanish Imperial Economy*. Edited by Jacques A. Barbier and Allan J. Kuethe. Manchester, 1984.

Lampros, Peter James. "Merchant-Planter Cooperation and Conflict: The Havana Consulado, 1794–1832." Ph.D. diss., Tulane University, 1980.

Llaverías y Martínez, Joaquín. *La comisión militar ejecutiva y permanente de la isla de Cuba*. Havana, 1929.

———. *Contribución a la historia de la prensa periódica*. 2 vols. New York, 1957–59.

López Sánchez, José. *Tomás Romay y el origen de la ciencia en Cuba*. Havana, 1964.

Lovett, Gabriel H. *Napoleon and the Birth of Modern Spain*. 2 vols. New York, 1965.

Luz y Caballero, José de la. *De la vida íntima*. 2 vols. Havana, 1945.

Madden, R. R. *The Island of Cuba*. London, 1849.

Marichal, Carlos. *Spain (1834–1844): A New Society*. London, 1977.

Medina, José T. *La imprenta en la Habana, notas bibliográficas*. Santiago de Chile, 1904.

Mitjans, Aurelio. *Estudio sobre el movimiento científico y literario de Cuba*. Havana, 1890.

Monte, Domingo del. *Escritos de Domingo del Monte*. Introduction by José A. Fernández de Castro. 2 vols. Havana, 1929.

Morales y Morales, Vidal. *Iniciadores y primeros mártires de la revolución cubana*. Havana, 1931.

Moreno Fraginals, Manuel. *El Ingenio: complejo económico social cubano de azúcar.* 3 vols. Havana, 1978.

———. *The Sugarmill: The Socioeconomic Complex of Sugar in Cuba, 1760–1860.* Translated by Cedric Belfrage. New York, 1976.

Murray, David R. *Odious Commerce: Britain, Spain and the Abolition of the Cuban Slave Trade.* Cambridge, 1980.

Neal, Clarice. "Freedom of the Press in New Spain, 1810–20." In *Mexico and the Spanish Cortes, 1810–1822: Eight Essays.* Edited by Nettie Lee Benson. Austin, Tex., 1966.

Novísima recopilación de las leyes de España. Madrid, 1805.

Ortiz Fernández, Fernando. *Recopilación para la historia de la sociedad económica habanera.* Havana, 1924.

Otero, Gustavo Adolfo. *El periodismo en América.* Lima, 1946.

Pérez Cabrera, José Manuel. *Historiografía de Cuba.* Mexico, 1962.

Pezuela, Jacobo de la. *Ensayo histórico de la Isla de Cuba.* New York, 1842.

Remak, Henry H. H. "West European Romanticism: Definition and Scope." In *Comparative Literature: Method and Perspective.* Edited by Newton P. Stallknecht and Horst Frenz. Carbondale, Ill., 1961.

Roberts, Harmon Martin, Jr. "The Revival of Spain and the Development of Cuba, 1823–1830." Ph.D. diss., University of Miami, 1977.

Rodríguez, Iraida, ed. *Artículos de costumbres cubanos del siglo XIX: Antología.* Havana, 1974.

Roig de Leuchsenring, Emilio. *Los escritores.* Havana, 1962.

———. *Los periódicos: el papel periódico de la Havana.* Havana, 1962.

———. *Los periódicos: los continuadores del Papel periódico.* Havana, 1962.

Rumeu de Armas, Antonio. *Historia de la censura literaria gubernativa en España.* Madrid, 1940.

Saco, José Antonio. *Colección de papeles científicos, históricos, políticos y de otros ramos sobre la isla de Cuba.* 3 vols. Paris, 1858. 1858.

Salas y Quiroga, Jacinto de. *Viajes de D. Jacinto Salas y Quiroga.* Havana, 1964.

Schulman, Ivan A., and Erica Miles. "A Guide to the Location of Nineteenth-Century Cuban Magazines." *Latin American Research Review* 12:2 (1977): 69–102.

Schulte, Henry F. *The Spanish Press, 1470–1966: Print, Power, and Politics.* Urbana, 1968.

Shafer, Robert J. *The Economic Societies in the Spanish World.* Syracuse, 1958.

Smith, Anthony. *The Newspaper: An International History.* London, 1979.

Suárez y Romero, Anselmo. *Francisco.* Introduction by Eduardo Casteñeda. Havana, 1970.

Tacón y Rosique, Miguel. *Correspondencia reservada del Capitán General Don Miguel Tacón.* Edited by Juan Pérez de la Riva. Havana, 1963.

Talmon, J. H. *Romanticism and Revolt: Europe 1815–1848.* Norwich, 1968.

Thomas, Hugh. *Cuba: The Pursuit of Freedom.* New York, 1971.

Thompson, James Westphal. "The Origin and Development of the Newspaper." *The Rice Institute Pamphlet* 17 (1930).

Torre Revello, José. *El libro, la imprenta y el periodismo en América durante la dominación española.* Buenos Aires, 1940.

Trelles, Carlos. *Bibliografía cubana del siglo XIX.* 8 vols. Matanzas, 1911.

Turnbull, David. *Travels in the West.* London, 1840.

Valdés, Antonio José. *Historia de la isla de Cuba y en especial de la Habana.* Havana, 1964.

Villaverde, Cirilio. *Cecilia Valdés o la loma del angel.* 2 vols. Madrid, 1971.

Vitier, Medardo. *Las ideas en Cuba.* Havana, 1938.

Wellek, René. "The Concept of Romanticism in Literary History." In *Concepts of Criticism.* Edited by Stephen G. Nichols, Jr. New Haven, Conn., 1963.

Zaragoza, Justo. *Las insurrecciones en Cuba.* 2 vols. Madrid, 1872.

INDEX